The Family as Basic Social Unit

The Family as Basic Social Unit

Living Out Catholic Social Teaching

Kevin Schemenauer

Foreword by John S. Grabowski

The Catholic University of America Press
Washington, D.C.

A few pages in chapter 4 were previously published as "Hating One's Family: Reading Luke 14:26 in the Context of Luke's Gospel," in *Human Families: Identities, Relationships, and Responsibilities*, ed. Jacob M. Kohlhaas and Mary M. Doyle Roche, College Theology Society Annual Volume, 66 (Maryknoll, NY: Orbis Books, 2021), 100–11. This text is used with permission.

The paper used in this publication meets the minimum requirements of
American National Standards for Information Science—
Permanence of Paper for Printed Library Materials, ANSI Z39.48-1992.

∞

Cataloging-in-Publication Data available from the Library of Congress
ISBN (paperback): 978-0-8132-3-7947
ISBN (hard cover): 978-0-8132-3-8548
ISBN (ebook): 978-0-8132-3-7954

Dedicated to Frances, Gabriel, Dominic, William, and Felicity Schemenauer

Contents

Acknowledgments

This book has been long in the making and is the fruit of a rich personal and academic interdependence I share with others. I would like to thank Marian University for a mini-grant that helped me purchase books in the beginning stages of my research. During my research and writing, Saint Meinrad Seminary and School of Theology provided generous and crucial support in the form of two one-semester sabbaticals, during which I developed ideas and completed a draft. New Wine, New Wineskins, and College Theology Society provided occasions for sharing early stages of my research. The members of those societies encouraged my work and gave me hope that the manuscript has a contribution to make. I am thankful to the publishers who have granted permission to use portions of previously published work. Some of the quotes I use from Pope Francis's writings in chapter 3 resemble "The Works of Mercy: Francis and the Family," *Journal of Moral Theology* 6, no. 2 (June 2017): 32–47. A few pages in chapter 4 rely heavily on "Hating One's Family: Reading Luke 14:26 in the Context of Luke's Gospel," originally published in *Human Families: Identities, Relationships, and Responsibilities*, ed. Jacob M. Kohlhaas and Mary M. Doyle Roche, College Theology Society Annual Volume, 66 (Maryknoll, NY: Orbis Books, 2021), 100–11. Finally, some quotations from Francis de Sales and Dietrich von Hildebrand in chapter 6 resemble "The Infused Virtue of Simplicity: St. Francis de Sales and Dietrich von Hildebrand," *Logos* 20, no. 3 (Summer 2017): 95–121.

I am thankful to the anonymous reviewers who worked with The Catholic University of America Press to provide careful feedback as the manuscript approached the final stages of writing. I am thankful to the staff at The Catholic University of America Press, especially John Martino for his remarkable professionalism, patience, and support during writing and reviews and his insights during the editing process.

Thank you to John Grabowski for writing the foreword to this book. John was my graduate professor and dissertation director. I have long been impressed with the breadth and depth of John's reading and his commitment to the Church. It is a great honor to me that he has framed and introduced my work.

My work also is the fruit of teaching Catholic social ethics for the past fifteen years. I am thankful to the hundreds of students at Marian University and Saint Meinrad Seminary and School of Theology who have engaged these topics with me in the classroom.

Finally, my academic interest in the social character of the family largely reflects my own family's attempt to live out Catholic social teaching in our unique circumstances. While I have respected the intimacy of family life in the examples I provide, the concrete challenges and joys of our shared life together account for much of the hard-earned wisdom herein contained.

Foreword

Saint John Paul II in his "Letter to Families," written during the international year of the family in 1994, taught that the family is "the way of the Church" as she continues her ministry in the contemporary world.[1] The term "way" here recalls its use in the New Testament to denote Christianity itself (cf. Acts 9:2; 18:25; 24:22). To be a disciple, to be called and healed by the Lord, is to follow him on the path or road (*hodos*) that he himself walks (see Mark 10:52). Thus, families are a key part of the path that the Church is called to walk as she follows her Lord. Families are integral to the Church's life and mission; she cannot respond to the call given to her without attending to and ministering to them.

Yet at the same time the Church is composed of families, which are living cells in the body of Christ that she constitutes. As miniature or domestic churches, they participate in Christ's priestly, prophetic, and kingly offices.[2] Seen in this way, they are not just objects of the Church's evangelizing mission but are called to be active subjects in it, especially by taking the lead in the Church's outreach to other families.[3] The Church cannot live without the families that comprise her and whose activity animates her just as cells give life to a body.

These ideas that have blossomed in postconciliar Catholic life and theology have deeper and far older theological roots. They are found in the history of salvation. In his apostolic exhortation on the family, *Amoris Laetitia*, Pope Francis observes that

> the word which appears most frequently in the Old Testament after the name of God (YHWH, "the Lord"), is "child" (*ben*, "son"), which is itself related to the verb "to build" (*banah*). . . . These images reflect the culture of an ancient society, yet the presence of children is a sign of the

1 John Paul II, Letter to Families *Gratissimam Sane* (February 2, 1994), 2.

2 See John Paul II, Apostolic Exhortation *Familiaris Consortio* (November 22, 1981), 49–50.

3 Pope Francis teaches that "the new evangelization calls for personal involvement on the part of each and every one of the baptized. Every Christian is challenged, here and now, to be actively engaged in evangelization." Apostolic Exhortation *Evangelii Gaudium* (November 24, 2013), 120. In his apostolic exhortation *Amoris Laetita* (March 19, 2016), he applies this to Christian families, which "by the grace of the sacrament of matrimony, are the principal agents of the family apostolate" (200).

> continuity of the family throughout salvation history, from generation to generation.[4]

In other words, salvation history is carried forward by the building up of families across time. One of the purposes of biblical genealogies in both the Old and New Testaments is to trace the unfolding of God's promises and their fulfillment across the generations. The principal actors in the history of salvation are families that are called, formed, and indeed "built," by God. The covenants into which the Lord enters with humanity—whether with Adam, Noah, Abraham, Moses, or David—are covenants with the "houses" or families of these men. In and through these families, even in their brokenness, God walks with His people, bringing His plan of salvation to fulfillment.

This divine accompaniment is seen throughout scripture. In forming the people of Israel, the Lord forms a family of people called out of the nations of the earth set apart to worship God and obey the terms of the covenant expressed in the Torah. More specifically, Israel is God's own family: it is in a familial relation with its Lord. For this reason, Moses sprinkles blood on both the altar (representing God) and the people in their covenant ratification ceremony at the base of Mount Sinai (see Exod. 24:6–8). Blood in the scriptures is a symbol of life. To sprinkle the same blood on the altar and the people indicates that they share a common life—they are family. It is not accidental that the primary images for the covenant between YHWH and Israel in the teaching of many of the prophets are familial, often nuptial (see, e.g., Hosea 1–3, 4; Jer. 2, 3, 30, 31; Ezek. 16, 23) but sometimes filial (see, e.g., Hosea 11:1; Jer. 3:14; Isa. 1:2, 30:9). In the New Testament, the Church as the reconstituted Israel is also described as the Bride of Christ and thus as belonging to the family of God. And as firstborn Son, Christ, who is Son by nature, shares His inheritance with us, us sons and daughters through the grace of adoption (cf. Rom. 8: 14–17; Heb. 12:5–12).

In the incarnation, God entered the world in a human family. The Son of God has a human mother and a human foster father. He went into exile with his family as a refugee. He prayed with them, was obedient to his human parents, ate at their table, and learned a trade at their hands. In his public ministry, far from repudiating His own family, Jesus lauded their

4 Francis, *Amoris Laetita*, 14.

example. In teaching that his "mother and . . . brothers are those who hear the word of God and act on it" (Luke 8:21b),[5] Jesus is not dismissing his parents. Scripture tells us that Saint Joseph heard the Lord speak to him in dreams and heeded what the Lord said, taking Mary as his wife and fleeing with her and their son to Egypt to escape from Herod's murderous plans (see Matt. 1:20–21; 2:13). Mary, Luke goes out of his way to tell us, pondered the events of her Son's life (such as the finding in the Temple) in her heart (see Luke 2:19). Thus, both Joseph and Mary are presented to us in scripture as people who heard and kept the Word of God while serving as the earthly parents of the Word Incarnate.

Nonetheless, Jesus does challenge what could be a kind of idolatry of the family in the culture of his day. Thus, he teaches that it is impossible to prefer mother, father, husband, wife, sister, or brother to him and still be his disciple (see Luke 9:59–62, 14:26–27; Matt. 8:21–22). Allegiance to Christ must take precedence over all earthly loves and attachments. Jesus's followers themselves form a kind of spiritual family constituted by faith, and their spiritual bonds are stronger even than relations of kinship (cf. Mark 3:33–35; Luke 8:19–21). The waters of Christian baptism are indeed thicker than blood.[6] In a Christian family, the members are united by both kinds of connection—natural and spiritual.

Why does God build His people into a family? Christian revelation tells us that God Himself exists in a family-like communion of love between coequal divine persons. God the Father, from all eternity, pours Himself into the person of His Divine Son who is His perfect image and eternal Word. Their mutual love breathed forth for one another is so intense that it constitutes the divine person of the Holy Spirit. That is why John Paul II referred to both the Holy Trinity and the family, which is its icon, as a communion of persons (*communio personarum*).[7] In His love for us, God seeks to form us to be like Himself, capable of the self-gift of love in relationships of communion. The family—whether the family into which we are born, the family we form through marriage, or the family of the Church—is the principal place where this occurs.

5 Biblical citations in this foreword are taken from the NABRE.

6 The phrase is drawn from the title of Jana Marguerite Bennett's insightful book, *Water Is Thicker Than Blood: An Augustinian Theology of Marriage and Singlehood* (Oxford: Oxford University Press, 2008).

7 See John Paul II, *Gratissimam Sane*, 6.

It is for all these reasons that "family is the way of the Church." Families constitute the Church and the Church herself is a larger family formed by God so that we can become like Him. It is little wonder that the Church has devoted so much of her attention to teaching about this subject.

But over the last 130 years, there is an area to which the Church's magisterium has devoted even more attention. That area is Catholic social teaching, which concerns the "temporal aspects of the common good," especially "economic and social matters," and stretches from the years "when the Gospel encountered modern industrial society with its new structures"[8] to the present day.

The relation between the Church's teaching on family and her social teaching is sometimes contested. Some commentators see them as pulling in opposing directions with different methodologies and diverging concerns. A better reading is that they should be understood as complementary and mutually supportive, grounded in a common understanding of the dignity of persons.[9] For example, the understanding of marriage as an indissoluble union between a man and a woman ordered to the good of spouses and children, has real and tangible benefits for children, women, and men, including social and economic ones. Faithful, fruitful marriage can be an engine that lifts people out of poverty, helps them flourish, and transforms human communities in positive ways.

But this is not the full story. Kevin Schemenauer shows us that there is a deeper and far richer interface in these bodies of teaching. In *The Family as Basic Social Unit,* he cross-pollinates Catholic social teaching with the Church's teaching on family, resulting in a far richer description of the family as both social and socializing. For example, he takes the Church's vision of the dignity of work and applies it to the often-invisible sphere of labor in the household. In so doing, he gives visibility and form to the oft-heard feminist cry that housework is real work and should be seen as such. Sibling conflict and violence is analyzed through principles of peacemaking. Anyone raised with siblings can attest that questions of violence and peace are not just for the battlefield: they have a place within the walls of the family home. The works of mercy can be practiced in a household as well as by a

8 *Catechism of the Catholic Church,* §§ 2420–21.

9 Erika Bachiochi, "Conclusion: Reflections on the Kinship between Catholic Sexual and Social Teaching," in *Women, Sex, and the Church: A Case for Catholic Teaching*, ed. Erika Bachiochi (Boston: Pauline Books and Media, 2010), 179–92.

family serving together outside of their home. This is a way that the family can share in the kingly office of Christ who "did not come to be served but to serve and to give his life as a ransom for many" (Mark 10:45).

If families are cells within the body of Christ and within human society, then, like the cells of the human body, they are permeable. Schemenauer foregrounds this permeability in his analysis of the social interdependence of the family. As a socially interdependent unit, the family is susceptible to the toxic influences that float through human societies. The book outlines this phenomenon in vivid detail in its examination of the effect of consumerism on human relationships and the home. Consumerism helps drive the distortion of sexual desire and views of love before and after marriage. The results are grim. We are left with what Pope Francis has called a "culture of the ephemeral" in which people think that they can move from one romantic attachment to the next as easily as "blocking" someone on their phone or social media feeds.[10] It also helps fuel the commodification of sex in the ubiquitous pornography industry and its toxic spillover into mainstream advertising. Consumerism also feeds what Pope Francis has labeled our throwaway culture and John Paul II described as manifestations of a culture of death, in which even persons are seen as disposable, as in abortion or euthanasia.[11] Schemenauer's analysis adds a wider context to these prophetic identifications of threats to the family in Church teaching, helping us see them as expressions and symptoms of deeper currents in Western culture.

But if the family is open to the influences of the wider culture, it can also influence that culture. Families are the basic cell of human society—not just of the Church. Families can positively impact the culture around them. Schemenauer highlights the virtue of simplicity as a way to unite the family's social engagement in their communities and the wider world with the love of God, which is the telos of the family's life. By avoiding cooperation with evil in the society around them and living simply, families can practice their own form of asceticism and provide a witness to the excesses of the consumer culture around them. Families are also uniquely situated to engage in various forms of social ministry to those in need outside the walls of their homes. This book highlights various ways families can actively contribute to the common good on the local and global levels.

10 See Francis, *Amoris Laetitia*, 39.

11 See, for example, Pope Francis, Angelus Message, January 29, 2023; John Paul II, Encyclical Letter *Evangelium Vitae* (March 25, 1995), 19–20.

By looking at the family through the lens of Catholic social teaching, Schemenauer brings into focus much more clearly the challenges and opportunities facing Christian families in the twenty-first century. While vulnerable to negative forces in the culture around them, these families have a distinct mission to form their members in a life centered on the love of God that pours forth into a social mission in their wider communities. This richer and more textured picture of family can be an aid to those who live in families and to those who minister to them.

As God walked with families in unfolding His plan for our salvation in the pages of scripture, He walks with them still in and through the Church. This book helps us see more clearly why and how family remains "the way of the Church" in her life and mission in the world.

John S. Grabowski
The Catholic University of America
March 19, 2024: Feast of St. Joseph, Husband of Mary

Introduction

THE NEED TO CLARIFY THE FAMILY'S SOCIAL ROLE

Swiss theologian Hans Urs von Balthasar famously discussed the moment a small child becomes self-aware in response to his mother's smile. Far from making ourselves by an individual act of thinking or willing, Balthasar explores how we receive our experience of self through the loving gaze of our mother, or more broadly, our families. Balthasar explains, "The child responds to a directive that cannot in any way have come from within its own self. . . . The entire paradise of reality that unfolds around the 'I' stands there as an incomprehensible miracle: it is not thanks to the gracious favor of the 'I' that space and the world exist, but thanks to the gracious favor of the 'Thou.'"[1]

No one denies, of course, that parents smile at their children, and that their children respond—but in identifying "the mother's smile" as the primordial experience of being human, Balthasar gives attention to a foundational reality that can too easily be overlooked. The goal of the present book is to examine a similarly foundational but overlooked experience—the family's social character. The social experience of families is so literally "familiar" that it hardly bears noticing. One might hear striking statements about family life—such as the popes' repeated affirmations that "the family is the basic cell of society"[2]—nod one's head, then continue on living life as if the family's social character was evident and not in need of further analysis. Ethicists—whose job is to pay attention to the deep structures of moral and social life—should not be willing to accept this state of affairs. Since families are foundational, one does well to clarify the social character of family life. Why is the family a vital cell of society? If the family is a basic social unit, then in what sense is it basic and in what sense is it social? What is the relationship between families and other social institutions? What is the relationship between one's responsibilities to family and to broader social needs?

1 Hans Urs von Balthasar, "Movement Toward God," in *Explorations in Theology*, vol. 3, *Creator Spirit* (San Francisco: Ignatius Press, 1993), 46.

2 See e.g., John Paul II, Apostolic Exhortation *Familiaris Consortio* (November 22, 1981), 46. Unless otherwise indicated, citations to papal and other Vatican documents in this book are to the versions of these documents found at www.vatican.va.

What does the foundational character of the family mean for those who do not maintain family relationships or who are deeply harmed by family life? How does the Christian faith impact the social character of the family?

Few people would deny that the family is a community or that families are interdependent with other social communities. Without critical reflection, however, one can easily pick and choose different dimensions of the family's social role and ignore others, as suits one's ideological purposes. Application becomes inconsistent and misleading. One might approach an issue like abortion by arguing that family is merely "private," but then emphasize the family's social interdependence in promoting social welfare programs. Alternatively, one might stress the family's social interdependence in public discourse about the definition of marriage, but then speak as if families were merely private in their economic choices. Such picking and choosing overlooks the whole reality—that the family is both a community and interdependent with other social communities. Economic decisions have various social influences and implications; so do abortions. Social welfare programs do not relieve individuals of their unique familial responsibilities; neither do legal definitions of marriage.

The goal of this book is to fill out a complete picture by reflecting on the family's social role and character. My intended contribution is twofold. First, I seek to provide language to make explicit and clear claims about the family's social role that often remain implicit and undefined in Catholic social ethics. Specifically, I propose that two claims—the family is internally social, and the family is socially interdependent—help clarify the family's social role. I derive these two claims from the bedrock affirmation of Catholic social teaching that the family is a basic social unit. As a social unit, it is internally social, and as a basic unit, it is socially interdependent with other larger communities. My purpose in proposing these two claims will not be to stage a dialectic argument with any scholars who might take an opposing view of one or the other. Instead, I hope to convince the reader through the clarity and consistency of these claims as I present them. That is, my first contribution is language and clarity. The task is to offer a succinct and insightful formulation that will help scholars and moral agents understand what these claims about the family's social role actually mean and how they might be applied.

My second contribution is creative and constructive. I demonstrate how applying these two claims (the family is internally social and socially interdependent) is enlightening for family ethics. In highlighting the internally social character of family life, one sees how the richness of the Catholic social tradition offers much wisdom and guidance to individuals concerning their everyday interactions with family members. One can exercise preferential care for the poor[3] to one's children or grandparents. A Catholic framework for work sheds light on household labor. Practices of peacemaking assuage family tensions. One can perform works of mercy toward one's spouse, grandparent, or child. In highlighting the socially interdependent character of family life, one sees the need to cultivate a supportive social structure for one's family. One sees the great gift of childcare assistance, vibrant parish communities, humane job opportunities, and stable political structures. One sees the struggles of those couples who pursue jobs that are geographically isolated from extended family or supportive networks of friends.

I propose that vigilance in applying the family's internally social and socially interdependent character is crucial for family ethics. This proposal implies two things: scholars often overlook one of these two claims, and attentiveness to these two claims is helpful for family ethics. Indeed, the second implication is the more important one—if thinking about the family as internally social and socially interdependent does not prove helpful, then perhaps scholars would be right to overlook them. Accordingly, I intend to focus on how these claims are applied, rather than on documenting who may have overlooked them and why. In other words, my focus is constructive and creative—to present a fruitful application of the claims that the family is internally social and socially interdependent. Accordingly, my scholarship focuses on those authors who are offering creative and constructive accounts of the family's social role; in dialogue with such scholars, my focus is to show how maintaining that the family is internally social and socially interdependent is fruitful for family ethics.

At this point, some terminological clarification seems necessary. "The family" is a contested term, after all.[4] Why employ the term "family" rather

3 While Catholic social ethicists often employ the language of a "preferential option for the poor," I employ instead the phrase "preferential care for the poor." I have found that the word "option" causes confusion, leading some people to see care for the poor as an option or to think that one should prefer those who struggle with poverty over others. When I use the phrase "preferential care for the poor," I am trying to highlight that the dignity and needs of those who struggle with poverty can be overlooked because they lack voice and power, and so individuals and groups should work intentionally to recognize and serve the poverty of others.

4 When I employ the phrase "the family," I am speaking in theoretical or universal terms. I employ the phrase "a family" when I want to indicate a personal element or when I present a concrete example or application.

than "household," a term that has biblical roots and often presents a more accurate description of the basic social community? To be sure, the word family can mean a variety of things. In general, by family, I mean a community related by marriage, conception, and adoption.[5] Family speaks to those relationships that often are foundational and remain whether we choose them or not.[6] I do not mean this definition to separate the family from other social communities but to highlight the unique mission and responsibility one has to family members. The definition moves beyond the husband-wife-children nuclear family since parents also have parents and siblings, children often also have spouses and children, and many families include single parents or divorced and civilly remarried parents. I intentionally leave unanswered the question of where the circles of family connections end. While a husband and wife come from two different families and then form a new family in marriage, the spousal relationship and the parent-child relationship also are locations where family converges.[7] From the perspective of the child, the original families are different sides of his family—the mother's side and the father's side. Moreover, many speak of the parents of one's spouse as one's mother- and father-in-law. Often, family connections are layered. Cousins share the same grandparents, but also aunts and uncles; one's parents are aunt and uncle to one's cousin and one's siblings are also cousins to one's cousin. In other cases, family connections are more singular. The parents of the spouses share their child with their child's in-laws, and perhaps share grandchildren, but do not share cousins, or uncles, or nephews. Are the two sets of grandparents in the same family? They may not self-identify in that way, but they also may experience familial bonds with each other when they gather to celebrate their grandchild's baptism, or birthday, or graduation, and laugh with each other about the goodness and eccentricities of their children and grandchildren. In any case, they are each a member of the grandchild's family.

5 Donald Miller highlights marriage, blood, and adoption. Donald Miller, *Concepts of Family Life: From Vatican II through 'Christifideles Laici'* (San Francisco: Catholic Scholars Press, 1997), 177.

6 Second Vatican Council, Pastoral Constitution on the Church in the Modern World *Gaudium et Spes*, 25, in *Vatican Council II: The Conciliar and Post Conciliar Documents*, ed. Austin Flannery, rev. ed. (Collegeville, MN: Liturgical Press, 1975), 926.

7 See, for example, Second Vatican Council, *Gaudium et Spes*, 52, in Flannery, *Vatican Council II*, 956: "The family is the place where different generations come together and help one another to grow wiser and harmonize the rights of individuals with other demands of social life; as such it constitutes the basis of society."

In this definition, I am not considering close friends to be family. One might say that a friend is like a brother or that a mentor is like a mother, but these attributions work only by analogy. In distinguishing friendship from family, I am not indicating a separation. Friends impact family life. Moreover, the distinction between family and friends does not imply that family relationships are always more foundational and formative or that relationships with one's family are necessarily more intimate than friendships. In fact, the reverse often is the case. In some cases, I will employ the term "household" to indicate foundational living arrangements that are not necessarily rooted in family connections. The language of household is significant for understanding scripture and the call to frame family commitments in relation to the family of God. A good deal of what I say has implications for other communities of formation, like friendships, neighborhoods, parishes, and the workplace. I am highlighting the family because one cannot focus on all communities at once, but also because family members have a unique social mission and responsibility toward one another, a responsibility that has implications for one's responsibilities to God and society.

OVERLOOKING THE FAMILY'S SOCIAL ROLE

While my focus is creative and constructive rather than historical and argumentative, I will spend a little time in this introduction providing some background for the tendency to overlook the family's social role at the level of application. One reason for the divergence between theory (i.e., the family is a basic social unit) and application (e.g., the family is an isolated refuge lacking broader social responsibilities) has to do with the history of academic moral theology. First, from the seventeenth into the middle of the twentieth century, Catholic moral theology focused on the minimum obligation implied by moral laws.[8] Influenced by nominalism, the moral manuals emphasized God's will as manifested through moral laws. Unlike spiritual theologians, who are concerned with contemplation and holiness, the task of the manualists, and therefore moral theology, was to clarify the minimum obligations of the moral life. Like books of jurisprudence, the manuals focused on the ethical precedents for how moral laws have been applied in the past. Their answers often failed to consider the specific moral agent's character and the action's circumstances. The manualists affirmed

8 Servais Pinckaers, *Sources of Christian Ethics*, trans. Sr. Mary Thomas Noble, OP (Washington, DC: The Catholic University of America Press, 1995), chapter 11.

as universal guidance what might apply only in distinct circumstances, and usually dwelled on what not to do.

While moral theologians today rightly challenge the nominalism and minimalism of the manuals, other dimensions of the manuals remain influential. Challenging questions and novel themes continue to set the scholarly agenda. Questions arise and scholars seek the service or honor of clarifying matters. Is artificially delivered food and water ordinary care? Is it morally acceptable to carry out drone strikes against supposed terrorists? Can one switch the tracks of a trolley car so that the trolley will run over two people instead of five? Pressures to present and publish encourage scholars to seek the novel (e.g., the ethics of an aboriginal community or rare family models). Focus on novel and confusing questions often means that more common concerns (e.g., how do spouses navigate household and childcare labor) rarely attract the gaze of moral theologians.

The academic specialization that encouraged manualists to focus on minimum obligations, while allowing spiritual theologians to reflect on contemplation and holiness, has only intensified even if today's moral theology shelves are not stocked with moral manuals. Graduate students often specialize their research in order to complete a dissertation and prepare themselves to be contributing members of a theology department. Newly minted theologians are specialists in a specific subdiscipline of moral theology and often in the writings of one author within that subdiscipline. Social ethicists take a different course than sexual ethicists. Each subdiscipline serves a niche role. Catholic social ethics focuses on large social structures, often impersonal, but with broad and far-reaching consequences. Sexual ethicists focus on specific sexual questions. The location of family ethics in the subdisciplines of moral theology is often not clear, and academic specialization leads to unfortunate contradictions. For example, social ethicists affirm in the abstract the family's crucial social role but then at the level of application, since social ethics is focused on large social structures, that role is largely overlooked. Sexual ethicists offer detailed analysis of the object and intention of an action but often overlook how family dynamics and broader social influences impact sexual ethics. How do economic factors, for example, impact moral agents' reflections on what entails a serious reason to postpone conception or whether to employ contraceptive acts, sterilization, or fertility monitoring as a way of avoiding pregnancy?

The tendencies of moral theology to focus on the novel, the controversial, and the specialized all work to prevent the application of the family's social role to concrete action. Most family interactions are mundane and do not fit neatly into social ethics or sexual ethics. The problem of separating the family from the social is exacerbated by cultural tendencies toward individualism and ethical distortions of personalism and conjugal love. In a context of individualism, self-asserted individual rights are extended to the family, which is viewed as a private, isolated community free to define the meaning of marriage, the role of children in marriage, and human flourishing.[9] Distorted personalist theologies of marriage sometimes support these isolated accounts of marriage. Beautiful articulations about how spouses can image God's love or about the distinctiveness of each marriage can suggest that nuclear families are a perfect community, complete in themselves. If families are socially detached and self-defining, then application of Catholic social ethics to family life seems self-contradicting or voluntary at best. Further, private, isolated families bear no responsibilities to broader society. To be a family is to do what one wants without external constraints, support, or responsibilities.[10]

This separation of the isolated-private from the public hides the family's social character but also reflects a deprived account of privacy. The good of privacy is not self-asserted radical individualism, but respect for and protection of human agency and intimacy. Privacy does not necessarily contradict sociality.[11] Privacy often requires social support, and private decisions can have far-reaching social implications. Private corporations and religious communities, for example, require public goods and infrastructure and thereby, even beyond their specific mission, bear responsibilities toward society. The family is private in the sense that civil society and the state should respect the human agency and intimacy of family life, only intervening in cases of urgent need or when individuals are gravely harming

9 See, for example, Brent Waters's reflections on how individualism and contract theory impact conceptions of marriage and family life. Brent Waters, *The Family in Christian Social and Political Thought* (New York: Oxford University Press, 2007).

10 The false dichotomy between the private and the public leads to various negative consequences. If a religious community is merely private, then one can reduce religious freedom to the right to worship. Moreover, public figures who have no expertise in political matters, such as athletes, actresses, and social influencers, have a forum for political discourse while individuals are encouraged not to discuss "divisive" matters like faith and politics in "private" relationships with family and friends.

11 Drawing on Aquinas, Leo XIII makes a distinction between private societies and public societies. Leo XIII, Encyclical Letter *Rerum Novarum* (May 15, 1891), 37–38, in *Catholic Social Thought: The Documentary Heritage*, ed. David O'Brien and Thomas A. Shannon, rev. ed. (Maryknoll, NY: Orbis Books, 2016), 34.

the agency or intimacy of other family members. Nevertheless, the family is a community and therefore social. The success of families depends on public goods, and families bear social responsibilities to civil society, the Church, and the state.

Many Catholic social ethicists propose that Catholic social ethics is the Church's best-kept secret, and many Catholic sexual ethicists note that US Catholics seem to act without noticeable differences from their non-Catholic counterparts. Given the lack of focus on common family challenges, it should be no surprise that academic Catholic social ethics and sexual ethics seems to have had limited formative influence on Catholics. Do Catholic ethicists have something to offer families who struggle to discern how to act in concrete situations? I believe that they do. While in some sense, every Catholic is a moral theologian, insofar as they live and act and therefore have an account of how to respond to God's invitation of love, academic moral theologians have unique opportunities for intellectual formation, and therefore a responsibility to reflect thoughtfully and fruitfully and to teach and guide others in living more fully the Gospel.[12] Many Catholics are focused on their personal and work lives and do not have the opportunity to study the Catholic social tradition. I do not expect that the present book on its own will cause a renewal in the social lives of US Catholic families. However, I am deeply convinced that Catholic social ethics presents a treasure of wisdom for Catholic families as they attempt to be a basic social unit. The challenge in applying Catholic social ethics to family life is to provide guidance that is relevant without becoming overly specific in a way that overlooks genuine differences of opinions or divergences in circumstances. When I provide examples, I attempt to model the fruitful application that can occur when one reflects on how Catholic social ethics relates to the basic social unit.

CONSTRUCTIVE CONTRIBUTIONS

Indeed, the time is ripe for theological reflections on and the application of the family's social role. The field of moral theology has turned toward virtue ethics, which highlights the role of communities of formation, including families. More than ever in the history of the Church, married theologians are teaching Catholic social ethics and recognizing that families have a spe-

12 John Paul II, Encyclical Letter *Veritatis Splendor* (August 6, 1993), 113.

cific social role and responsibility. Moreover, isolated definitions of marriage, sometimes supported by naïve theologies of love, have not served families well.[13] A fuller account of marriage, attentive to the social dimensions of family life, is necessary. My own work is deeply indebted to theologians who have challenged isolated definitions of marriage and argued that everyday family life is an essential part of Catholic social ethics. I engage a handful of those authors now for two reasons. First, I want to express my gratitude for their work, which has greatly enhanced my understanding of these themes. Second, a synthesis of their work clarifies the goals of my own research. In some cases, I assume conclusions that they have established. Since I am attempting to build on their work, one is able to see my goals more clearly in relation to that work.

Lisa Sowle Cahill was a pioneer in reflecting on the family's social role. She analyzes the relationship between families and other social communities, including the Church. Cahill argues that biblical and patristic early household churches, and certain contemporary African American Catholic communities, model Christian family life in that their care for kin is contextualized by the family of God.[14] The task of caring for kin extends beyond nuclear families and other social boundaries and involves a service to the common good, especially care for the poor. Cahill applies the social analysis of power dynamics and patriarchy to reflect critically on Christian accounts of family life.[15] Cahill describes the family as an institution that is interdependent with various other communities of civil society. This interdependence means both that the family is formed by culture but also that it is called to be socially transformative.[16] In highlighting the essentially social character of the family, I want to build on her insight that the family

13 The COVID-19 pandemic has painfully highlighted the dangers of social isolation.

14 Lisa Sowle Cahill, *Family: A Christian Social Perspective* (Minneapolis: Fortress, 2000), chapters 2 and 5.

15 In describing the personal experiences that influence her work, Cahill highlights the frequent invitations she received to speak on women's roles and her early and ongoing interest in questions of patriarchy. Cahill, xiii.

16 Concerning how culture influences the family, Cahill writes, "Historically, the so-called Christian family has often been co-opted by existing social structures, especially those that reproduce economic and gender inequities." Cahill, 83. Concerning how the family should transform society, Cahill posits that "in my view, the Christian family is not the nuclear family focused inward on the welfare of its own members but the socially transformative family." Cahill, xii. See also her analysis of the Puritans: "The genius of the Puritans, however, is to see that society can be transformed, that civil institutions at the grassroots can be enlisted as agents of change." Cahill, 79.

is an institution of civil society that relates with other communities of civil society, expand her reflections on how culture influences family life by articulating how consumerism impacts family life, and clarify that, in addition to being a means to social transformation, families also are internally social.

My own work is not as focused on or attentive to questions of power as Cahill's. She frames a series of relationships—between husband and wife, laity and magisterium, family and civil society—in terms of power. She argues that Christ and early Christian household churches challenged the social power of ancient families, but she encourages present-day families to recognize and employ their power to transform society through service to the common good and care for the poor. My focus is not on how much social power families exercise but on clarifying the role of families in civil society and in service to Christ. While families often presented obstacles to Christian life in the early Church, the challenge was not necessarily their concern for the social status or social power of family, but the treatment of the family as a veritable idol. Adults, for example, who struggle to provide for the basic needs of their family are rightly focused on enhancing their family's social status and power. In arguing for the social character of the family, I do not seek to increase the power of socially detached families over and against the market or the state, but to challenge and guide families toward faithfulness to Christ, which concerns one's (social) responsibility to family members but also implies service to the common good and care for the poor. While Cahill describes the family as a community of civil society, implying its essentially social character, her emphasis is that the life of the family as a collective institution carries with it certain social consequences. Whereas my focus is the internally social and socially interdependent dimensions of family life, Cahill's focus is the impact of patriarchy on family life and the responsibility of families to serve the poor.

Cahill concludes by clarifying that the social concerns that are present outside a family can be difficult to sustain. Often, it seems that the most we can do is be understanding of different kinds of families and "to offer our time and resources rather sporadically to help other families in trouble or to make community life better. We are too consumed with our own family's well-being, which for some of us seems very, very difficult to secure."[17] I try to address this tension between family responsibilities and broader social service in chapter 7 but also highlight the continuity between service to the

17 Cahill, 137.

social community of one's family and service to those outside one's family. Accordingly, the social mission of the Christian faith need not be sporadic for those with family responsibilities but can permeate their whole lives.

David Matzko McCarthy argues that families should not close in on themselves but should open themselves to broader communal connections and support.[18] He focuses on developing a neighborhood economy of gift giving but also notes the importance of broad communities of kinship and friends. A family is not private in the sense of being a closed, affective refuge from a competitive world. Rather, families should be open, cultivating necessary, even if messy, communal bonds of support. McCarthy's focus is to promote the open family, that is, a recognition of the broader social and economic context of family life and openness to complicated interactions with neighbors, extended family, friends, and the Church. He successfully and thoroughly critiques the false ideal of a closed family, that is, the pursuit of family life as a romantic, affective refuge, self-sufficient and independent from a competitive world. His focus is appropriately placed on culturally dominant and idealistic notions of the closed family.

In critiquing isolated and private notions of family life, McCarthy's general argument tends toward highlighting the social character of the family. He emphasizes gift exchange over contractual exchange, and he notes that the isolation of the closed family finds application within families as well. He also frequently speaks of a household economy and highlights the social, economic, and political role that the family continues to serve despite the prominent ideal of family isolation. Despite the language of isolated family ideals, the inescapable social role of families quietly remains. McCarthy affirms that "the familial, in other words, is the political."[19]

Although McCarthy is critical of models of isolated family life, since his emphasis is to highlight the need to move beyond the closed family, he understandably focuses on the neighborhood economy and not on the social resources and social character internal to communities of kinship. His challenge for families to move beyond themselves into their neighborhood overshadows his insights about the social nature and resources of the family. Consequently, his response to the closed family ideal risks implying that more is always better when it comes to interacting with neighbors and

18 David Matzko McCarthy, *Sex and Love in the Home: A Theology of the Household*, 2nd ed. (London: SCM Press, 2004).

19 McCarthy, 11.

friends.[20] McCarthy offers important corrective guidance for those influenced by isolated family ideals, but the risk is that in challenging the private-public divide by highlighting the need for interaction in one's neighborhood, one overlooks the unique responsibilities one bears toward one's family and the distinctive social character of family life.

The invitation to cultivate broader communities of support in an economy of gift exchange also risks becoming another ideal that is unattainable for many who lack the neighborhood structures of support, trust, and reciprocity that McCarthy highlights. Individuals missing the kind of neighborhood McCarthy describes can draw on the social resources of their family even while recognizing that such support will be critically incomplete without broader structures of support. I propose that an emphasis on the family's internally social character need not endorse a private, isolated, nuclear family. Articulating the internally social character of the family can help, for example, to critique the closed, nuclear family by helping to clarify why individuals are inclined to overestimate the social support provided by a nuclear family.

McCarthy also takes a critical stance toward personalism. He defines personalism as I-thou–focused relationships separated from broader economic, cultural, and political realities. McCarthy convincingly demonstrates that separating spousal and parent-child relationships from these broader contexts leads to problems. Nevertheless, the personalism he often engages is shallow.[21] One need not choose between personalist concerns and attentiveness to broader social realities. Instead, by clarifying the communal dimension of the person, one sees more clearly the relationship between human individuality and personal relationships set within broader economic, cultural, and political contexts. One should be concerned with the person one is engaging, but this concern need not be exclusive and should reflect the socially fecund character of love. Personalism has highlighted with greater clarity how the dignity of the person revealed in Christ is the

20 While his emphasis is on the context of the neighborhood, McCarthy also highlights dependence on extended family and friends. While McCarthy's family seems to have found their support and dependence in relation to their neighborhood, he recognizes that other households might find community in extended family or friends. The central idea is that the family is not an isolated community.

21 In his introduction, McCarthy writes, "Personalist philosophy, along with the modern spirit of individualism, tends to set the household upon a foundation of affective and non-pragmatic (i.e. utopian) relations." McCarthy, 5.

foundational principle of Catholic social ethics. This dignity motivates care for family and neighbor alike.

Florence Caffrey Bourg reflects on the family as a domestic church. As a little church, the family shares in the social mission of the Church to the world. Drawing on sacramental theology, ecclesiology, and virtue ethics, Bourg highlights that the mission of the Church needs concrete application in everyday life, which for many means primarily application in family life.[22] Everyday family life has spiritual and social significance. Like Bourg, I will highlight the relevance of everyday family life. However, whereas Bourg applies sacramental theology and ecclesiology to the family, I apply Catholic social ethics. Whereas Bourg clarifies how the family is a domestic church, I clarify how it is a distinct social community. Whereas Bourg identifies everyday family life as sacred, I identify the everyday as social.

Julie Hanlon Rubio is another pioneer in reflecting on the social role of family life. Working from the "dichotomy" of personal family life and public life, one can see in the work of Hanlon Rubio the gradual construction of a bridge connecting the two sides. In her 1997 article, "Does Family Conflict with Community?," Hanlon Rubio engages authors who argue that spending time at work or in social ministry detracts from family life. Hanlon Rubio challenges the dichotomy of personal and public by arguing that social engagement in work and politics does not undermine family life but rather enhances it.[23] In a 2002 article, "The Dual Vocation of Christian Parents," she argues that not only is it acceptable for parents to serve the broader society but that they have a responsibility to do so.[24] Against an isolated, romantic narrative of marriage, Hanlon Rubio argues in her 2010 book, *Family Ethics: Practices for Christians*, that marriage is a personal-social reality. She proposes that family practices, such as eating and tithing, are worthy of

22 Although Bourg highlights the social character of the family in her reflections on the family as domestic church, at times she focuses on the social implications of family life rather than the social character of family life. For example, in affirming that marriage and family are always public affairs, she highlights how the teaching role of the family has "many public repercussions" and that family breakdown has "social costs." Florence Caffrey Bourg, *Where Two or Three are Gathered: Christian Families as Domestic Churches* (Notre Dame, IN: University of Notre Dame Press, 2004), 90. Bourg's emphasis in this section is like that often found in Hanlon Rubio's work, discussed below. The family is social not so much because it is social in and of itself but because family practices have social consequences.

23 Julie Hanlon Rubio, "Does Family Conflict with Community?," *Theological Studies* 58, no. 4 (December 1997): 597–617.

24 Julie Hanlon Rubio, "The Dual Vocation of Christian Parents," *Theological Studies* 63, no. 4 (December 2002): 786–812.

attention in social ethics because these practices have social consequences and because families are called to social action outside the home.[25] Then, in her 2016 book, *Hope for Common Ground: Mediating the Personal and the Political in a Divided Church*, Hanlon Rubio argues that local communities occupy a crucial space for common ground in the space between individuals and the state.

One sees in *Hope for Common Ground* movements toward seeing family as internally social but also the dichotomizing of the family and the social that frames Hanlon Rubio's work and concerns. In early sections of *Hope for Common Ground*, Hanlon Rubio includes the family as a community located in the space between the personal and the public.[26] Placing the family between the individual and the public suggests that the family is internally social. However, Hanlon Rubio struggles to remove herself from the dichotomy that she so insightfully challenges.[27] In the conclusion of this same work, she places family on the personal side of a personal-public dichotomy. She writes, "Focusing on the local entails a willingness to shift some energy away from politics. . . . It also entails shifting some energy away from the personal, for though our interactions with family and friends, along with efforts to evangelize individuals, are important manifestations of Christian commitment, we are called to take more responsibility for others."[28]

25 Julie Hanlon Rubio, *Family Ethics: Practices for Christians* (Washington, DC: Georgetown University Press, 2010).

26 Julie Hanlon Rubio, *Hope for Common Ground: Mediating the Personal and the Political in a Divided Church* (Washington, DC: Georgetown University Press, 2016), 57, 64, 69, 77. This affirmation is reminiscent of chapter 2 of her *Family Ethics*, titled "Between the Personal and the Political," which reflects on the family as a community. However, in *Family Ethics*, her emphasis is not on how family life is social but on showing how some parents were and can be agents of social change outside the family and how family practices have social consequences.

27 Hanlon Rubio seems aware of this unnecessary dichotomy. In note 4 on page 60 of *Family Ethics*, she writes, "The distinction between public and private is murky, and while I am employing the terms as they are commonly used, I do not mean to suggest here that family life is wholly private. As I hope to make clear, I am arguing for the social significance of daily practices, thus challenging the idea that 'private' life is devoid of 'public' or social significance." Nonetheless, her use of the common terms remains her framework. One sees similar language distinguishing the public from the private in church documents, such as John Paul II's *Familiaris Consortio* (5, 9).

28 Hanlon Rubio, *Family Ethics*, 228–29; see also the last paragraph of the book, where she writes, "The important work on structural change being done by committed theologians, Catholic organizations, and politicians can and must continue, just as evangelization efforts aimed at individuals and families should always flourish. However, in the face of impasses on marriage, poverty, abortion, and end-of-life care, it would be prudent to move some energy to a different social space" Hanlon Rubio, 232.

In the end, the dichotomy between the personal and the public remains in place, with the family placed on the side of the personal and therefore not the social. While Hanlon Rubio convincingly argues that family practices have social consequences, that families have social responsibilities, and that the family has a formative character, her tendency is to argue that families are called to be both personal and social rather than to show that the separation of personal and public is an inadequate framework for thinking about the family's social role. While her work opens avenues for exploring the social character of the family, she often overlooks how family life is internally social. The dual vocation of parents at times feels like a dualism in life, according to which one is a part-time private parent whose private actions occasionally carry social consequences and a part-time public worker. I propose that parents engage in social work when they are intentional about the social consequences of family practices, work for financial gain, and serve the poor, but also when they live fruitfully the internally social character of family life.

Pope Francis is another clear companion for the project of analyzing the family's social character and responsibilities. One refreshing aspect of Francis's ministry is the way he makes the Gospel accessible to everyday lives. He invites his audiences to reflect on what the Gospel asks one to do for one's coworker, children, or neighbor. He notes the foundational character of families for social ethics in his writings, but he does much more than merely mention that the family is the basic social unit. His preaching and speeches are filled with examples from everyday family life. Since the family is basic and foundational, these everyday challenges put the Church's best-kept secret into the everyday lives of the faithful.

Cahill, McCarthy, Bourg, and Hanlon Rubio have opened the field of social ethics and family ethics and have covered much ground. Cahill shows how families are one community of civil society that interacts with other communities of civil society. McCarthy critiques the false ideal of a closed family. Bourg highlights the socially formative character of family life and the ethical relevance of everyday family life. Hanlon Rubio demonstrates how common family actions have social implications and argues that individuals have social responsibilities beyond family commitments.

The work of these authors has directed me away from some potential pitfalls. Drawing on scripture and tradition, Cahill clarifies that the goal for Christian family ethics is not merely to increase the social power of one's family but to contextualize one's family within the family of God. Cahill highlights Christian responsibilities to serve the common good and the poor. McCarthy's analysis clarifies that any reflection on the internally social character of the family should be cautious to avoid the limitations of closed family models. Bourg highlights the formative character of the family and the significance of the mundane. Hanlon Rubio shows that public service and employment can enhance family life and that family practices are an appropriate subject matter for Catholic social ethics.

My own work assumes the ground that these authors have established. While I engage their central themes, I do not see the need to rewrite their books. I adopt Cahill's insight that families are one community of civil society among others. I assume McCarthy's critique of isolated, private accounts of family life. I do not see the need to argue that everyday family life is an appropriate topic for moral theology since Bourg and Hanlon Rubio have already done so. My emphasis is twofold. First, I seek to provide a formulation of the family's social role that is succinct and insightful; namely, that the family is internally social and socially interdependent. These claims help to clarify, qualify, and balance the academic discussion of the family's social character. Second, I seek to demonstrate the fruitfulness of applying these two claims to family life.

I see my work as a work of integration showing how social ethics has relevance for family ethics. I intend with this book to challenge both social ethicists and family ethicists. For the family ethicists, my claim is that since the family is a basic *social* unit, families can learn a great deal about their everyday family interactions from the Catholic social tradition. For the social ethicists, my claim is that since the family is a *basic* social unit, one crucial way to make social ethics more obviously relevant is to clarify the social character and role of families.

OUTLINE

The two basic concepts—the family is internally social and socially interdependent with other social communities—will structure my reflections. The first three chapters focus on the former claim and the final four chapters focus on the latter. Chapter 1 develops the central unifying principle—the family is a basic social unit, with emphasis on its internally social character. The family's internally social character is self-evident. The family is a community of persons and therefore social. To see the family's internally social character more clearly, one needs to see how it is distinctly social. Family relationships have an enduring and intimate character that transcends personal choices. Since marriage unites families, family communities often are socially robust, including various and diverse dimensions of social life. The Christian faith enhances and clarifies the internally social character of family life. Divine love provides the origin, meaning, and end of familial communion. Families are called to image God's love, not as perfect and private, but as a specific participation in theological charity. Finally, families serve the ecclesial mission of family formation. Parents have a unique responsibility to form children in social virtues and Christian discipleship.

Chapters 2 and 3 draw out the implications of the family's internally social character. In chapter 2, I propose that the Catholic social principles developed in the social encyclical tradition provide a rich framework for reflecting on everyday family life. An application of Catholic social principles to everyday family life helps families to become communities of life and love that are active in their social mission. Catholic social principles are specific enough to provide both language and prudential guidelines for everyday family life but general enough to respect the unique circumstances of each family. To demonstrate the fruitfulness of Catholic social principles for family interactions, I apply the dignity of work and peacemaking to family interactions. I show especially how Catholic social ethics illuminates reflections on household labor and violence between siblings.

Since my focus is to highlight how the Catholic social tradition illuminates everyday family life, I reflect in chapter 3 on how individuals can perform works of mercy toward their family members. Highlighting the tension that can exist between social ethics and family commitments, I ask the question of whether service to family members is a matter of justice and therefore not of mercy. After providing a brief history of the works of mercy, I theologically frame a work of mercy in relation to God's mercy rather than in contrast to justice. Accordingly, I propose that individuals can perform works of mercy toward their family members insofar as they act in participation with God's mercy. Moreover, since key biblical passages for mercy employ familial language and analogies, I argue that mercy in the family is crucial for the intelligibility and accessibility of the biblical witness.

Part 2 focuses on the socially interdependent character of families. In chapter 4, the transition chapter, I show how the family's internally social character highlights its interdependence with other social communities. Individuals, even in the context of extended family connections, require social opportunities for growth and development outside of their families.

Families need the support of political stability, economic opportunities, infrastructure for communication and transportation, healthcare, and civil society to allow the free pursuit of personal interests and friendships.

After reflecting broadly on the interdependence of families with other social communities in chapter 4, I provide an example of interdependence in chapter 5 by analyzing how consumerism impacts families' ability to live out their social mission. While the Church presents a bold vision of living as a basic social unit, one will miss the challenge of that vision if one does not come to terms with the obstacles that consumerism presents to family life. Indeed, one of the reasons that Catholic social teaching is often called "a secret" is that, in many locations, consumerism has a stronger moral influence on the faithful than does the Christian faith. Many families are sympathetic to serving others but do not do so because they are busy, dissatisfied, and in debt. Further, analysis of sexual and medical ethics remains severely limited without attentiveness to the pervasive influence of consumerism. The pervading influence of consumerism has had a significant and, in important ways, corruptive influence on the way one understands spousal love, marriage, and the having and rearing of children.

Since the interdependence of a family with other social communities is both positive and negative, in chapter 6, I provide a theological framework for analyzing a family's communal engagement. Many challenges facing individuals concern how their families should or should not interact with other social communities. I begin with the infused virtue of simplicity, arguing that simplicity is a way of life united in the love of God. This means that the goal is neither more nor less interaction with social communities but uniting one's engagement in the love of God. I propose that the tradition of moral cooperation offers helpful categories for individuals discerning the proper social engagement of their family. I analyze moral cooperation next to questions of moral formation, moral appropriation, and the common good and situate the analysis in the framework of a family's interdependence with other social communities. I conclude the chapter by reflecting on family practices that help unite social engagement in the love of God. One sees in the complexity of the world and one's life an opportunity to grow into and to express love of God and neighbor.

Finally, in chapter 7, I develop a framework for discerning a family's involvement in social ministry. Models of social ministry often fail to account for the unique social resources and skills that many families possess. I develop a framework suited to those with family responsibilities by holding together two points of tension: the tension between family responsibilities and the Gospel call to serve the poor, and the tension between service in embodied communities and service to those outside of one's embodied community. I analyze four ways in which families can engage in social ministry working from the family outward, reflecting on the possibilities of the integration of and tension between family responsibilities and broader social service. I begin with instances in which family relationships motivate participation in social service. I then move to service in a family's embodied communities such as the neighborhood, workplace, or parish. Third, I reflect on indirect and direct aid to those with urgent needs outside of a family's embodied communities. Finally, using the case study of Catholic Worker families, I analyze centering one's family on social ministry. These various forms of social service highlight the Gospel call to care for the poor and clarify that families should discern how, not whether, they will serve the broader community.

PART I

The Internally Social Character of Families

1

The Internally Social Character of Families

Catholic social encyclicals and the writings of Catholic social ethicists contain many compelling and beautiful statements about the family's social character: the family is the basic social unit, the vital cell of society, the future of humanity.[1] Despite the frequency of such statements, church teachings and academic theologians often say little about what these statements mean and how one can apply them concretely.[2] The social character of the family often is highlighted, and then overlooked.[3]

As I explained at the outset of the book, I propose to clarify the claim that the family is a basic social unit with two additional formulations: the family is internally social and socially interdependent. This first part of the book is dedicated to the internally social character of families, and this first chapter is dedicated to elucidating what I mean by "internally social character."

The family is internally social. This claim is self-evident; the family by necessity consists of more than one person and is therefore social. Few would deny the family's internally social character. The challenge, however, is to apply this insight consistently and concretely to family life in contexts

1 See, for example, Pope John Paul II, Apostolic Exhortation *Familiaris Consortio* (November 22, 1981), 42, 46, 86.

2 Some rare exceptions are the recent work integrating family ethics and social ethics referenced in the introduction, as well as John Paul II's *Familiaris Consortio* and Pontifical Council for Justice and Peace, *Compendium of the Social Doctrine of the Church* (Washington, DC: United States Conference of Catholic Bishops, 2005); Pope Francis, Postsynodal Apostolic Exhortation *Amoris Laetitia* (March 19, 2016); and Brian Benestad, *Church, State, and Society: An Introduction to Catholic Social Doctrine* (Washington, DC: The Catholic University of America Press, 2011).

3 See, for example, Thomas Massaro's popular textbook, *Living Justice*. Massaro mentions family as one of the key themes of Catholic social teaching. In his two-page discussion of the family, he writes that it is the most basic unit and the first cell of society. He affirms that larger institutions cannot substitute for the important social roles played by families and that the well-being of society depends on the well-being of families, which is a crucial community for virtue formation. Thomas Massaro, *Living Justice: Catholic Social Teaching in Action*, 3rd ed. (Lanham, MD: Rowman and Littlefield, 2016), 91–93. Beyond these two pages, however, the family is almost completely absent from the text even while the subtitle of the book is "Catholic Social Teaching in Action."

that are often obscured by contrasting, individualistic accounts of family. In this chapter, I clarify how the claim that the family is internally social is distinct from an individualistic viewpoint wedded to a social contract theory of marriage. To clarify the internally social character of the family, I proceed in three steps. First, I describe how the family is internally social, highlighting how it is distinctly and robustly social. Second, I examine ideas that challenge the family's internally social character. Affirming this character will do little if individualistic conceptions of family life remain more prominent in ethical application. Finally, I provide a theological analysis of the family's internally social character. I propose that Christ's emphasis on the "family of God" clarifies and enhances the family's internally social character by highlighting the familial call to image God as a communion of persons and the mission of family formation.

A BASIC AND DISTINCT SOCIAL COMMUNITY

In affirming that the family is internally social, I mean first of all that it is more than a random collection of individuals. Indeed, family is foundational to human existence, and therefore social interaction. Aristotle writes in his *Politics* that "there must be union of those who cannot exist without each other, that is, a union of male and female for the sake of procreation."[4] Similarly, Aquinas speaks of a self-evident natural inclination to sexual intercourse and the education of offspring.[5] Without the propagation of the human species, earthly social communities would cease to exist. Further, from the beginning of their existence, children stand in social relationship to their parents and other family members.[6] Despite occasional ideas going back to Plato's *Republic* to separate procreation completely from education—to raise children as wards of the state—the family, in whatever permutation, persists as the primary locus for housing and raising children throughout the modern world, just as it did in ancient times.

4 Aristotle, *Politics*, I.2, in *Aristotle: Selected Works*, trans. Hippocrates G. Apostle and Lloyd P. Gerson, 3rd ed. (Grinnell, IA: The Peripatetic Press, 1991), 559.

5 Thomas Aquinas, *Treatise on Law* (Washington, DC: Regnery, 1956), I-II, q. 94, a. 2.

6 Because it is self-evident, the family's internally social character is a reality from which one can derive arguments about important matters. For example, one basis on which the bishops of Vatican II argue for religious freedom is the family's social character: "Every family, in that it is a society with its own basic rights, has the right freely to organize its own religious life in the home." Second Vatican Council, Declaration on Religious Freedom *Dignitatis Humanae* (December 7, 1965), 5, trans. Laurence Ryan, in *Vatican Council II: The Conciliar and Post Conciliar Documents*, ed. Austin Flannery, rev. ed. (Collegeville, MN: Liturgical Press, 1984), 803.

The foundational social character of family life is one of the distinct aspects of the family's social character. In *Gaudium et Spes*, the bishops highlight another; namely, that family ties go beyond free choice.[7] McCarthy similarly observes that one often does not have the family one imagined one would have, writing that "family life is largely about acceptance rather than choice."[8] One does not get to choose one's parents, siblings, children, grandparents, aunts and uncles, or cousins. While one makes a free decision to begin a spousal relationship or to adopt a child, even here, once one becomes a spouse or a parent, the social bonds that are thereby generated go beyond personal choice. Individuals are socially bound to family members by marriage, conception, and adoption. In marriage, conception, and adoption individuals make social commitments that establish lasting relationships with others. Even when these relationships break down, bonds remain. A father who leaves his family remains the children's biological father. Even those who pursue divorce and civilly remarry often refer to their previous spouse as their ex-husband or ex-wife. Family relationships transcend personal choice.

The enduring character of family relationships is naturally supported. The social commitment of marriage binds two individuals to one another. This bond is strengthened when spouses maintain a household together, share sexual intimacy, and become parents together. The relationship between parent and child is strengthened by the originating role of the parent. A parent is connected to a child as source, and the act of co-creating implies responsibilities to the child, who is vulnerable and in need of relationship and care. A mother's relationship to her child is strengthened further by the physical union of pregnancy and the intimacy of nursing.

In addition to their foundational and enduring character, families also are unique in their social complexity. In the family, one sees executive

7 Second Vatican Council, Pastoral Constitution on the Church in the Modern World *Gaudium et Spes*, 25, in *Vatican Council II: The Conciliar and Post Conciliar Documents*, ed. Austin Flannery, rev. ed. (Collegeville, MN: Liturgical Press, 1975), 926. Cahill contrasts the family of modern liberal individualism focused on personal choice with a Catholic, covenantal-sacramental approach to family relationships that recognizes biological and material forms of human interdependence and thereby goes beyond personal choice. Lisa Sowle Cahill, *Family: A Christian Social Perspective* (Minneapolis: Fortress, 2000), 133.

8 David Matzko McCarthy, *Sex and Love in the Home: A Theology of the Household*, new ed. (London: SCM Press, 2004), 205. See also Stanley Hauerwas's proposal that "we no more know the person we marry than we know ourselves." Stanley Hauerwas, *The Hauerwas Reader*, ed. John Berkman and Michael Cartwright (Durham: Duke University Press, 2001), 513.

leadership, lawgiving, lobbying, law enforcement, judgment, physical borders, a language of the common good, communication, conflict, diplomacy, compromise, security concerns, economics, social roles, work, religion, various forms of poverty, education, skills training, moral formation, voluntary associations, integration with and dependence on other communities, culture, identity, friendship, food, recreation, beauty, art, music, exercise, hospitality, trust, success, failure, competence, mistakes, celebrations, and multiple generations.[9] While any group has a social character, few communities have the robust social character of the family. Families are not only self-evidently and foundationally social but often robustly so.

The family provides various kinds of relationships that form individuals in social virtues and vices.[10] The bishops of the Second Vatican Council observe that in a family, individuals can "help one another to grow wiser and harmonize the rights of individuals with other demands of social life; as such it constitutes the basis of society."[11] To highlight the social formation that occurs in a family is to highlight that families are a location for practicing social ethics. Individuals develop social virtues and vices in their family interactions because family interactions are social. As Paul Furfey notes, while family interactions prepare individuals for broader social action, a family also provides a context for the "personal practice of social virtues."[12]

Spouses fulfill a social role and function in running a household together. They need to care for the home and in some cases the yard, pre-

9 The authors of *Gaudium et Spes* highlight that a family is a place where "different generations come together." Second Vatican Council, *Gaudium et Spes*, 52, in Flannery, *Vatican Council II*, 956. As such, a family provides a unique opportunity to impart religious, cultural, and family traditions and wisdom over generations. Francis observes that the married couple

> 'shares plans, trials, expectations and concerns; they learn care for one another and mutual forgiveness. In this love, they celebrate their happy moments and support each other in the difficult passages of their life together. . . . The beauty of this mutual, gratuitous gift, the joy which comes from a life that is born and the loving care of all family members—from toddlers to seniors—are just a few of the fruits which make the response to the vocation of the family unique and irreplaceable,' both for the Church and for society as a whole. (Francis, *Amoris Laetitia*, 88; the internal quotation comes from Synod of Bishops, Fourteenth Extraordinary General Assembly, *Relatio Finalis* [October 24, 2015], 49–50).

10 Pontifical Council for Justice and Peace, *Compendium of the Social Doctrine of the Church*, 213.

11 Second Vatican Council, *Gaudium et Spes*, 52, in Flannery, *Vatican Council II*, 956.

12 Paul Furfey, *Fire on the Earth* (New York: Macmillan, 1936), 94. The quotation is cited by Julie Hanlon Rubio in *Hope for Common Ground: Mediating the Personal and the Political in a Divided Church* (Washington, DC: Georgetown University Press, 2016), 69.

pare food and clean dishes, wash and fold clothes, and care for family members. They must weigh expenditures and balance budgets. Spouses must regularly discern and communicate family roles and duties and develop skills necessary to constitute a functioning, and if possible, thriving, family community. Pope John Paul II, in his discussion about marriage preparation programs, notes the importance of preparing the engaged persons for productive, communal skills. He writes that beneficial marriage preparation programs will "acquaint those concerned with correct methods for the education of children and will assist them in gaining the basic requisites for well-ordered family life, such as stable work, sufficient financial resources, sensible administration, notions of housekeeping."[13] Couples discerning marriage do well to ask themselves if they can effectively run a household together.

McCarthy offers an expanded analysis of how family roles and duties are necessary for a productive household.[14] His focus is to highlight that family life is more than affective connections.[15] A family is a community whose functioning requires productive activity like buying clothes and providing transportation. The completion of these and other tasks requires "a set of roles and practices" and the "attainment of skills, proximate ends, and overriding purposes."[16] In highlighting the importance of social roles in a family, McCarthy is careful to clarify that the requirement of family roles and duties should not imply that women fulfill only submissive family roles. Many spouses find the task of differentiating spousal roles without undermining the dignity of women challenging in part due to history. Too often,

13 John Paul II, *Familiaris Consortio*, 66. David Matzko McCarthy highlights how family roles and duties are necessary for a productive household in *Sex and Love in the Home* (154–61).

14 McCarthy, *Sex and Love in the Home*, 154–61.

15 While McCarthy contrasts affective connections with productive work, I propose that the productive work required of family life clarifies the nature of spousal and familial love. When the authors of *Gaudium et Spes*, John Paul II, and Francis challenge spouses to live as a community of love, they are inviting them to something more than sexual attraction. See Francis, *Amoris Laetitia*, 284. Spousal and familial love often require daily, even seemingly monotonous and mundane self-giving: "All members of the family, each according to his or her own gift, have the grace and responsibility of building, day by day, the communion of persons, making the family 'a school of deeper humanity.'" See John Paul II, *Familiaris Consortio*, 21. See also Second Vatican Council, *Gaudium et Spes*, 49 and 52, in Flannery, *Vatican Council II*, 956. Spousal love involves a commitment of the will but also the affective fruit of sharing lives together in the management of a household. A failure of self-giving, particularly on the part of men, is by contrast often cited as an important source of marital stress and breakdown.

16 McCarthy, *Sex and Love in the Home*, 158.

women have been reduced to the role of bearing children in pregnancy and doing the thankless, private work of caring for children, while men have fulfilled public roles and received public recognition. One might conclude from this that injustice flows from a conception of family roles. When families are inflexible about the roles individuals serve, it is often the case that some family members receive public honor and praise while others receive thankless task after thankless task.

To overcome this challenge, McCarthy distinguishes between gender roles and family roles. To functionally run a household, one needs to assign and commit to different tasks. One spouse buys groceries and cooks. The other spouse washes dishes and does the laundry. One spouse wakes up more frequently in the night with the newborn. The other spouse wakes up early with the toddler and cares for the older children. McCarthy argues that even if one accepts common gender-related generalizations, such generalizations do not clearly require or exclude men and women from performing various family roles.[17] Still, one should not dismiss the natural and cultural influences that impact how men and women exercise family roles. In most social contexts, women disproportionately bear the burden of childcare, even as social and political efforts have been made to treat men and women as if they were the same. In the end, McCarthy proposes that the challenge concerning gender and family roles is "to take the procreative goods of sex seriously without reducing gender differences to a simple division of roles."[18]

CHALLENGES TO THE FAMILY'S INTERNALLY SOCIAL CHARACTER

Many social ethicists have commented on how the family was once the preeminent social institution, whereas now individuals often view families as an emotional haven in a heartless world.[19] This narrative is often repeated in part because it offers explanatory power for many challenges facing families today. Donald Miller proposes that, into the early twentieth century,

17 McCarthy roots his distinction between gender-related roles and family roles theologically in scripture, arguing that scripture offers a complex presentation of the relationship between gender-related and social roles. McCarthy, chap. 9.

18 McCarthy, 191.

19 Donald Miller, *Concepts of Family Life: From Vatican II through "Christifideles Laici"* (San Francisco: Catholic Scholars Press, 1997), 22. See also Mary M. Doyle Roche, *Schools of Solidarity: Families and Catholic Social Teaching* (Collegeville, MN: Liturgical Press, 2015), 3.

families handled "employment; health and mental-health care; education and socialization; social control; religion; recreation; marrying; reproduction; identity; affection and love; and the protective care of children, the frail, the disabled, and the chronically ill."[20] Miller writes that by the mid-1950s "the family's responsibilities were reduced to two: reproduction and identity, affection, and love."[21]

While contemporary accounts of marriage and family differ, Brent Waters shows how the framework of social contract theory proves to be illuminating and compelling for framing popular discourse about marriage.[22] However, social contract theory provides little to no foundation for the social and political character and role of family life. In fact, social contract theory threatens to undermine the social character and role of marriage and the family—if marriage is merely a social contract between two individuals in the pursuit of individual fulfillment, then marriage and family life is more a private manifestation of self-expression protected from public concerns than a basic social community. If marriage is merely a social contract, then one can leave the union when one's fulfillment no longer appears to be served. Social contract theory thus promotes a twofold undermining of childhood. First, children are vulnerable and struggle to represent themselves in social contracts; adult interests tend to take precedence. Second, since having children, like all things, is framed in terms of individual self-fulfillment, parents can enjoy the children they have conceived but need not feel burdened to rear them.[23] Children become a consumer option available for spouses who enjoy children.

Under social contract theory, Waters notes, the responsibility of child-rearing moves from parents to the state, which has a triple motivation to control the rearing of children. First, parents cannot be compelled to raise their children since such a requirement could undermine the parents' freedom to seek self-fulfillment. Second, children are formed in foundational ways in their childhood and so the future of society depends on their formation. Third, parents cannot be trusted to form children in the social contract virtues of tolerance and acceptance. Therefore, the state and public

20 Miller, *Concepts of Family Life*, 23.

21 Miller, *Concepts of Family Life*, 24.

22 Brent Waters, *The Family in Christian Social and Political Thought* (New York: Oxford University Press, 2007); see also Edward Hadas, *Counsels of Imperfection: Thinking through Catholic Social Teaching* (Washington, DC: The Catholic University of America Press, 2021), 332–44.

23 Waters, *The Family*, 68–76.

professionals need to take primary responsibility for the rearing and education of children.[24]

In this system, parents have limited authority over and responsibility to their children. Children are a source of enjoyment for the parents until they become adults and then they become like other citizens, mature adults freely pursuing self-fulfillment. In rural contexts, where children provide free labor on the farm, children are a great resource encouraging parents to have children. In more urban settings, however, children are an economic and personal drain. Newborns wake up throughout the night, toddlers need their diapers changed, children need to be fed and clothed, adolescents are moody and ungrateful. Outside of personal enjoyment or free labor, it is not clear why, in a social contract framework, parents would want children and would make the sacrifices necessary to raise them well. Indeed, in countries where this theory has significant influence, birth rates are seen to plummet.

Marriage and family seem to have little role in social contract theory. Especially in cultures where individuals can choose their professions and seem able to move from one social class to another, the family's social power seems to be in decline. One might conclude from all of this that the family's social character was a historical contingency that is now being left behind. One might even rejoice in the decreased social power of families, which tended to locate power in familial patriarchs. Literature, the stage, and film—when they look back to history at all—are full of stories of young people oppressed by traditional family structures who are liberated by a more modern, romantic outlook oriented to self-fulfillment, and often matriarchs or patriarchs who learn the error of their ways.

One should be careful, however, about concluding from these historical narratives that a social role for marriage and family has come to an end. Neither contract theory, the desire to decrease the social power of familial patriarchs, nor a recognition that many families do not possess the social power of past generations imply that families have therefore become merely private and not social. Families are internally social—they consist of more than one person, they are foundational for human existence, they entail bonds that transcend human choice, and they often are socially robust.

Recognizing the internally social character of families helps provide nuance to the powerful historical narratives about the family's social decline. In recognizing the internally social character of family life, one sees more

24 Waters, 77–84.

clearly how families retain social tasks and social power even in locations where marriages are defined as private social contracts and where familial power seems to be waning. While families in the United States, for example, often do not exhibit the social power commonly seen in families throughout most of human history, the social influence of the family (for good or for ill) remains strong despite, or in some cases because of, the breakdown of family life. Further, even in cultures in which movement away from the social class of one's family is a hope or a possibility, the social and financial status of one's family remains a significant factor determining the opportunities available to children.[25] Family life impacts the safety of one's community, the education one receives, the safety nets that allow one to take risks, and one's exposure to religion.[26] Adults who can enter into social contracts were first vulnerable children who needed relationships with and care from other human persons. Many individuals continue to find themselves bound to and responsible for their parents, siblings, and children. In other words, despite efforts to eliminate the natural bonds, roles, and responsibilities of family relationships, these bonds continue to express themselves. Social contract theory does not account sufficiently for the social roles of marriage, the intimate bond of spousal union, and the vulnerability of a child who needs to receive love and care in a stable community. As the bishops of the Second Vatican Council affirm in *Gaudium et Spes*, "the strength and vigor of the institution of marriage and family shines forth time and again."[27]

A family is not a private, isolated entity but a community of persons that moves individuals out of anonymity. Pope Francis notes:

> The family is the primary setting for socialization, since it is where we first learn to relate to others, to listen and share, to be patient and show respect, to help one another and live as one. . . . In the family, we learn closeness, care and respect for others. We break out of our fatal self-absorption and come to realize that we are living with and alongside others who are worthy of our concern, our kindness and our affection.[28]

25 See Robert Putnam's *Our Kids: The American Dream in Crisis* (New York: Simon and Schuster, 2015).

26 Stanley Hauerwas writes "Notre Dame and its sister institution Saint Mary's . . . were rightly used by Catholic families who sent their sons and daughters in the hopes that they would meet someone of approximately the same social class and religious background to marry. That is arranged marriage under the illusion of choice." Hauerwas, *The Hauerwas Reader*, 513.

27 Second Vatican Council, *Gaudium et Spes*, 47, in Flannery, *Vatican Council II*, 949.

28 Francis, *Amoris Laetitia*, 274.

Julie Hanlon Rubio describes how a family meal, for example, can lead family members out of their isolation. She explains that around the table, family members learn how to communicate, compromise, and tolerate: "The practice of eating civilizes and stretches us because it teaches people to participate in something larger than themselves."[29] Hanlon Rubio's discussion of the family table provides a concrete example of the family's social nature. Family life, which includes activities like sharing a meal, is not an isolating community but possesses social resources to move individuals beyond a focus on personal choices and desires to concern for cultivating a community of persons with others. Because it is social, the family is not a location for anonymous self-seeking, but as John Paul II notes, "a complex of interpersonal relationships"[30] that possesses "formidable energies capable of taking man out of his anonymity."[31] Marriage (and with it the family) "elevates and perfects the social dimension of existence."[32]

The challenge, however, is not merely to affirm that the family is a community that involves a complex set of relationships requiring productive roles. One can give intellectual assent to such a position and then forget about this insight in the face of powerful historical narratives about the family's social decline. In locations where socially detached definitions of family life permeate, the tendency in social and sexual ethics is to note the family's social role but then default to accounts of isolated family life. To benefit richly from insights about the family's social character, one must make an intentional and conscious effort to recall the family's social character in moral analysis. A full documentation of this tendency to overlook the family's internally social character goes beyond the scope of the present inquiry. I will simply provide one example from the work of Julie Hanlon Rubio, who has otherwise done as much as anyone to advance the notion of the family's social character.

Hanlon Rubio often frames her discussions of family in terms of a private-public dichotomy. In a discussion on social service outside of the family, Hanlon Rubio argues that married couples should make social service outside the family a priority and that this service should continue,

29 Julie Hanlon Rubio, *Family Ethics: Practices for Christians* (Washington, DC: Georgetown University Press, 2010), 143–44.

30 John Paul II, *Familiaris Consortio*, 15; see also *Amoris Laetitia* (74), where Francis speaks about "the entire network of relations that [husband and wife] build with their children and the world around them."

31 John Paul II, *Familiaris Consortio*, 43.

32 Francis, *Amoris Laetitia*, 205.

although perhaps in new forms, even after spouses are blessed with children. She challenges families to move beyond "their comfortable isolation to encounter those on the margins of life."[33] Drawing on the work of John Kavanaugh, she describes how encountering those outside of one's family who bear the wounds of humanity can remind us of "our most dependent fragile-beginnings, or our diminishment and dying, of our ultimate inability to manage and control either our bodies or our world."[34]

While a dichotomy between a comfortable, insular family life and one dedicated to social ministry may form a rhetorically compelling way to encourage families to broaden their service experience, this dichotomy in most cases is false and risks presenting a misleading image of family life and life outside of family interactions. One could just as well imagine the reverse scenario in which service to one's family requires one to move beyond the comfortable isolation of one's job, hobbies, or even social ministry to engage more fully in familial relationships.[35] In *Amoris Laetitia*, Francis proposes that married life is not a model supporting a lifestyle of comfortable isolation but a model for overcoming it.[36] As Jana Bennett insightfully argues, for the Christian, no state of life is consistent with a life of comfortable isolation: "It is not the case that one begins to live a Christian life of holiness only when a choice has been made for marriage or for celibacy. On the contrary, that choice is part of the Christian's entire orientation toward God, desire for God, and desire to do God's will."[37] One sees more

33 Hanlon Rubio, *Family Ethics*, 209.

34 Hanlon Rubio, 209. Hanlon Rubio is drawing on the work of John F. Kavanaugh, *Following Christ in a Consumer Society* (Maryknoll, NY: Orbis Books, 2006), 189.

35 Lisa Sowle Cahill writes, "Despite an ethos of individualism, humans rarely in fact live in isolation. Therefore, before calling for more and stronger community, we must recognize that humans typically *do* live in communities; the question is what kind of communities we create and who is accepted within them." *Family*, 102. Similarly, McCarthy:

> Contractual social relations and market utility shape the dominant narrative of home, but on this standard, many households do not succeed. The ideal suburban home brings the benefit of social autonomy and various pleasures of leisure, but many aspiring families do not attain self-sufficiency and security. The middle-class family, by and large, is motivated and structured by a therapeutic individualism that advances the economic interests of its members while cultivating love and compatibility through non-utilitarian activities (i.e., fun). But there are households (perhaps most) that occupy spaces outside the dominant narrative, on the fringe, or at an indeterminate point between failure and success. (McCarthy, *Sex and Love in the Home*, 89–90).

36 Francis, *Amoris Laetitia*, 162.

37 Jana Marguerite Bennett, *Water Is Thicker Than Blood: An Augustinian Theology of Marriage and Singleness* (Oxford: Oxford University Press, 2008), 134.

clearly that family life is not merely comfortable isolation when one recognizes the internally social character of the family community and thereby sees care for family members as a kind of social service.

Private notions of family life not only prevent individuals from serving those with urgent needs in the broader community; they also leave individuals ill prepared to relate to those needs in one's family community. Individuals might attempt to cultivate a life in which their family life is an experience of comfortable isolation from the urgent needs and concerns of the world. They might wish to find in their family relations a life of comfortable isolation. Instead, they will find their family, each member of which is at their own stage of development and experiencing their own emotions, hardships, and sins as well as growth, blessing, and grace. Individuals or families trying to maintain the familial image of private refuge will inevitably deny one another's struggles or look to place blame on others. Francis writes,

> Faced with a crisis, we tend first to react defensively, since we feel that we are losing control, or are somehow at fault, and this makes us uneasy. We resort to denying the problem, hiding or downplaying it, and hoping that it will go away. But this does not help; it only makes things worse, wastes energy and delays a solution. Couples grow apart and lose their ability to communicate.[38]

The ideal of a private, isolated, perfect family can only set families up for failure. A family is not a gathering of self-seeking, perfect individuals but a community that develops the person's social nature through joys, struggles, productive tasks, challenges, and vulnerability.[39]

Highlighting the internally social character of the family not only offers us accurate descriptions of social needs and struggles in the family but also allows us to see more clearly the social resources it provides. Kavanaugh and Hanlon Rubio are right to highlight how providing service to the urgent needs of those outside the home challenges families to move beyond "their comfortable isolation to encounter those on the margins of life."[40] Such ministry can shake individuals out of a shallow complacency and offer perspective on life. However, one should not suggest that the education and

38 Francis, *Amoris Laetitia*, 233.

39 Francis repeatedly expresses concern about the stifling character of false family ideals. See, for example, *Amoris Laetitia* (106, 113, 122, 209–10, 218, 221, 232–37, 325).

40 Hanlon Rubio, *Family Ethics*, 209.

formation that results from attending to the needy neighbor is not available to those who care for needy family members. Certainly, one does not need to engage in social ministry to encounter one's most dependent and fragile beginnings, or one's diminishment and dying, or one's ultimate inability to manage and control either one's body or one's world. To do that, one need only try to put a baby to sleep, witness the death of one's sister, or attempt to guide a toddler or a teenager experiencing puberty. In recognizing the social character of the family, one sees more clearly that the relationship between care for family and care for the needy neighbor need not be so disconnected. Rather, care for the poor in one's family demands practices, a sense of responsibility, and formation that can stand in harmony or integration, just as it can stand in contrast, with care for one's needy neighbor.[41]

To be sure, both Kavanaugh and Hanlon Rubio recognize that family life is far from a life of comfortable isolation.[42] I turn to their writings with a spirit of gratitude, but draw attention to how even these authors, who are so attentive to interpersonal family challenges, struggle to keep the internally social character of families in mind at the level of concrete application. I propose that the real dichotomy is between a life of isolated comfort and a life of service, both within and beyond the family, not between private family life and public social ministry. The primary tension is not between caring for family members and caring for those in the broader community with urgent needs, but between a life oriented around caring for people and one focused on practices of consumption or an excessive prioritization of social and financial security. This fundamental distinction in attitude applies whether the family's social power is waxing or waning. My goal is not to exalt the family against other social institutions, but to highlight that the family is internally social, and thus I seek to clarify its social role in relation to other social communities. The Christian faith helps on both fronts, as I explain in the next section.

THE CHRISTIAN FAITH AND THE FAMILY'S SOCIAL ROLE

Revelation and Christian tradition enhance and clarify the social role and character of family life. In this section, I highlight especially the familial call to image God's love and the ministry of familial formation. In the process,

41 In *Familiaris Consortio* (69), John Paul II describes the relationship between intimate home life and building up Church and society as a harmony rather than a balancing act.

42 See, for example, Hanlon Rubio, *Family Ethics* (4, 66–93).

I also warn against reading this familial call through a socially detached conception of family. In addition, I briefly engage Gospel passages in which Christ seems to have disregard for family commitments. I turn first to the theme of communion. One sees in this theme of communion an intimate relationship between family life and the Gospel. Divine communion is the origin and end of family communion, and family communion participates in and provides a fitting analogy to divine communion.

Familial Communion as Divine Image

The human person is *creatio ex nihilo* by divine love and called to participate in and manifest that love through human communion. John Paul II proposes that human beings image God when they live as a communion of persons.[43] This call to communion speaks to the origin, meaning, and end of human life, and familial communion is a unique manifestation of human communion. The divine origin of familial communion is beautifully portrayed in Genesis: "God created man in his image, in the divine image he created them; male and female he created them. God blessed them, saying: 'Be fertile and multiply'" (Gen. 1:27).[44] Human life, sexual union, and the capacity to procreate are gifts of creation originating in divine love.

In the Christian tradition, the family's origin in divine communion contextualizes the end and meaning of family communion. The author of Revelation presents the vision of an eternal wedding banquet in which God marries His people (chap. 21). The goal of Christian life is union with divine love and citizenship in the kingdom of God, not an increase in familial social status or even familial communion.

In biblical times, the social significance of families was assumed. Lisa Sowle Cahill writes, "Individual identity is defined primarily in relation to the family and its social place; it consists of the duties, responsibilities, and prerogatives one holds within one's family and by virtue of one's family role in the social network."[45] The framework of divine communion as superior to

43 For John Paul II, the familial image of God is a specific expression of the more fundamental image of God present in any human community of persons. He proposes that to say humans image God as a communion of persons "constitutes perhaps the deepest theological aspect of everything one can say about man." John Paul II, *Man and Woman He Created Them*, trans. Michael Waldstein (Boston: Pauline Books, 2006), 164.

44 All biblical citations in this book are to the New American Bible.

45 Cahill, *Family*, 19; see also Samual L. Adams, *Social and Economic Life in Second Temple Judea* (Louisville: Westminster John Knox Press, 2014), 8.

this familial social structure helps to explain some of the challenging familial passages in the synoptic Gospels where Christ seems to dismiss the importance of family commitments.[46] Christ moves His audience from familial or household commitments to the family of God. For example, in chapter eight of the Gospel of Luke, Jesus's mother and brothers cannot reach Him because of the crowd. Christ states, "My mother and my brothers are those who hear the word of God and act on it" (Luke 8:21; see also Luke 9:59; 11:27–28; 12:52–53; 14:26; 21:16). Family commitments are a great good, but they should not replace one's commitment to God or undermine Christian discipleship. Since Christian commitment aims at union with God, one should order family relationships toward hearing the word of God and observing it. The divine origin and end of familial communion cautions disciples against making one's family and the social status of one's family into an idol.

Families, however, are more than an idol to avoid. An intimate and permanent family communion provides a fruitful analogy to divine communion. John Grabowski notes how Old Testament prophets use the language of marriage to articulate God's love and to remind the faithful of their covenantal commitment to God.[47] Christ's preaching about the family of God (e.g., Luke 8:21) seems to assume that his readers' experiences of maternal and fraternal relationships will communicate the intimate bond shared by citizens of the kingdom of God: "Luke shows that family commitments can provide relationships and language that enlighten Christian discipleship. Further, the sacrifice of family relationships illustrates well the radical demands of Christian discipleship since, in risking rejection from one's household, one risks the loss of much that is good."[48]

46 The Gospel of Luke presents two of the more dramatic statements. In Luke 14:26, Christ proclaims, "If anyone comes to me without hating his father and mother, wife and children, brothers and sisters, and even his own life, he cannot be my disciple" (see the parallel and somewhat tamer passage at Matt. 10:37). In Luke 21:16, Christ prophesies, "You will even be handed over by parents, brothers, relatives, and friends, and they will put some of you to death" (see also Matt. 10:21). For more discussion of these and other similarly challenging texts, see Cahill, *Family*, 18–47; Julie Hanlon Rubio, *A Christian Theology of Marriage and Family* (New York: Paulist Press, 2003), 45–64; and Andrew S. Jacobs, "'Let Him Guard Pietas': Early Christian Exegesis and the Ascetic Family," *Journal of Early Christian Studies* 11, no. 3 (2003): 265–81.

47 John S. Grabowski, *Sex and Virtue: An Introduction to Sexual Ethics* (Washington, DC: The Catholic University of America Press, 2003), 51.

48 Kevin Schemenauer, "Hating One's Family: Reading Luke 14:26 in the Context of Luke's Gospel," in *Human Families: Identities, Relationships, and Responsibilities*, ed. Jacob M. Kohlhaas and Mary M. Doyle Roche, College Theology Society Annual Volume 66 (Maryknoll, NY: Orbis Books, 2021), 109. https://orbisbooks.com/collections/series-college-theology-society/products/human-families.

The Christian faith challenges a family community to image and be a witness of triune love and Christ's love for the Church. To represent God's love to the world is no small task; it is a call that the bishops of the Second Vatican Council deservingly describe as a social apostolate.[49] The intimate, life-giving, and enduring character of family relationships make families a uniquely fitting image of God's love. One needs to be careful here, however, to avoid affirming naïve ideals. Like all analogies of God's love, the family analogy will necessarily and dramatically fall short. A theology highlighting the familial analogy of divine love is especially vulnerable to harmful ideals when paired with culturally dominant accounts of a "happy" isolated family. To say that a family is called to image divine love does not mean that its members experience their family as an affective refuge without tension, disagreement, limitations, and struggle. Such a reading of the family image presents false expectations for individual family members and a crushing yoke for a family community. As Francis notes, "There is no need to lay upon two limited persons the tremendous burden of having to reproduce perfectly the union existing between Christ and his Church."[50] If one associates only peace, joy, and fulfillment with divine love, then one will be unprepared to handle situations when family life does not seem peaceful, joyful, and fulfilling. These false expectations become particularly problematic when one believes that one's family embodies divine love simply because it is a family. Rather, as Francis highlights, "Marriage as a sign entails 'a dynamic process . . . , one which advances gradually with the progressive integration of the gifts of God.'"[51]

Families can model triune love and Christ's love for the Church only in an embodied and fitting way. In seeking to be a communion of persons, families must, so to speak, "put on flesh." In this sense, the family image functions more as a description of a loving family than a description of the nature of or even one's primary focus for family life. One should not use one's family members to represent God's love to the world as if one's family members were merely billboards for God's love. Rather, individuals love their family members because of their shared human dignity and the responsibility that flows from family relationships. Moreover, one can seek

49 Second Vatican Council, Decree on the Apostolate of Lay People *Apostolicam Actuositatem* (November 18, 1965), 11, in Flannery, *Vatican Council II*, 778.

50 Francis *Amoris Laetitia*, 122.

51 Francis, 122; internal quotation is from John Paul II, *Familiaris Consortio*, 9.

to imitate divine love in one's family without attempting to maintain the façade of perfection. Francis writes, "If I expect too much, the other person will let me know, for he or she can neither play God nor serve all my needs. Love coexists with imperfection. It 'bears all things' and can hold its peace before the limitations of the loved one."[52] Imaging divine love in a human family will involve asking for forgiveness, struggling to be patient, and finding ways to challenge others in love rather than anger.

When families are asked to image God's love, they are being asked no more than to live out their Christian commitment. All Christians are called to live in theological charity; that is, to allow God's love to animate their lives. God's faithful love provides the model and the strength for families to love one another.[53] Families image God's love not because they are perfect but because God shares His love with those who accept that love. Those who focus on family commitments are not distinct from other Christians in being called to live in the image of God's love. A family, however, does present a unique context for imaging God as a communion of persons because of the enduring and often intimate character of family relations. To say that a family images God's love highlights that God is a communion of persons. One manifestation of Christian charity is to participate in the communion of persons by fostering in one's family a community of persons: "In the end, marital spirituality is a spirituality of the bond, in which divine love dwells."[54]

Sometimes family commitments and living in God's love seem to stand in tension. Familial commitment requires preferential love for a few, whereas theological charity implies loving God and all others in God. If one views family relations as socially detached, then the preferential character of familial relationships may indeed stand in tension with charity. Individuals following this view serve their family without concern for or responsibility to those outside of one's family.[55] David Matzko McCarthy, however, notes how

52 Francis, *Amoris Laetitia*, 113.

53 John Paul II highlights in *Familiaris Consortio* (12) how God's faithful love provides a model for spouses.

54 Francis, *Amoris Laetitia*, 315.

55 See, for example, Soren Kierkegaard:

> *Erotic love and friendship are preferential and the passion of preference*. Christian love is self-renunciation's love and therefore trusts in this *shall* [love one's neighbor]. To exhaust these passions would make one's head swim. But the most passionate boundlessness of preference in excluding others is to love only the one and only; self-renunciation's boundlessness in giving itself is not to exclude a single one. . . . Consequently, Christianity has misgivings about erotic love and friendship because

a theology of communion clarifies the relationship between family commitments and theological charity. The universality and selflessness of Christian love must continue with respect to community: "Familial love is not an early stage on the way to more mature universal or disinterested love. Rather, the love of family is basic to the love of God, to universal love, and to the church's role as a sacrament of God's love in the world."[56] The end of charity is not disinterested relationships and self-destruction, but the cultivation of divine and human communion. Familial love may be, but need not be, an obstacle to God's love. Families can image God's love through the cultivation of human communion. Concern for familial communion, in charity, opens to further communion with God and all others in God.

In mediating the family image of divine love and the call to divine and human communion, John Paul II focuses in *Familiaris Consortio* on four tasks of the family: to be a loving community of persons, to have and raise children, to participate in society, and to share in the Church's mission.[57] Family life concretely images God's love by cultivating communion in these four ways. These four social tasks challenge families to move beyond obligational minimalism and private isolation.

John Paul II's articulation of its four tasks presents a bold vision for the family's social role that moves beyond culturally controversial prohibitions. More than simply avoiding divorce, spouses are called to foster a loving community of persons. More than simply avoiding recourse to contraception, sterilization, or abortion, spouses are called to be prudentially and generously open to any children God gives them as well as diligent in raising those children. More than simply refraining from breaking the law in pursuing their private interests, spouses are called to participate in the life of society. More than simply attending Sunday Mass, spouses should share in the Church's mission. A family should provide a witness of God's love, but it provides this witness by building community through concrete acts of love expressed through everyday joys and struggles.

---

preference in passion or passionate preference is really another form of self-love. (Soren Kierkegaard, *Works of Love: Some Christian Reflections in the Form of Discourses*, trans. Howard and Edna Hong [New York: Harper and Row, 1962], 65)

56 McCarthy, *Sex and Love in the Home*, 11; see also 127–39.

57 John Paul II, *Familiaris Consortio*, 18–64. The pope's articulation of the four tasks of marriage remains the most comprehensive treatment of the family's social character and role in magisterial teaching. See also Brian Benestad's commentary on the four tasks in *Church, State, and Society*, chap. 7.

The witness of familial love is not typically what one associates with evangelical action in the Church. Families need not stand on a soapbox or knock on doors to preach the Gospel. Individuals perform concrete acts of love for those who are nearby, and by doing so they intentionally build a familial communion of persons. While focused on those that family members seek to serve, these concrete actions and communal building provide a silent, overflowing witness of community, and thereby an evangelical witness of God.

Formation in the Family

In addition to imaging God through communion, family members also play a crucial social role in providing for the moral and spiritual formation of their members.[58] By living in God's love, all Christians are called to be concerned with the salvation of souls. This Christian commitment rooted in the sacrament of baptism is further specified for many in the sacrament of marriage. In marriage, spouses publicly commit to a unique concern for each other's salvation. This ecclesial mission of spousal formation is not merely an obligation, but a sacramental and ecclesial sanctioning and support of spousal love, whose intimacy typically carries formative significance. Reflective of spousal intimacy and permanence, the apostolate of spousal formation is different from the task of a teacher or a spiritual director. Spouses form one another as permanent companions and equals rather than as temporary guides or superiors. The potential for spousal formation grows over the course of marriage as spouses get to know one another, struggle with each other's limitations, benefit from the security of a stable relationship, and understand that challenges from one's spouse come from within a broader and deeper context of love. This social and formative role specified by spousal love and sacramental marriage is one among many reasons why marriages between spouses unable to have children still express the social significance and internally social character of the family.[59]

58 In his 1891 encyclical letter *Rerum Novarum*, Leo XIII proposes that the family is a unique location where one can change hearts. Protecting and supporting the foundationally formative character of the family and the stability that such formation requires is a central concern for Leo XIII permeating his discussion of private property, just wage, just working conditions, and socialism. Hanlon Rubio highlights Leo XIII's emphasis on family life as a location for virtue formation in *Family Ethics* (40–43).

59 Those spouses who do not become pregnant despite a desire for children still retain the ecclesial mission to perform concrete acts of love, build family community, and lovingly challenge their spouse to grow. See, for example, Second Vatican Council, *Gaudium et Spes* (50).

The familial social mission that receives the most prominence in the Christian tradition, and speaks most directly to the social role and responsibility of family life, is the spousal mission to have and raise children.[60] This social mission reflects the very nature of the institution of marriage and married love, since marriage and spousal love are "ordered to the procreation and education of the offspring and it is in them that it finds its crowning glory."[61]

This social mission, so necessary for the existence and functioning of society, is clarified and in some ways elevated in the Christian faith. One can see more clearly the essential connection between conjugal union and procreation when one sees that at an even more fundamental level, love is fruitful.[62] God's love overflows into creation. Through appreciation of creation and participation in the grace of redemption, spousal love committed in marriage is morally and spiritually fruitful for the spouses. Procreation is a participation in the loving fruitfulness of creation and in the loving fruitfulness of a spousal love committed in marriage. The begetting of new life actualizes the fruitfulness of spousal love but also, and more fundamentally, involves a divine intervention in which God creates a human soul out of nothing. In procreation, God invites spouses to participate in an action that only God can perform, namely, creation. The procreation of children is no mere duty or obligation but a great honor and an ecclesial mission.[63] Children are entrusted to parents by God through procreation, and through infant baptism the mission to raise children is sanctioned by the Church and ratified by the parents. This mission requires much more than joining egg and sperm. Through their marital promises and their choice to unite sexually, spouses commit to the ecclesial mission of raising children in a community of love.

The ecclesial apostolate to form children reflects and emphasizes the need for the stability of marriage. The bishops of the Second Vatican Coun-

60 Florence Caffrey Bourg provides a collection of magisterial statements highlighting the family's educational role in *Where Two or Three Are Gathered: Christian Families as Domestic Churches* (Notre Dame, IN: University of Notre Dame Press, 2004), 43–45.

61 Second Vatican Council, *Gaudium et Spes*, 48, in Flannery, *Vatican Council II*, 950; see also *Gaudium et Spes*, 50.

62 Francis highlights the need to expand notions of marital fertility; see *Amoris Laetitia* (80, 165, 184).

63 Janet Smith convincingly argues in her commentary on *Gaudium et Spes* and *Humanae Vitae* that parenting is better understood as a mission than a duty; see especially Janet Smith, *Humanae Vitae: A Generation Later* (Washington, DC: The Catholic University of America Press, 1991), 136–40.

cil note that although marriage receives its stability from a human act, after consent is given, the marriage no longer depends on human decision alone, precisely because it involves a commitment to the good of one's partner and children and to the good of society.[64] Francis proposes that the indissolubility of marriage "should not be viewed as a 'yoke' imposed on humanity, but as a 'gift' granted to those who are joined in marriage."[65] In the context of a stable family, spouses and children develop their social identity in relation to their family community, they develop trust in others, and they can take healthy risks knowing that their family unit remains a supportive foundation. One must work through the challenge of family community because one's parents, siblings, and children will be there again tomorrow and the next day.

The ecclesial apostolate to form children also highlights the fundamental character of parent-child relationships and the foundational experiences of early childhood. As with spousal relationships, parent-child relationships often involve an intimacy that lends itself to formative influence. Social scientists verify the conventional wisdom highlighting the importance of parent-child relationships.[66] Perhaps one sees this insight most clearly when something goes wrong with a child. If a child is acting out or struggling with psychological illness, others want to know about the family situation and the relationships shared between the child and his parents. Parents, whether they realize it or not, speak to the origins of their children. Insofar

64 Second Vatican Council, *Gaudium et Spes*, 48, in Flannery, *Vatican Council II*, 950; for more discussion on why marriage is more than a personal choice, see Cahill, *Family* (133). John Paul II also argues that in addition to the good of children, indissolubility is crucial because the family is a sign of the faithful love of God. *Familiaris Consortio*, 20. Sociological research highlights the central role that stable family relations have on childhood development. Hanlon Rubio cites studies highlighting the negative impact of divorce on children. *Family Ethics*, 18. Cahill cites studies highlighting the negative impact of single parents and absent fathers at *Family* (112), citing Sara McLanahan and Gary Sandefur, *Growing Up with a Single Parent: What Hurts, What Helps* (Cambridge, MA: Harvard University Press, 1994), 38.

65 *Amoris Laetitia*, 62. Francis is quoting from Synod of Bishops, Third Extraordinary General Assembly, *Relatio Synodi* (October 18, 2014), 14. See also *Amoris Laetitia* (205), where Francis writes that marriage "benefits children by offering them the best context for their growth and development."

66 See, for example, Samuel Essler, Natalie Christner, and Markus Paulus, "Longitudinal Relations between Parental Strain, Parent-Child Relationship Quality, and Child Well-Being during the Unfolding COVID-19 Pandemic," *Child Psychiatry and Human Development* 52 (August 2021): 995–1011; Elizabeth Votruba-Drzal and Eric Dearing, eds., *The Wiley Handbook of Early Childhood Development Programs, Practices, and Policies* (Malden, MA: John Wiley and Sons, 2017), chapters 5–7; and Nicole Letourneau and Martha Hart, *Parenting and Child Development: Issues and Answers* (East Sussex, UK: Waterside, 2020).

as parents love their children before such love can be earned, parents reflect for their children God's gift of love.[67] Francis states it well, "A person's affective and ethical development is ultimately grounded in a particular experience, namely, that his or her parents can be trusted. This means that parents, as educators, are responsible, by their affection and example, for instilling in their children trust and loving respect."[68] Trust and loving respect open the child to developing relationships with others and with God.

Both fathers and mothers contribute to instilling trust and loving respect in their child. Parents who live together in marriage show through their relationship with one another "the value of reciprocity, of respect for differences and of being able to give and take."[69] In their commitment to one another, spouses present a model for the possibilities of married life.[70] One can recognize the need for the father's presence while also maintaining the unique role that mothers play in the early months of life.[71] The capacity of women to become pregnant and breastfeed their children does not imply that fathers should be absent from their children or that society and culture should limit a woman's social role to being a wife and mother. Building on the work of the Second Vatican Council, both John Paul II and Francis express concern about social and cultural tendencies that have limited a woman's role to wife and mother. John Paul II speaks against discrimination toward childless wives, widows, separated or divorced women, and unmarried mothers, and he calls for vigorous pastoral care to overcome this discrimination.[72] Francis further argues that gender does not imply certain roles.[73] He writes,

> It is possible, for example, that a husband's way of being masculine can be flexibly adapted to the wife's work schedule. Taking on domestic chores or some aspects of raising children does not make him any less masculine or imply failure, irresponsibility or cause for shame. Children have to be

67 Francis, *Amoris Laetitia*, 166. Francis is quoting from his Catechesis of February 11, 2015.

68 Francis, *Amoris Laetitia*, 263; see also 172.

69 Francis, 172.

70 Francis, 208.

71 Second Vatican Council, *Gaudium et Spes*, 52, in Flannery, *Vatican Council II*, 956; John Paul II writes at *Familiaris Consortio* (25) that the presence of the father is irreplaceable; see also, Francis, *Amoris Laetitia*, 55, 175.

72 John Paul II, *Familiaris Consortio*, 23.

73 Francis, *Amoris Laetitia*, 175. See also McCarthy, *Sex and Love in the Home*, chap. 9.

> helped to accept as normal such healthy "exchanges" which do not diminish the dignity of the father figure. A rigid approach turns into an overaccentuation of the masculine or feminine, and does not help children and young people to appreciate the genuine reciprocity incarnate in the real conditions of matrimony. Such rigidity, in turn, can hinder the development of an individual's abilities, to the point of leading him or her to think, for example, that it is not really masculine to cultivate art or dance, or not very feminine to exercise leadership.[74]

Gaudium et Spes, John Paul II, and Francis thus emphasize that the social importance of motherhood should not thwart women's legitimate social advancement or prevent women from adequate access to public functions.[75]

Part of the tension between valuing motherhood and providing social opportunities for women is diffused when one recognizes parenthood as serving a social role rather than a socially detached role.[76] One need not contrast a private, socially detached motherhood with social opportunities for women. Rather, recognizing the social role of motherhood (and fatherhood) should allow for integration of rather than an opposition between "private" family life and public life. Many parents experience that their children open up new opportunities and motivations for friendships, communal living, civic engagement, political action, and religious engagement. Indeed, it is even a common complaint in many churches that social activities revolve so much around families with children that people in other states of life feel marginalized. While parenthood should never serve as a litmus test for other social roles, neither should it be socially dismissed or viewed as a social negative. The tasks and skills necessary for parenting develop vital social virtues.

One of the reasons why parent-child relationships are fundamental is that children interact with their parents during the impressionable first experiences of early childhood.[77] As Francis writes, "Certain inclinations

74 Francis, *Amoris Laetitia*, 286.

75 Second Vatican Council, *Gaudium et Spes*, 52, in Flannery, *Vatican Council II*, 956; John Paul II, *Familiaris Consortio*, 23.

76 Drawing on Christopher Lasch's *Haven in a Heartless World*, McCarthy highlights in *Sex and Love in the Home* (186) that housekeeping in the late nineteenth and early twentieth centuries was intensely social.

77 See, for example, Proverbs 22:6: "Train a boy in the way he should go; even when he is old, he will not swerve from it." See also Aristotle, *The Nicomachean Ethics*, trans. David Ross (Oxford: Oxford University Press, 1998), I. 4, pp. 5–6.

develop in childhood and become so deeply rooted that they remain throughout life, either as attractions to a particular value or a natural repugnance to certain ways of acting."[78] Psychologists and cultural wisdom highlight the fundamental importance of family history and family wounds.[79]

Nonetheless, although the foundational character of early childhood is broadly recognized, this formation, like the social importance of family life, is an insight often highlighted and then overlooked. C. S. Lewis opens *The Abolition of Man* with "I doubt whether we are sufficiently attentive to the importance of elementary text-books."[80] Since early experiences are foundational, should we not dedicate effort and resources to early formation and honor those who care for young children? Since early experiences are vitally important, the souls of individuals and the future of society are in the hands of parents, daycare providers, and elementary school teachers.

In *Amoris Laetitia*, Francis dedicates a full chapter to rearing children.[81] He encourages parents to be patient, to be attentive to their child's journey, to allow their children to surprise them, to cultivate trust, to allow children to learn for themselves, to encourage children to say please and thank you, to show appreciation for their children, to discipline but not to discourage, to propose small steps, to guide children in use of social media and in making prudent economic decisions, and to find age-appropriate ways to teach children about their sexuality.[82] Francis provides an invitation for further reflection and emphasis on the formative years of childhood.

The responsibility to care for children in their formative years falls not exclusively but primarily on parents.[83] As baptized Christians who

78 Francis, *Amoris Laetitia*, 274.

79 See, for example, Glenn R. Schiraldi, The *Adverse Childhood Experiences Recovery Workbook* (Oakland: New Harbinger Publications, 2021), chaps. 1–3.

80 C. S. Lewis, *The Abolition of Man* (New York: Macmillan, 1947), 13.

81 Francis writes, "Since the educational role of families is so important, and increasingly complex, I would like to discuss it in detail." Francis, *Amoris Laetitia*, 259.

82 Francis, 259–90.

83 Second Vatican Council, *Gaudium et Spes*, 48, in Flannery, *Vatican Council II*, 950–51. When Pius XI reflects on educating youth in his 1929 encyclical, *Divini Illius Magistri*, he draws from a surprising source:

> The Supreme Court of the United States of America, in a decision on an important controversy, declared that it is not in the competence of the State to fix any uniform standard of education by forcing children to receive instruction exclusively in public schools, and it bases its decision on the natural law: the child is not the mere creature of the State; those who nurture him and direct his destiny have the right coupled with the high duty, to educate him and prepare him for the fulfillment of his obligations.

have specified their commitment of faith to be open to having and raising children through their marriage vows, who have renewed that commitment through the parental promises at infant baptism, who speak to the origin of the child as co-creators through their sexual union, who maintain intimate relationships with their children, and who care for or are present to children in the formative years, parents have the primary responsibility to form their children.[84] The stability of parent-child relationships also allows parents to draw on the child's personal history to guide the child forward.[85]

Since parental responsibility to form children extends to faith formation, parents exercise a crucial formative mission for the Church.[86] Mitch and Kathy Finley reflect on the implications of this mission by suggesting that formation in parenting is like developing proficiency in "practical ministerial skills."[87] Parents are called to show children that the foundation of life is goodness and love.[88] Like missionaries evangelizing the unchurched, parents often offer the first presentation of faith to their children. Parents have the delicate challenge of presenting the faith in the native language of their children. This requires more than bringing their children to Mass on Sundays. Parents must teach their children to recognize God's presence and

---

(Pius XI, Encyclical Letter *Divini Illius Magistri*, 37 [December 31, 1929], citing the US Supreme Court decision in the *Oregon School Case*, June 1, 1925)

The decision in the *Oregon School Case* highlights not only the right but also the high responsibility that parents have to educate their children. See also Pius XI, *Divini Illius Magistri*, 34; Code of Canon Law, 793, 1136. See https://www.vatican.va/archive/cod-iuris-canonici/cic_ index_ en.html.

84 John Paul II affirms that "since parents have conferred life on their children, they have a most solemn obligation to educate their offspring." *Familiaris Consortio*, 36. This is a direct quote from Vatican II's Declaration on Christian Education *Gravissimum Educationis* (October 28, 1965), 3; see also Francis, *Amoris Laetitia*, 16.

85 Bourg, *Where Two or Three are Gathered*, 124.

86 John Paul II speaks of the parental education of children as an ecclesial mission and a ministry through which the Gospel is radiated. *Familiaris Consortio*, 38–39; see also 21, where the pope speaks of forming children as a ministry of service, and his "Letter to Families" (February 2, 1994), 16. Lisa Sowle Cahill provides a similar insight from Martin Luther: "Married people 'can do no better work and do nothing more valuable either for God, for Christendom, for all the world, for themselves, and for their children than to bring up their children well.'" *Family*, 65; reference from Luther, "Sermon on the Estate of Marriage."

87 Mitch Finley and Kathy Finley, *Christian Families in the Real World: Reflections on a Spirituality for the Domestic Church* (Chicago: The Thomas More Press, 1984), 80.

88 John Paul II proposes that parents are called to be a visible sign of God's love to their children in *Familiaris Consortio* (14).

to accompany their children as they seek to identify and respond to God's call. They introduce their children to the community of faith. They provide the child's first encounters with prayer. They answer probing questions from children who are naturally curious and uninhibited about God and the supernatural realm. Since a significant part of child formation occurs through the child imitating his parents, parents provide an important ministry of witness as well. Beyond promoting positive foundational experiences, parents also are called to journey with and guide their children to help them grow and mature in their faith.

John Paul II writes that parents should present all of the topics necessary for their children's gradual Christian maturation.[89] Among other things, this requires that parents form their children in the social responsibilities of the Christian faith.[90] The family is a school of social virtue and social living.[91] In the social community of the family, children learn how to interact with others.[92] They also should discover in the witness and invitation of their parents the need to participate in civil society, and especially to care for the poor.[93]

To properly see the ecclesial and social mission of education and formation, parents need to move beyond seeing their family as an isolated refuge from the broader society. Education and formation involve challenges and struggles and require time. If these challenges do not fit into the affective refuge model, parents might be inclined to hire out the education and formation of their children. They might withdraw from the process of formation, thinking that the parish will form their children through religious education or Catholic school, or they might let the teachers, peers, and coaches in a public school system form their children. However, even though parents need support from the broader community in educating their children, they should not excuse themselves from their educational responsibilities. Perhaps, more accurately, parents cannot excuse themselves from forming their children. As Francis writes, "Parents always influence the moral development of their children, for better or for

89 John Paul II, 39.

90 Pius XI, *Divini Illius Magistri*, 36; John Paul II, *Familiaris Consortio*, 2, 36; the latter of these sections quotes from Second Vatican Council, *Gravissimum Educationis* (3); see also *Gravissimum Educationis*, 1.

91 John Paul II, *Familiaris Consortio*, 37, 42; see also Francis, *Amoris Laetitia*, 195.

92 John Paul II, *Familiaris Consortio*, 2, 60; see also Francis, *Amoris Laetitia*, 195.

93 John Paul II, *Familiaris Consortio*, 37; see also Cahill, *Family*, 55–56.

worse."[94] Since parents speak to the origin and identity of a child, they necessarily form their children, even by their absence when they do not interact with their children at all.

In living out the ecclesial mission to form children, parents find themselves both the evangelizers and the evangelized. Highlighting the responsibilities of children to parents, John Paul II writes that children contribute love, respect, and obedience.[95] Small children often inspire parents with their faith and their innocence. They believe what they do not see, and they move on quickly from their wrongdoings. Francis praises the humility, trust, and spontaneity of children.[96] In their impressionable stages, children often act like a mirror revealing to their parents the kinds of values and commitments parents are modeling to their children. Examining the opposite side of John Paul II's insight, I propose that children also contribute to their parents' growth through their selfishness, disrespect, and disobedience. Children challenge their parents to grow through the struggles they bring, the opposition they offer, and the conflict that they generate as siblings.[97] While children often have an inspiring purity and innocence, the Church also reminds us that children struggle with the effects and the allure of sin. Parents grow as disciples and as teachers as they face the unexpected, everyday challenges that community with their children brings.

Parents and children also form one another through the process of aging and dying. Both parent and child discover anew through this process that parents, who are foundational for their children, also are "vulnerable and dependent."[98] In aging and death, both children and parents can witness to a human dignity that goes beyond personal autonomy and social contributions.[99] Respect and care for the elderly flow from human dignity but

94 Francis, *Amoris Laetitia*, 259. See also Second Vatican Council, *Gravissimum Educationis* (3), which affirms that "parents must be acknowledged as the first and foremost educators of their children. Their role as educators is so decisive that scarcely anything can compensate for their failure in it." This quotation also appears in John Paul II, *Familiaris Consortio* (36).

95 John Paul II, *Familiaris Consortio*, 21; see also *Amoris Laetitia* (17), where Francis connects the responsibility of children toward their parents to the Fourth Commandment.

96 Francis, *Amoris Laetitia*, 18.

97 Francis writes in *Amoris Laetitia* (315): "Living in a family makes it hard for us to feign or lie; we cannot hide behind a mask." Of course, today family members are more likely to try to hide behind a screen, so to speak, by disengaging from one another to interact with media and social media.

98 Francis, 48.

99 Something similar could be said about care for siblings. Francis writes that "having siblings provides opportunities to learn how to help and care for others." *Amoris Laetitia*, 195.

also gratitude and historical consciousness. Care for the elderly, especially one's parents, honors parents for being co-creators with God and for the sacrifices they have made throughout their lives for their children's well-being. It is no surprise that societies influenced by the social contract theory of marriage and the private refuge view of families struggle with humane care for the elderly, and pressure builds for assisted suicide and euthanasia. Beyond the time and effort that families contribute to caring for the elderly, which makes a real impact on the social welfare of a society, there is a spill-over effect in the culture from caring families to a general reverence for the elderly and the dignity of the human person.

Care for the elderly also serves the secondary but crucial role of bridging the generation gap.[100] The elderly form younger generations through their hard-earned wisdom and their historical memory. Francis observes:

> Very often it is grandparents who ensure that the most important values are passed down to their grandchildren, and 'many people can testify that they owe their initiation into the Christian life to their grandparents.' Their words, their affection or simply their presence help children to realize that history did not begin with them, that they are now part of an age-old pilgrimage and that they need to respect all that came before them.[101]

This generational memory provides both individuals and societies a context and location for their own challenges and struggles. Contrary to the social contract theory, which views each family as generated merely by personal choice, families who retain this historical memory allow communities to plan and grow because they know their starting point.

CONCLUSION

The family is internally social. At a basic level, this is self-evident. The family is a community and therefore internally social. Moreover, families are distinctly social in that family relationships transcend personal choices. Families also often involve intimate relationships. Spousal union, the bonds between mother and child naturally developed in pregnancy and nursing, the relationship between father and child, and the bonds among siblings tend to be familiar in addition to being familial. Since marriage unites differ-

100 Francis, 192.

101 Francis, 192; the internal quotation comes from Synod of Bishops, *Relatio Finalis* (18).

ent families, family relationships often are socially robust, involving various elements of social life. Family interactions rarely involve an experience of comfortable isolation; instead, they often challenge individuals to move beyond isolated autonomy.

While few challenge that families are internally social, the influence of social contract theory presents a compelling explanation for why the family's social character is so often overlooked or minimized. If marriage is merely a contract between two individuals seeking their self-fulfillment, then marriage will last only while it satisfies both individuals. Moreover, in social contract theory, children are merely a consumer option for spouses who think they might enjoy children. Parents bear only a passing responsibility to raise or form their children, tasks that might undermine the pursuit of individual fulfillment and which are assumed as much as possible by the state, especially through public schooling. Social contract theory thus challenges the family's internally social character but does so at great cost. Social contract theory fails to account for the enduring bonds of familial relationships and the great social good of having and raising children, and it ultimately leads to a breakdown in historical memory and care for the elderly as well.

While Jesus in the Gospels challenges individuals who would make their family community an idol, the Christian faith does not eliminate the family's social role but, rather, clarifies and enhances it. Because families are social, the social mission of the Christian faith applies, among other places, to interaction amidst one's family. Families are called in a unique way to form a community of love and thereby participate in and image the model of God's love within concrete life, as messy as it may be in a fallen world. Finally, family members have a unique mission of formation to help one another develop as humans and to grow closer to God, a mission that includes the mutual influence of spouses and the influence of children on their parents as well as the more obvious role of parents in the formation of their children. This ecclesial mission includes the responsibility to form one another in faith and in social virtues. Family members should model and guide in their treatment of one another how to live with justice and mercy.

Because the family's social role is foundational to human life and social analysis, I propose that social ethics and family ethics will greatly benefit from highlighting and applying the family's social role to various situations. Unfortunately, the family's social role is often mentioned but then overlooked in application. To overcome this challenge, two things are necessary.

First, one must clarify the social role of families. Second, one must demonstrate how the application of the family's social role enlightens and enriches ethical analysis. In this chapter, I have explored the first half of the first of those tasks, clarifying the meaning of the family's internally social character. I take up the question of clarifying and then applying the family's socially interdependent character in the second part of the book. In the remaining chapters of part one, I focus on applying the family's social character to family life, showing how Catholic social principles and the works of mercy illuminate everyday family interactions. The fruitfulness of this chapter's clarification, I believe, becomes evident in these applications. The call to image God in the family is shown not to be a stifling ideal far from the daily struggles of people today, but instead the path marked by mercy that allows each member of the family to grow and experience the gift of divine love.

2

Catholic Social Principles and Family Life

APPLICATION OF SOCIAL PRINCIPLES

One variation on the Church's claim that the family is a basic social unit is the formulation of *Apostolicam Actuositatem* that calls it "the primary vital cell of society."[1] This phrase suggests a biological metaphor—just as a living body is made up of various types of cells, so the "body politic" is constituted primarily by families of various sizes and shapes. Such a vision is in contrast with modern individualism, which tends to atomize society by regarding familial and other relationships as incidental, while the relationship between the individual and the person is fundamental. One danger of the metaphor, however, is that it can cause us to exaggerate the difference between sociality within the family (the intracellular relationships, as it were) and sociality between families (the intercellular relationships). Having clarified in the prior chapter that the family is internally social, the goal of this chapter will be to examine that internally social character.

To this end, in this chapter I illuminate interactions within the family by applying principles from Catholic social ethics that are usually only expounded at the level of the wider society. These social principles are a good place to start, as they are a central element of Catholic social ethics. They are specific enough to provide guidance but broad enough to allow application to varying situations. The most commonly cited principles are the dignity of the individual, the common good, subsidiarity, solidarity, preferential care for the poor, the dignity of work, and peace. These form the language and foundation by which Catholic social ethicists reason and debate. If families are indeed internally social, one would expect these principles to apply to family interactions.

1 Second Vatican Council, Decree on the Apostolate of Lay People *Apostolicam Actuositatem* (November 18, 1965), 11, in *Vatican Council II: The Conciliar and Post Conciliar Documents*, ed. Austin Flannery, rev. ed. (Collegeville, MN: Liturgical Press, 1984), 779.

While the application of social principles to the family is not typical in academic Catholic social ethics, in the last thirty years, with the resurgence of virtue ethics, some ethicists have highlighted the need to apply these ethics to everyday life.[2] The growth of virtue ethics has led to debates among social ethicists concerning the most effective way to implement Catholic social ethics in order to transform society: changes to the social structure or virtue formation in local communities. While I focus on family interactions, I am not thereby siding with virtue formation over social structures. Attentiveness to virtue formation and social structures are both essential for social ethics. Formation without just structures leaves virtuous individuals few opportunities to act out their good habits. A manager who was well formed in her upbringing may want to pay her coworkers a living wage but may be prevented from doing so by company policy. A single father who desires to provide for his children through gainful employment will struggle to do so if getting a job means receiving less compensation than welfare benefits would provide.

On the reverse side, Catholic social ethics risks becoming armchair analysis or pub talk if application focuses only on what business and political leaders should do, especially if those business and political leaders have been raised in a culture that prioritizes self-seeking competition.

Different moments and different personal callings will require different emphases on social structures or virtue formation. I want to make an appeal to those inclined to focus on social structures to see that if the family is internally social, then Catholic social principles have application to family life as well. I also want to make an appeal to those focused on virtue formation in local communities to see how Catholic social principles provide an invaluable resource for everyday family interactions and therefore assist virtue formation.

If audiences are to understand and live out Catholic social ethics, social ethicists need to provide moral analysis that illuminates daily challenges, and for many, family interactions are a key location of those challenges. One will miss this realm of Catholic social ethics if one limits social analysis to

2 For a discussion on the recent increase in attention to virtue, see David Cloutier and William C. Mattison III, "The Resurgence of Virtue in Recent Moral Theology," *Journal of Moral Theology* 3, no. 1 (January 2014): 228–59. For examples of moral theologians reflecting on concrete, everyday challenges, see Julie Hanlon Rubio, *Family Ethics: Practices for Christians* (Washington, DC: Georgetown University Press, 2010) and Florence Caffrey Bourg, *Where Two or Three Are Gathered: Christian Families as Domestic Churches* (Notre Dame, IN: University of Notre Dame Press, 2004).

social structures and defines the family as private and socially isolated. Moral theologians and committed Christians have many good reasons to reflect on how Catholic social principles apply to family life. The most fundamental reason is that the well-being of the family depends on the insights contained in those principles. Many ethical dilemmas facing individuals involve interactions with family members. Since the family is a social community, Catholic social principles provide a rich resource that illuminates family relationships.

For example, human dignity reminds individuals to show care for a whining two-year-old, a grandparent who is losing mental and physical capacities, a socially awkward sibling, an argumentative teenager, or a self-serving cousin. The common good provides individuals with a language to understand the need to complete household chores even if they do not receive a direct personal benefit from their work. Subsidiarity clarifies how parents help their kids dress themselves and informs how to assist family members who often lose things or struggle with addiction. Solidarity informs the need to stay in contact with family members, especially when they are struggling or disagreeable. Dignity of work informs how to respond to a six-year-old who wants to help make supper, or how individuals value household labor and employment for financial compensation. Preferential care for the poor informs how to care for family members who are ill, little, ignorant, or not successful or efficient at certain tasks. Peace informs how to handle disagreements between spouses, unwanted interventions from parents, or violence between siblings.

Society and social ministry also benefit from an application of the social principles to everyday family life. The formation of family members in social virtues overflows into society. If individuals are not able to see the need to care for family members in their poverty and vulnerability, or they do not see the need to avoid violence in handling injustices in their families, then the Church will have little capacity to convince political and business leaders to implement the preferential care for the poor and peace in their executive decisions. Catholic social ethics would be a little less of a "secret" if parents formed children at a young age to think about the tradition's social principles in terms of their everyday lives. Moreover, family examples serve a pedagogical function. Household applications are broadly relatable and understandable. The principles are reinforced when individuals see them alive in their everyday interactions. Family applications do not establish a new understanding of social principles but can help overcome reductive approaches to the principles. The complexity of family life helps demonstrate the nuance of Catholic social principles for those learning them. The permanence of family relationships requires that one move beyond easy, short-term answers, and the pull between various loving familial relationships highlights the full demands of and need for discernment in applying the principles.

In this chapter, I will analyze two Catholic social principles—the dignity of work and peace—and show how they illuminate everyday family life. I have chosen work and peace for three reasons. First, these two principles are foundational in important ways. John Paul II writes in *Laborem Exercens* that "human work is a key, probably the essential key, to the whole social question."[3] Peace, on the other hand, frames the human telos. Second, these two principles provide crucial insights into fundamental family struggles that often remain hidden. Those operating out of an isolated family framework rarely give household work the respect it deserves. Violence and injustice frequently fester when they are kept hidden in a family. Third, and more practically, I cannot cover all of the social principles in one chapter and since I cover many of them in other chapters, I will limit myself to these two here. For each principle, I will highlight its central features and provide examples of how it illuminates specific family interactions.

THE DIGNITY OF WORK AND HOUSEHOLD LABOR

Family life has held a central place in the Catholic social tradition's discussion of work. In *Rerum Novarum*, Leo XIII persistently roots his critique of harsh working conditions in his concern for the family. He notes how long working hours, child labor, and socialism prevent parents from raising their children well.[4] He highlights that wages should allow workers to provide for their families and that workmen's associations should provide for widows and orphans.[5] Labor practices have a dramatic impact on family life, for good and for ill. A job supports family life when it pays a family

3 John Paul II, Encyclical Letter *Laborem Exercens* (September 14, 1981), 3, in *Catholic Social Thought: The Documentary History*, ed. David J. O'Brien and Thomas A. Shannon, rev. ed. (Maryknoll, NY: Orbis Books, 2016), 381.

4 Leo XIII, Encyclical Letter *Rerum Novarum* (May 15, 1891), 9–11, 29, 33, in *Catholic Social Thought: The Documentary Heritage*, ed. David O'Brien and Thomas A. Shannon, rev. ed. (Maryknoll, NY: Orbis Books, 2016), 18–19, 28–29, 31. Note that there are various editions of *Rerum Novarum* and that the manner for numbering sections differs considerably between them.

5 Leo XIII, *Rerum Novarum*, 34, 36, 41, in O'Brien and Shannon, *Catholic Social Thought*, 31–36.

wage, allows workers to develop as people, and provides time off. By contrast, long hours, injustice in the workplace, and inadequate compensation can be devastating to family life.

In highlighting the internally social character of the family, however, my emphasis is on household work completed by family members. I propose that household labor is work. The present need to make this argument is somewhat unique in human history. For centuries, the home was the primary location of work. The term economy comes from the Greek *oikos*, meaning household. Only with industrialization in the eighteenth and nineteenth centuries did a separation between work and the home become widespread. Work began occurring more often in urban factories than the home, and working hours prevented laborers from engaging in work at home. Labor unions and labor rights legislation in many contexts have moderated working hours and given laborers some time for household work but have not overcome the lingering separation of work and the home.[6]

Many challenges and moral dilemmas of family life relate to household labor: How should parents balance work outside of the home with work inside of the home? Is each spouse doing his or her fair share around the house? How can we promote greater opportunities and equality for women in work outside of the home without undermining the honor due to men and women who focus on household labor? How can we cultivate a child's desire to work and contribute to the family community? When should we seek or accept assistance from others and when should we complete tasks on our own?

Since I am treating two principles in one chapter, my account of each can only be broad. The primary goal is to show how Catholic social principles enlighten family interactions, and so I do not seek to develop a definitive theology of work. The secondary goals are to show how family applications of social principles help to increase the relevance and influence of Catholic social ethics by highlighting the family's role in social formation, the pedagogical accessibility of family examples, and the nuance that comes from the family's social complexity and loving relationships.

It is possible to see how the Catholic tradition on work enlightens family life when one sees more clearly the nature of work and the crucial insight in the Catholic social tradition that work ought to develop the person. I will

6 Yves Simon, *Work, Society, and Culture*, ed. Vukan Kuic (New York: Fordham University Press, 1971), 77–83.

reflect on three features of work: work as an activity that earns money, work as fulfilling obligations, and work as human activity. Related to these three features, I will highlight central themes from the papal social encyclicals that develop a theology of work focusing on just wage, the development of the person in work, just working conditions, and worker associations. Then, I will apply this framework to specific questions related to household labor. What is a just wage for household labor? How do young children model how work can develop the person? Do individuals who focus on household labor endure unjust working conditions? What is the role of worker associations for household labor?

The word "work" can mean various things. One can speak of blue-collar and white-collar work, household work, a work of art, or the work of salvation. Since most perceived disagreements are truly misunderstandings, one does well to clarify one's use of the word "work" before beginning. Rather than provide a single definition of the word, I will provide three that I have synthesized from both the Catholic social encyclical tradition and from common uses of the term.

The first definition of work is activity aimed at financial gain. This category refers primarily to those who are contracted by an employer to complete some activity for financial compensation but also includes those who are self-employed. In this understanding of work, financial compensation motivates one's commitment to work. Even if the work is enjoyable (at least in some respects), one would not complete the work or at least not in the same way without the financial benefits that accrue from it. This seems to be the operational understanding of work when people ask questions like "What do you do for a living" or "Does your spouse work?" In other words, what do you do to provide for yourself and your family and does your spouse work outside of the home for financial compensation?

A "living wage" is an essential concept in the Catholic social tradition. The *Compendium of the Social Doctrine of the Church* proposes that "they commit grave injustice who refuse to pay a just wage or who do not give it in due time and in proportion to the work done."[7] John Paul II highlights the social significance of a just wage when he writes in *Laborem Exercens* that "a just wage is the concrete means of verifying the justice of the whole socioeconomic system and, in any case, of checking that it is functioning

7 Pontifical Council for Justice and Peace, *Compendium of the Social Doctrine of the Church* (Washington, DC: United States Conference of Catholic Bishops, 2005), 302.

justly."[8] If individuals cannot provide for their families through their full-time jobs, then they will need to work multiple jobs, rely on the generosity of others, or go without basic resources. In the Catholic social encyclical tradition, a living wage is compensation that allows a single-income family living frugally to provide for their needs and to save a little for security and property.[9] A living wage considers not only the dollar amount shown on one's paycheck and the local cost of living but also benefits like health insurance, disability insurance, retirement contributions, and others related to one's business, such as product discounts or stock options.

The reduction of work to financial gain, however, presents an impoverished account of labor. John Paul II calls this reduction "economism," which he notes is a form of materialism. Economism overlooks the personal dimensions of work. Rooting his reflections in Christ's work as a carpenter, John Paul II argues that the basis for determining the value of human work is "the fact that the one who is doing it is a person."[10] Especially in contexts where honor derives from wealth, a framework that limits work to financial benefit has significant impact on how one values (or disvalues) household labor. Since activities that aim to care for the house or children often do not carry explicit financial benefits, cleaning house, making food, washing dishes, folding laundry, and caring for children do not qualify as work in this framework. These activities are to be performed by those who are not able to do the allegedly "real" work of making money. Operating within a framework emphasizing financial gain, individuals may incorrectly think that gainful employment has greater importance and that those who make more money in the family therefore have greater dignity and should have greater authority over family matters. However, if work has dignity because of the dignity of the laborer, then household work, whether that be a father folding the laundry, a sweeping job done poorly by a nine-year-old, or a partially burnt meal cooked by a teenager, has dignity because the work is done by a human person.

Reducing work to financial gain leads to confusing contradictions. One provides a great social service if one runs a daycare for eight children, and

8 John Paul II, *Laborem Exercens*, 19, in O'Brien and Shannon, *Catholic Social Thought*, 406.

9 Leo XIII, *Rerum Novarum*, 4, 34–35, in O'Brien and Shannon, *Catholic Social Thought*, 15, 31–33.

10 John Paul II, *Laborem Exercens*, 6, in O'Brien and Shannon, *Catholic Social Thought*, 385. Leo XIII also highlights the work of Christ as a carpenter in *Rerum Novarum* (20), in O'Brien and Shannon, *Catholic Social Thought* (23).

if the daycare is financially successful, then one is publicly recognized as having marketable skills. Older siblings who receive money for providing part-time childcare or mowing lawns for other families likewise are providing a social service that demonstrates a strong work ethic. However, if a person cares for his own eight children or watches younger siblings or mows the lawn for his own family, then he is merely assisting a private, isolated family or, at best, developing skills that may be useful later in gainful employment. John Paul II observes that family members who "bear the daily burden and responsibility for their homes and the upbringing of their children" often work "without proper recognition on the part of society and even of their own families."[11] The reduction of work to financial gain is one reason among others for this lack of appreciation.

The second definition of work is activity for which one has a responsibility or an obligation to complete. This definition includes but also expands the first definition. In the context of gainful employment, work understood as obligation includes work that one feels responsible for completing even if it is not required by contract or necessary to receive one's paycheck. If work is the fulfillment of one's responsibilities, then household labor is a kind of work. Care for one's house and children often is work done out of obligation. Individual family members are responsible for providing shelter, food, and clothes for other family members. One makes a meal for the family, for example, not because the wages are great but because one feels responsible for providing food for one's spouse, children, or parents.

That household labor is a kind of work involves a rephrasing of the work-family balance question. In addition to obligations at one's place of employment, individuals also have responsibilities toward family members. If individuals perceive family life as a private refuge from work, they will be confused and frustrated in those times when family obligations are more exhausting than work done for gainful employment. The work-family discernment often is less a balance of work and nonwork and more a balancing of different kinds of work. Seeing household labor as work helps to explain the weariness that many parents experience. Accordingly, in seeing family responsibilities as work, one recognizes more clearly the need for leisure in one's life. Perpetual movement from one kind of work for which one is responsible to another kind of work is exhausting. Josef Pieper emphasizes the need for time and activity that go beyond both what one is

11 John Paul II, *Laborem Exercens*, 9, in O'Brien and Shannon, *Catholic Social Thought*.

obligated to complete and what has primarily a practical orientation. Even if one finds fulfillment in one's work, something new is added when one engages in an activity that one is not obligated to complete. One is truly free to engage in the endeavor for its own sake, expressing one's creativity and enjoying the process.[12]

The third definition is the broadest—work is human activity. John Paul II proposes in the preamble of *Laborem Exercens* that "work means any activity by man, whether manual or intellectual, whatever its nature or circumstances."[13] Work includes building a sidewalk, formulating legislation, participating in a meeting, and changing a diaper. If work involves all activity, then even prayer and liturgy involve a kind of work—a participation in Christ's salvific work.[14] Instead of arguing that one should not allow one's work to invade the Lord's Day, John Paul II takes a hopeful and evangelical approach to the relationship between work and prayer. He highlights the power of God and argues that the movement should go from prayer to work.[15] God's work should permeate the rest of the work week. In his meditations on the early chapters of Genesis, John Paul II proposes that the *imago Dei* relates to a call to work; that is, to subdue the earth.[16] In human work, the person encounters the gift of creation and can act as a co-creator with God. John Paul II, referencing *Gaudium et Spes*, proposes that "awareness that man's work is a participation in God's activity ought to permeate, as the Council teaches, even 'the most ordinary everyday activities.'"[17]

Two of the great insights of John Paul II's *Laborem Exercens* are that the dignity of work is rooted in the dignity of the worker and that work is

12 Josef Pieper, *Only the Lover Sings: Art and Contemplation*, trans. Lothar Krauth (San Francisco: Ignatius Press, 1990), 19–27; see also Josef Pieper, *Leisure: The Basis of Culture*, trans. Gerald Malsbary (South Bend, IN: St. Augustine's Press, 1998).

13 John Paul II, *Laborem Exercens*, preamble, in O'Brien and Shannon, *Catholic Social Thought*, 378.

14 John Paul II, *Laborem Exercens*, 27, in O'Brien and Shannon, *Catholic Social Thought*, 417–18.

15 John Paul II, *Laborem Exercens*, 25, in O'Brien and Shannon, *Catholic Social Thought*, 413–14.

16 John Paul II, *Laborem Exercens*, preamble, in O'Brien and Shannon, *Catholic Social Thought*, 378. The theme of subduing the earth permeates the encyclical.

17 John Paul II, *Laborem Exercens*, 25; the internal quotation is from Second Vatican Council, Pastoral Constitution on the Modern World *Gaudium et Spes*, 34, in *Vatican Council II: The Conciliar and Post Conciliar Documents*, ed. Austin Flannery, rev. ed. (Collegeville, MN: Liturgical Press, 1975).

essential to the human person.[18] While recognizing that work in a fallen world inevitably involves toil and noting that work should allow one to provide for one's family, John Paul II also presents a vision in which work authentically develops the person. In one's work, one can learn new insights, cultivate new skills, exercise human agency, offer input on the best way to do things, provide services to society, foster a community of persons, express gratitude for the gift of creation, and participate in the sanctification of the world. The opportunity to develop one's person through one's work is crucial since many individuals spend most of their lives working in some capacity.

To protect the dignity of the worker and to organize work with the person's development in mind, the Catholic social tradition has argued for just working conditions. First, the working conditions should be safe. The air should be clean to breathe and safety precautions should be available to minimize physical dangers. Individual workers should have protocols to report and address harassment and abuse. Furthermore, working hours should be appropriate to the nature of the work and the capacity of the worker, allowing the worker time for prayer, family, and leisure. Workers should receive adequate breaks.

In developing the person, the workplace also should provide an environment for cultivating relationships between coworkers. The Catholic vision for worker associations is a community that gathers for collective bargaining, sharing fellowship, sharing best practices, and providing aid in times of need. Collective bargaining highlights the vulnerability that many wage-earners experience when they are agreeing to a work contract with their employer. By joining with other workers in an association, the community of workers has stronger negotiating power to insist on a living wage and just working conditions. Collective bargaining is attentive to the ways that power dynamics contribute to injustices. Justice and the common good should form the framework for analyzing the negotiating power of workers.[19] The association is attentive to issues of power insofar as they relate to the association's pursuit of justice in the workplace. The focus is to cultivate a just community of workers, not to increase the self-serving power of one group over another.

18 John Paul II sets out this theme in the opening chapters of *Laborem Exercens* and returns to the insight as a foundation for various ethical claims throughout the encyclical. In his encyclical letter *Veritatis Splendor* John Paul II lists refining and developing the riches of the material world and contemplating beauty, along with the natural inclinations highlighted in Thomas Aquinas's account of the natural law. John Paul II, Encyclical Letter *Veritatis Splendor* (August 6, 1993), 52.

19 John Paul II, *Laborem Exercens*, 20, in O'Brien and Shannon, *Catholic Social Thought*, 408–9.

Beyond collective bargaining, worker associations should cultivate a community of persons in which coworkers develop friendships through their common work and their pursuit of shared goals. Coworkers should assist one another so that together they can more effectively serve the community. Accordingly, workers should cultivate their trade by collaborating with one another about effective methods and providing training for those in need. As a community of workers, individuals also should temporarily accept extra responsibilities to assist other workers who are ill or need to care for or grieve the loss of family or friends.

Just Wage and Household Labor

If everyday family activities are a kind of work and work demands a living wage, does that mean that one needs to provide wages for every household activity completed? No. Distributive justice involves the distribution of resources from the group to individuals based on their proportion of need in addition to their contribution. A two-year-old does not need to earn his room and board through his household labor. Individuals have a responsibility to provide food, shelter, and basic medical care for their children and parents regardless of how well the children and parents contribute to household work. Moreover, since the dignity of work is rooted in the human person, and not financial gain, work is not limited to financial benefit. Individuals have responsibilities toward their children and parents, for example, that go beyond financial considerations.

By rooting one's reflections on work in the dignity of the person, one can show respect for all work, including household work, in a variety of ways that go beyond financial compensation. The community can express gratitude for household work, make sure laborers have the tools and resources to complete their work well, refrain from adding unnecessarily to the work that is required, honor the input of those who know the concrete demands of particular tasks, demonstrate the worthiness of the work by contributing to household work when possible, and fill in to provide breaks and support, especially in times of difficulty. Financial compensation, however, is one way among others to show respect for the dignity and importance of household labor. Distributive justice does, after all, consider proportionate contributions in addition to needs. Parents might take their children out to eat or provide a dessert after a long day of spring cleaning. Grandparents who provide childcare, or older children who do more than their fair share of household work or help with the family business, might justly deserve financial compensation.

Often, one spouse sacrifices her career for the sake of her spouse's career or to focus on care of the household. If the surrounding culture roots dignity in the public status of one's employment or the wages one receives, then those who focus on household work, especially when that work is defined as socially detached and often seems to include mindless duties, may question the significance of their work. Society and their families may fail, if not in theory, then in application, to recognize the significance of their work.[20] How does one respond to the challenges that often face those whose work focuses on household labor? One approach to this dilemma has been to accept without question the position that work has value only insofar as it is public, powerful, and profitable. According to this mindset, one might conclude that household work is only for those who are forced to do it, and that consequently one should avoid pregnancy because the demands of caring for children will sap one's mind and social status.

Another approach is to highlight the financial value of household work. Such work may not generate income, but it certainly lowers expenses. In a context that highlights finances, one could honor household work by attempting to calculate how much it would cost to hire out the household labor that family members complete. If one adds up the value of childcare, grocery shopping, cooking, washing dishes, laundry, cleaning house, mowing the lawn, landscaping, home maintenance and repair, tutoring, budgeting, financial planning, purchasing, and social planning, one quickly realizes the financial savings generated by household labor. Moreover, these activities allow other family members to work for financial compensation outside of the home. One way to recognize these financial contributions is to offer both indirect and direct financial compensation.

Considerations pertaining to a living wage for work outside of the home have indirect implications for those who focus on household labor. The income-earning spouse should receive adequate wages so that the other spouse can stay home to care for children and home if they desire to do so. Rather than receive a weekly wage, spouses who focus on household work should have access to the family's financial resources so they can meet their living expenses and healthcare needs, spend on professional development, and have opportunities for recreation and leisure. In many situations, the

20 John Paul II, *Laborem Exercens*, 9.

individual who focuses on household labor will be best positioned to exercise control over the family finances. They will understand the financial needs of the family, and they are just as likely to be competent in financial planning as those working outside of the home. Another way of manifesting financially the contributions of those focused on household labor is direct payment into a distinct account or to direct elective retirement contributions in the name of family members who have reduced the amount of their out-of-home work to focus on care of the household.

Limiting work to financial benefit, however, does not provide the full picture of household labor. While buying groceries and cooking a meal rather than eating out often dramatically decreases one's food bill, providing a meal to share at the table in one's home produces more benefits than simply saving money. One can share the joy of cooking with one's brother or tailor a meal for one's diabetic father. One need not worry about finding a parking spot or conversations that others might overhear. A teenager who is busy studying for exams can just show up, enjoy a meal and fellowship, and then return to work. Most household work bears significance beyond financial consideration and cannot be outsourced without significant loss: a mother's kiss goodnight to her child, washing the car with one's sister, a homemade card from a child, a surprise visit from an aunt, or a grandchild helping in the garden are activities that enhance the family community well beyond financial concerns. These actions enhance the communion of persons that is a family and thereby enhance the lives of each of its members. Because the family plays a central and foundational role in the formation of individual members, household labor, especially care for other family members, is one of the most formative and influential forms of work, even when no exchange of money occurs.

Child Development and Household Labor

If to be human is to work, then even young children are workers. In fact, children often serve as a strong reminder that work's dignity is rooted in the person working rather than the efficiency of the work. Children seek out household labor in order to develop skills, share fellowship, or enjoy the creative process. Maria Montessori observes that the concept of developing one's person through work is profoundly and beautifully on display in the first years of a child's life. Montessori marvels at the linguistic, mental, psychic, and physical growth that occurs in these first years: "For us, it is very difficult to conceive of the infant's mental power, but there can be no doubt how privileged it is."[21] Montessori proposes a revolution in which culture recognizes that the child is a "toiler" and that "the aim of his work is to make a man."[22] An infant absorbs the world in an unconscious but intelligent manner, and then through play and work makes those experiences conscious. Accordingly, Montessori stresses the importance of understanding childhood development and providing an environment that allows the child to cultivate their skills.[23]

Whereas in business, the development of laborers is one goal alongside maintaining financial sustainability and providing service to society, the primary focus of child labor in the home is personal development. Infants lie on their backs and do amazing ab workouts in preparation for rolling, crawling, and sitting. Toddlers put things in rows when they are learning about order and transfer objects from one container to another when they are working on small motor skills. When they are not otherwise distracted, small children often want to join their parents in housework. They want to help sweep the floor (or at least they like the idea of swinging a broom at dust and food on the floor). They want to rake leaves, mix ingredients, harvest fruits and vegetables, chop food with sharp knives, and sort laundry. This work relates to a skill or an identity they are trying to develop. They are exploring cause and effect, or developing fine hand motor skills, or demonstrating that they are getting bigger, more independent, and more responsible.

In addition to developing skills, small children also seek the fellowship and creative dimensions of work. I recall one time putting together wooden train tracks with my three-year- old son. He wanted a track with bridges and tunnels. I did not think he had the dexterity or patience to complete his vision and so I built it as quickly as I could so we could play with the completed track. As soon as I finished the first track, he wanted another, more complicated one. After the third track, I was weary and frustrated. Then, with some guidance from my wife, I realized that our son was more focused on enjoying the creativity and fellowship of the process than on having a completed track. When I approached the task with that same spirit, an activity that was a source of great frustration became an activity of great

21 Maria Montessori, *The Absorbent Mind*, trans. Claude A. Claremont (New York: Holt, Rinehart, and Winston, 1967), 26.

22 Montessori, 16–17.

23 Montessori, 8.

joy and creativity. The Catholic social tradition, which highlights human development, fellowship, and the creativity of work, gave my wife and me the language and clarity to fruitfully analyze what was happening. My son was observing my movements like an apprentice so he could replicate them in the future. He also enjoyed the fellowship of building with his father and the creativity involved in the process. I had taught in the classroom that efficiency is necessary but not sufficient in the workplace, but my young son taught me the need to move from theory to praxis. While I conceptually understood the theology of work, in practice I defaulted to my own formation and habits, which tended to reduce work to efficiency. Work can be more than efficiency. In addition to completing one's work diligently, one can enjoy fellowship with coworkers, students, and customers, and enjoy the cultivation of one's trade and the creative process of completing a job.

Household Labor and Just Working Conditions

The struggles of household labor are varied. Often, women disproportionately endure these burdens. Some women live in communities that highlight a woman's ability to nurture and be empathetic and overlook her capacity to reason and lead. In these contexts, women often lack access to education, financial resources, and opportunities for gainful employment that reflect their skills, interests, and personal discernment. Their social value is dependent on whether they marry, have children, and perform household labor well. They often suffer harassment and abuse. Other women live in communities that highlight the value of gainful employment and do not provide women resources for acknowledging and grieving the loss of time with child and home, or do not support those who choose to focus on the care of home and child. Others participate in a community of faith that describes motherhood vocationally but does not provide sufficient social support to overcome cultural tendencies downplaying the significance of household labor (associating value with public service and income) and does not provide a means to acknowledge and grieve the loss of gainful employment in which one can contribute to society, cultivate friendships with other adults, and receive a sense of public worth and approval.[24]

24 Mary Ellen Konieczny interviews mothers in two Chicago parishes, listening to their experiences of motherhood and analyzing how those articulations related to religious conceptions of motherhood in their faith communities. See especially her chapter on work in *The Spirit's Tether: Family, Work, and Religion among American Catholics* (New York: Oxford University Press, 2013), 184–233.

One could make parallel observations for fathers, grandparents, and children. Fathers also can experience tension related to household work. They may feel compelled to provide financially for their family and not have social outlets for grieving the loss of time with their family. Realizing that women often disproportionately endure the burden of household labor, men may feel guilty when they see, despite their best efforts to help with home and child, their wives struggling with household labor. Fathers who focus on household labor may struggle with a desire to provide financially or lack a supportive network of stay-at-home parents because they are excluded from mothers' groups and do not have men who understand their struggles. Various other family members also may endure the challenges presented by household labor. Some individuals struggle with caring for a terminally ill spouse or mentally ill sister. Others care for aging parents. Grandparents who have dedicated years to raising their own children are sometimes asked in their old age to care full-time for their grandchildren because their son or daughter is not present physically or psychologically to the children. Other times, parents intentionally or unintentionally require one child to complete more work than his or her siblings because of the child's age, skills, personality, or opportunities.[25] Since I am focusing on household labor and engaging socially detached definitions of family life, I will focus on the struggles of those who focus on care for child and home. While recognizing that women often endure disproportionately the burdens of household labor, I will analyze the question more broadly, since much of what follows also applies to fathers, grandparents, and children.

Since household labor is work, the workplace of the home should offer just working conditions. The work environment should be safe and free of prejudice and harassment. Responsible family members should make sure that vulnerable individuals who are helping to cook do not cut or burn themselves. The air should be relatively free from pollution. Individual members should not have to fear bombs, theft, or gang attacks. The household should be violence-free. Unfortunately, many families live in contexts that are not safe and many individuals endure situations in their family that are violent. When violence occurs in the workplace of one's home, the work

25 Victor Carmona notes, for example, that in families with mixed immigration status, children who lack citizenship often make sacrifices for siblings who have citizenship and therefore greater opportunities. See Victor Carmona, "Mixed-Status Families, Solidarity, and *Lo Cotidiano*," in *Sex, Love, and Families: Catholic Perspectives*, ed. Jason King and Julie Hanlon Rubio (Collegeville, MN: Liturgical Press, 2020), 208.

of life often becomes unbearable. To make matters worse, in a family, individuals lack a human resource protocol to address harassment and abuse. Injustice is defined as private and remains hidden. The surrounding communities need to help ensure that families enjoy a safe work environment and just means for addressing harassment and abuse in the family.

Moving from the work environment to the character of household work, one does well first to note why one might be inclined to overlook these injustices. First, one might make the mistake of thinking that when another has the primary responsibility, then further help is not needed. Especially in contexts that endorse individualism and private, isolated accounts of family life, one might be inclined to see household work as the sole obligation of those who chose to buy the house or conceive the children. Even if personal choice was not involved, family members, by virtue of their familial connections, are responsible for caring for individuals with special physical and psychological needs, or grandchildren or nieces and nephews who would otherwise be neglected. If one thinks that primary responsibility means sole responsibility, then one will overlook the harsh working conditions some individuals endure in their attempt to fulfill these domestic obligations.

Second, particular individuals might be expected to complete household work because of their sex, income, skill set, or personality. A son cares for dying parents because he is the oldest boy, or he lives closest to his parents, or he has a medical background. A mother quits her job and stays home with her newborn because she is a woman, or because her husband happens to make more money than she does. Parents ask their middle child to complete household chores because his personality disposes him to say yes and complete the job as requested. It is common to overlook the household work that is expected of family members. This oversight masks potential injustices in the workplace of the home. While the son who is expected to care for his dying parents may have attributes that dispose him well to serve his parents, some of which may increase his responsibility, he also may have other commitments to his faith community, family, or job that prevent him from exercising those attributes and responsibilities in this circumstance.

To limit decisions about household labor to particular personal attributes or circumstances without consideration of the larger context is to confuse input with discernment. A mother may bond with her child through pregnancy and nursing, but she may nonetheless lack the skills and disposition necessary for a life focused on household labor, or she may possess such skills and interests but also have skills and interests that better suit her to other work. Since the dignity of work is rooted in the human person, decisions about occupation and employment should work through the human agency and personal discernment of the individual worker. One should look to human agency and personal discernment rather than assume that a mother must stay home full-time because she is a woman or that the father must stay home because he makes less money than his wife. While personal responsibilities and communal resources and needs should rightly condition discernment as to the proper occupation, one moves toward enslavement the more a leader of a community denies a laborer's human agency, forcing undesirable labor on the laborer based on nation of origin, or skin color, or sex, when other more fitting and agreeable work is available.

Sometimes, however, one is responsible for completing work that one may not want to complete. A father needs to care for his infant throughout the night if he is a single parent or if his wife is on a business trip or vacation with friends. A son needs to care for his aging parents if no one else is willing to do so. A sense of responsibility for various household tasks, however, does not prevent one from needing sleep, or developing physical exhaustion or psychological imbalance. Julie Hanlon Rubio writes about the importance of listening to mothers whose commitment to household labor and childcare often involves isolation, exhaustion, anxiety, monotony, and guilt.[26] Human beings have limited energy and cannot work all day and all night. If a mother, or father, or another individual, spends the whole day caring, cooking, cleaning, doing laundry, consoling and intervening, playing, and enduring complaints without adequate sleep or breaks, then their work is not humanely sustainable. The phrase full-time parent or caregiver is a bit of a misnomer because household labor often requires more than a forty-hour work week. Especially when individuals are forced to complete endless work against their human agency or without support from others who could help, they endure unjust working conditions.

Certainly, individuals who care for young children or individuals with special needs will work long and hard. Expecting to log eight hours a day for five days a week will in most contexts be unrealistic. How then does one

26 Julie Hanlon Rubio, *A Christian Theology of Marriage and Family* (New York: Paulist Press, 2003), 101–5. Focusing on maternal mental health, Elisabeth Vasko asks, "Why are mothers with mental illness still hiding, and what does this hiding reveal about the body of Christ?" See Elisabeth T. Vasko, "'Mad Mothers, Bad Mothers': Resisting Stigma and Embracing Grace as Dis-ease," *Journal of the Society of Christian Ethics* 37, no. 1 (Spring/Summer 2017): 142.

construct household labor in a humane way? I will consider how the Catholic social tradition on human development and worker associations provides some resources. John Paul II highlights that one's work ought to develop the person. Workers should receive training for their work and have opportunities to complete various tasks that they can complete. Being expected to complete well work for which one lacks skills or understanding leads to an exercise in frustration and failure. Some forms of household labor are challenging because the individual worker feels incompetent to complete the work. Cooking may be stressful to someone who cannot cook well. Caring for a child with a mental illness or a parent with a terminal illness can be terrifying and frustrating if one does not understand the illness involved. Knowing a few things about child development can help in relating to children. Having the time and resources to cultivate skills that relate to one's household labor can provide a source of fulfillment. Since those who focus on household labor live in their workplace, they also need opportunities for personal development and leisure that are not necessarily tied to their work. Finding these opportunities for personal development often requires communal support.

Worker Associations and Household Labor

Catholic teaching on worker associations helps to articulate the kind of communal support that is necessary for household laborers. In the papal social encyclical tradition, worker associations offer possibilities of collective bargaining, fellowship, the cultivation of a trade, and communal support in times of need. Collective bargaining specifically serves the role of balancing power in the workplace. I propose that family members can gather together to serve a similar role in a family. Sometimes, family members use their power in a family for self-serving purposes. They demand more than they should from others or use their power to avoid household labor. A parent or older sibling may require a young child to be efficient in household labor when the child should be focused on developing their skills. An individual who makes money for the family may erroneously think they should be exempt from household labor. The Catholic social tradition's teaching on collective bargaining can help individuals identify when family members are misusing their power to require other family members to complete household labor, as when an uncle tricks his nephews and nieces into completing his work. Similarly, collective bargaining helps clarify what is happening when family members join forces to challenge other family members about their expectations for household work. Such negotiating could be a call to reason and justice, as when a mother and her children gather together to question the father or a specific child about unreasonable household labor demands. Sometimes, however, familial worker associations can focus on power beyond justice, such as when an older sibling convinces younger siblings to resist appropriate parental calls for assistance with household labor.

In the Catholic social tradition, workers also should cultivate fellowship with other workers. Models of family isolation might suggest that the family is a place of fulfillment rather than work and that one therefore should avoid household work as much as possible. When work is defined around an individual person rather than a community of laborers, one might focus on individual performance and efficiency rather than support for the overall well-being of the community. This emphasis on efficiency can be enhanced when individuals in a family are not secure in their communion with other family members or in their place in the family. They might attempt to avoid work or seek to establish their worth through competition in household labor, and thereby seek to highlight the limitations of others' work rather than helping others to develop life skills. Spouses might compete for the love of their children and children might compete for the attention of their parents. Siblings might feel threatened when their brothers or sisters can do things that they cannot. By framing household labor in terms of a community of workers and the cultivation of the trades of the household, individuals can focus on completing work well and helping others to do the same. Sharing best practices reminds household laborers that they live as a community of persons, and not as isolated individuals who establish their worth in the community by demonstrating superiority over others in the community. One should desire to help the other whom one loves and work together to contribute to the family community.

Finally, the community of laborers that is a family can support one another in their weakness and vulnerability. Individuals can be patient with family members who need instruction and experience and are not yet efficient in their work. When one family member is sick, struggling, or away, other family members can make sacrifices and temporarily complete their housework for them. The cultivation of household trades can occur through association with those in one's family as well as with those who run other households. Parents who stay home with their children, for example, can gather with other stay-at-home parents for play dates or a night out. They can talk shop and seek to understand one another's struggles and share best practices. They can discuss their struggles or even whether certain conditions are unjust and how to better advocate for their legitimate needs. They can engage in adult conversation about topics unrelated to their work. Since caring for family members often is more than a full-time job, caregivers will need some form of assistance from others. They might find assistance from extended family, friends, neighbors, babysitters, parishes, or state or civil programs.

Synthesis

Catholic social ethics has much to offer to families in their reflections on household labor. The dignity of work comes from the dignity of the laborer. In addition to earning income, work also involves the fulfillment of one's obligations, service to society, the cultivation of a community of workers, and the development or formation of the laborer. This broader vision helps to clarify that household labor is work and that this work is essential to the family and the common good. Seeing household labor as work reframes the question of a work-family balance and clarifies why many parents are exhausted from moving from one kind of work to another.

Catholic social ethics also clarifies the work of children and how caregivers can help children engage with their work more fully. By recognizing that the focus of work for small children is personal development, caregivers can see more clearly how to engage and form small children. The Catholic social tradition's emphasis on a living wage also highlights that household laborers should have access to financial resources so they can provide basic needs, allow for professional development, and provide opportunities for leisure. The Catholic social tradition on just working conditions and worker associations further enlightens family life. Opportunities for professional development, fellowship with other household workers, and support from the broader community are crucial resources for constructing a humane, and even fulfilling, framework for those who focus on household labor. Individuals should cultivate in a family a community of workers in which one cooperates with others to complete household tasks and help others develop the life skills necessary to complete household tasks. Families also need the support of other families and the broader community.

Since the family is internally social, the language of the Catholic social tradition contains crucial insights for everyday family interactions. Analysis of household labor in turn supports Catholic social ethics. The family plays a foundational, formative role, and this applies to formation in work. John Paul II writes that "the family constitutes one of the most important terms of reference for shaping the social and ethical order of human work. . . . The family is simultaneously a community made possible by work and the first school of work, within the home, for every person."[27] As the first school of work, the household forms how one thinks about work. In the home, one develops or fails to develop the soft skills so crucial for getting and maintaining a job.[28] Since family interactions are a central part of life for many people, explaining how the Catholic social tradition's insights about work apply to the family provides a pedagogical resource with which many can relate and a daily reminder of that tradition as they navigate work in the family.

PEACE

Whereas my discussion of work is rooted in principles articulated in the papal social encyclical tradition and applied to various family interactions, my discussion of peace is rooted in the developing theology of peacemaking. Contemporary debates related to just war theory and pacifism have tended to focus on whether one can, in justice, wage war. Peacemaking, on the other hand, focuses on nonviolent practices that help cultivate a sustainable social order.[29] Peacemaking focuses on breaking cycles of violence and engaging in the difficult work of gradually building accountability, reconciliation, trust, and shared cooperation in seeking social goals. Ethical analysis of violence in contemporary moral theology tends to focus on international violence between nations or among groups warring for control within a region or nation. Often overlooked in social debates about just war theory, pacifism, and peacemaking is another form of violence that is the most common, pervasive, devastating, and often hidden: domestic violence.

To show how social ethics illuminates family life, I intend to sketch out a theology of peace, summarize the practices of peacemaking, and then apply those practices to family interactions. In my application, I will draw

27 John Paul II, *Laborem Exercens*, 10, in O'Brien and Shannon, *Catholic Social Thought*, 391.

28 Julie Hanlon Rubio, *Hope for Common Ground: Mediating the Personal and the Political in a Divided Church* (Washington, DC: Georgetown University Press, 2016), 102–4, 138.

29 Lisa Sowle Cahill, *Blessed Are the Peacemakers: Pacifism, Just War, and Peacebuilding* (Minneapolis: Fortress, 2019); Glen H. Stassen, ed., *Just Peacemaking: The New Paradigm for the Ethics of Peace and War*, rev. ed. (Cleveland: The Pilgrim Press, 2008).

heavily on the work of psychologist Haim Omer. While much work is yet to be done, psychologists have made advances in studying and treating domestic abuse in the last fifty years. In fact, some psychologists have turned to principles and practices articulated in social ethics for guidance in treating domestic abuse. Omer is a leading figure in the use of nonviolent resistance as an aid for caregivers dealing with children acting violently. Following Omer's work, I will focus on the question of children who act violently toward siblings. I do so for three reasons. First and primarily, while Omer does not work explicitly from the Catholic tradition, his research offers a striking example of how ideas of peacemaking and nonviolent resistance found in the Catholic social tradition can enlighten family interactions. Second, Omer and others have recently argued that the violent actions of children against siblings seem to be the most common and overlooked form of domestic abuse. Third, focusing on how to guide parents in nonviolent resistance to children acting violently requires parents themselves to develop practices of peacemaking, thereby cultivating habits that are also resistant to spousal abuse, child abuse, and elder abuse. Since the practices of peacemaking are broadly applicable, the discussion of a more specific kind of violence helps to illustrate the practices of peacemaking in a way that is hopefully helpful in other domestic contexts.

Theology of Peace

In order to help develop a theology of peace, I turn to *Gaudium et Spes*, Dietrich von Hildebrand, and contemporary writings on peacebuilding. Among the three, the choice of Hildebrand is most likely in need of an introduction and explanation. Dietrich von Hildebrand was a philosophy professor in Munich when Adolf Hitler and the German National Socialist Party were gaining influence. Hildebrand recognized early the violent and inhumane implications of the movement's ideology and frequently challenged foundational ideas of the party. When Hitler came to power in Germany, Hildebrand fled to Austria and edited an anti-Nazi newspaper there until the German annexation of Austria. While editing this paper and enduring many threats to his life for the cause, he wrote *Transformation in Christ*, a book now recognized by many as a modern spiritual classic.[30] In

30 Dietrich von Hildebrand, *Transformation in Christ* (San Francisco: Ignatius Press, 1990). The book was originally published under the pseudonym "Peter Ott" to allow for its German publication.

the book, Hildebrand analyzes various spiritual attitudes and virtues that mark the lives of those who respond fittingly to the invitation of God's love. The thirteenth chapter is titled "Blessed Are the Peacemakers."

A theology of peace begins with God, who is peace. The *Compendium of the Social Doctrine of the Church* states: "Before being God's gift to man and a human project in conformity with the divine plan, peace is in the first place a basic attribute of God."[31] Peace in the human person is a resting in the warmth of God's love, which possesses a depth and a power that conquers all things. Peace is a remaining patient and calm in the hope of God's promises, in which one participates on earth while anticipating eternal fellowship with God and the communion of saints. The fullness of peace is a gift from God and not something that one can accomplish on one's own. Hildebrand writes, "We must not seek peace for its own sake, and on no account must we seek any and every kind of peace, but seek *God* and content ourselves with that peace which He alone can give our soul."[32] Peace is the fruit of right relationship with God. One should not settle for one's own cramped account of peace, attempting to turn God into a servant of one's mind.

The peace of God is a key theme in the witness of scripture. Kenneth Himes notes that the Hebrew *shalom* communicated a positive peace in which "the conditions for a flourishing communal life were in place for all to enjoy."[33] Peace features in key exchanges between Jesus and his apostles with respect to the events surrounding his death and resurrection. The *Compendium* states:

> On the eve of his death, Jesus speaks of his loving relation with the Father and the unifying power that this love bestows upon his disciples. It is a farewell discourse which reveals the profound meaning of his life and can be considered a summary of all his teaching. The gift of peace is the seal on his spiritual testament: "Peace I leave with you; my peace I give to you; not as the world gives do I give to you" (Jn 14:27). The words of the Risen Lord will not be any different; every time that he meets his disciples they

31 Pontifical Council for Justice and Peace, *Compendium of the Social Doctrine of the Church*, 488; this quotation is italicized in the original. See also Second Vatican Council, *Gaudium et Spes*, 78, in Flannery, *Vatican Council II*, 987.

32 Hildebrand, *Transformation in Christ*, 356.

33 Kenneth R. Himes, OFM, "Peacebuilding and Catholic Social Teaching," in *Peacebuilding: Catholic Theology, Ethics, and Praxis*, ed. Robert J. Schreiter, R. Scott Appleby, and Gerard F. Powers (Maryknoll, NY: Orbis Books, 2010), 268.

> receive from him the greeting and gift of peace: "Peace be with you" (Lk 24:36; Jn 20:19, 21, 26).[34]

Ubiquitous in Christian accounts of peace is the seventh beatitude, "Blessed are the peacemakers, for they will be called children of God" (Mt 5:9). Hildebrand notes how the scriptural testimony lives today in the life of the Church. He points to the kiss of peace that the faithful exchange before receiving communion. He also highlights that "*pax* is the motto of the Benedictines; *Pax et bonum*, that of the Franciscans."[35]

The peace that comes from God and is rooted in God's love motivates a person to live as an instrument of God's love and peace to others. Hildebrand writes, "The Lord says, not merely, 'Blessed are they who are at peace,' but, 'Blessed are the *peacemakers*.'"[36] This concern for others relates to social structures as well as personal relationships. Hildebrand articulates well how peace combines a patient trust in God with a hungering and thirsting for justice: "The lover of peace preserves his patience while waging a struggle. He *lets God decide* about whether he shall himself live to see that struggle crowned by victory; he conducts it without that violence which is the infallible mark of impatience."[37] Hildebrand observes the disarming strength of a peaceful spirit:

> Such a struggle is inscribed with the words of the Lord: "Father, forgive them, for they know not what they do" (Luke 23:34). For they who possess true inward peace irradiate peace even when fighting for the kingdom of God.... Such a style of warfare tends to disarm the antagonist and to communicate to him something of the serene calm that tints it; even to draw him irresistibly into the orbit of that victorious yet mild and redeeming light.[38]

Sustaining peace in the face of struggle is no easy challenge. Hildebrand notes the danger of "succumbing to the autonomous dynamism of hostility" and proposes that one must "never regard combative action as a neutral instrument which one may use freely if only it is ordained to an aim pleasing to God."[39] One must remain anchored in God's peace.

34 Pontifical Council for Justice and Peace, *Compendium of the Social Doctrine of the Church*, 491.

35 Hildebrand, *Transformation in Christ*, 338.

36 Hildebrand, 394.

37 Hildebrand, 354.

38 Hildebrand, 393.

39 Hildebrand, 353.

Peacebuilders offer concrete practices to help imbue one's struggle against injustice with the spirit of peace that Hildebrand discusses.[40] Since peacebuilding is an ethical framework with expanding edges, I will attempt to synthesize the literature recognizing that those who identify as peacebuilders each use slightly different terms and categories to frame the practice of peacebuilding. Lisa Sowle Cahill proposes that, whereas just war theorists and pacifists have long engaged in debates about whether war is ever morally acceptable, peacebuilding highlights goals commonly shared and practical measures that can help improve specific political and cultural conflicts.[41] One distinctive feature of peacebuilding is a holistic and comprehensive approach to peace. Peacebuilders attempt to identify the underlying causes of strife, seeking to understand a conflict's history and diagnose unjust structures and cycles of violence.[42] They cultivate transparency and accountability for those who act with violence or injustice. They then pool internal and external resources to employ nonviolent but forceful means to deescalate situations and challenge injustices. In line with the insight of *Gaudium et Spes* that "peace is more than the absence of war," peacebuilders take steps toward dialogue between conflicting parties, reconciliation and restoration, and long-term social sustainability.[43]

The insight that peace is more than the absence of war is foundational. As Kenneth Himes observes, "This negative understanding of peace is commonly found in popular discussion; when the shooting stops and active hostility ceases, we say there is peace."[44] In addition to popular notions of peace, ethicists and political leaders often focus on this negative conception of peace. Peace as absence of active conflict encourages focus on short-term state stabilization and material construction rather than on a more holistic, long-term, positive account of peace.[45]

40 The following synthesis on peacebuilding draws significantly from Cahill, *Blessed Are the Peacemakers*; Robert J. Schreiter, R. Scott Appleby, and Gerard F. Powers, eds., *Peacebuilding: Catholic Theology, Ethics, and Praxis*; Stassen, *Just Peacemaking*; and Marie Dennis, ed., *Choosing Peace: The Catholic Church Returns to Gospel Nonviolence* (Maryknoll, NY: Orbis Books, 2018).

41 Cahill, *Blessed are the Peacemakers*, vii–x, 1–6.

42 Cahill, 19.

43 Second Vatican Council, *Gaudium et Spes*, 78, in Flannery, *Vatican Council II*, 986–87.

44 Himes, "Peacebuilding and Catholic Social Teaching," 268.

45 Maryann Cusimano Love, "What Kind of Peace Do We Seek? Emerging Norms of Peacebuilding in Key Political Institutions," in Schreiter, Appleby, and Powers, *Peacebuilding*, 56–91.

Peacebuilding can be integrated with just war theory or pacifism but presents challenges to both. Peacebuilding highlights that the goal is peace, not victory, and demonstrates the various and effective nonviolent resources available to help people avoid the horror of war. Peacebuilding also recognizes that violence exists and demands a response. One cannot simply take a personal stance of nonviolence and rejoice in one's moral purity while perpetrators of horrendous violence continue to devastate their victims. Violence calls for forceful opposition.

The promise of eschatological peace helps peacemakers to frame their efforts. Hope in the Kingdom of God that is yet to come helps individuals avoid the destructive error of seeking utopias or a naivety about the effectiveness of peacebuilding efforts. Still, the yearning for eschatological peace motivates participation in that peace now through right relationship with God and through the cultivation of more just social structures. Peacebuilders recognize that efforts toward political peace on earth will inevitably include a combination of gains, losses, mistakes, and new insights. As the bishops of the Second Vatican Council state, "Peace will never be achieved once and for all, but must be built up continually. Since, moreover, human nature is weak and wounded by sin, the achievement of peace requires a constant effort to control the passions and unceasing vigilance by lawful authority."[46] Peacebuilding requires vigilance and persistence.

The work of peacebuilders often focuses on political violence between nations or warring groups within nations. Since they insist on a holistic approach, they discuss the need for all levels of society to be involved in the process of peacemaking, and they highlight the need to address various kinds of violence. Despite this holistic approach, peacebuilders rarely reference or apply their principles and practices to family life. This application is needed. Domestic violence is more common and more hidden than any other kind of violence. Whereas one's family should be a communion of persons that introduces one to the love of God, many instead experience in one's family spousal abuse, child abuse, elder abuse, and sibling abuse. The principles and practices of peacemaking offer rich resources for developing a response to domestic abuse.

46 Second Vatican Council, *Gaudium et Spes*, 78 in Flannery, *Vatican Council II*, 987.

Peacemaking and Sibling Violence

Ironically, although Catholic social ethicists have been reluctant to apply peacemaking to family life, some family therapists have seen in the sociopolitical practices of nonviolent resistance a framework for effectively treating domestic abuse. I will turn to the work of Haim Omer to show how principles and practices of peacemaking can help address domestic violence and also enrich family communion.

Haim Omer is a professor of psychology at the Tel Aviv University School of Psychological Science in Tel Aviv, Israel. He wrote a groundbreaking book in 2004 titled *Nonviolent Resistance: A New Approach to Violent and Self-Destructive Children* and continues to research and publish on related themes. In 2016, he wrote, with Eli R. Lebowitz, a review of various studies implementing nonviolent resistance to help caregivers reduce violent behaviors in children and adolescents.[47] The studies included treatment of children acting violently who had various diagnoses and lived in various cultural contexts (although the current research is focused on Israel and Europe). Nonviolent resistance has been employed by psychologists in school settings and to help caregivers in various situations, including caring for children who have anxiety disorders, particularly obsessive-compulsive disorder; children with adult entitled dependence; and foster care situations. Omer's synthesis of current studies concludes,

> Those studies demonstrated the efficacy of NVR [nonviolent resistance] across a variety of social and cultural settings. NVR was shown to be effective at reducing violence and other externalizing symptoms as well as parent-child escalation, and parental helplessness. NVR treatment also helped parents to increase their positive and caring gestures toward the child, often in situations in which such positive interactions had become unattainable because of chronic conflict. Treatment feasibility and acceptability were found to be high, as was parental satisfaction.[48]

I will leave to psychologists the task of discerning the effectiveness of nonviolent resistance in situations of domestic violence. Omer does acknowledge near the end of his review that nonviolent resistance therapy is

47 Haim Omer and Eli R. Lebowitz, "Nonviolent Resistance: Helping Caregivers Reduce Problematic Behaviors in Children and Adolescents," *Journal of Marital and Family Therapy* 42, no. 4 (October 2016): 688–99.

48 Omer and Lebowitz, 689.

relatively new and in need of further study: "NVR finds itself between the early and ripe stages recommended for the development of evidence-based practice."[49] Further, Omer limits himself to assisting caregivers who are struggling with children acting violently. He does not mention application to situations of spousal abuse or abuse of children, which would involve different dynamics.

Omer does provide, however, categories and examples for thinking about how social principles related to peacemaking could have application to the basic social unit. I will present Omer's summary of treatment steps, placing those steps in conversations with the principles and practices of peacemaking and then reflect on how peacemaking aids family well-being and how application of peacemaking to family life expands the success and influence of peacemaking.

Omer notes that parents of children acting violently often feel helpless and vacillate between responding violently themselves or giving in. Sometimes parents have originated the violence. This vacillation plays a role in cycles of coercion and escalation.[50] Responding violently provides an example and fuels future violence but giving in sets troubling precedents, suggesting that the violence is acceptable or at least a good way to get one's desired outcome. Parents feel helpless and angry, and they do not know what to do. A strategy of nonviolent resistance to their children's violence presents for many a meaningful alternative.

Omer and Lebowitz summarize standard treatment steps for nonviolent resistance. After establishing a working relationship with the client, the caregiver is given anti-escalation training. Caregivers imagine situations of conflict and practice responses that refrain from escalating the situation. Omer and Lebowitz write, "We have coined three phrases that illustrate the non-escalating stance of NVR, which parents should keep in mind: (a) 'Strike the iron when it is cold!'; (b) 'You can't control the child, but only yourselves!'; and (c) 'You don't have to win, but only to persist!'"[51] Anti-escalation aims at breaking the cycles of violence and coercion. The caregivers avoid responding in the heat of the moment and engage the issue when the parent and the child can think more clearly. Caregivers focus on what they can

49 Omer and Lebowitz, 699.

50 Omer and Lebowitz (693) write about *complementary escalation*, in which parental submission increases the child's demands and outbursts, and *reciprocal escalation*, in which hostility begets hostility.

51 Omer and Lebowitz, 695.

control; that is, their reaction. Anti-escalation training reframes a zero-sum battle for power into goals to resist and to seek gradual change over an extended time.

These anti-escalation efforts link well with the goals of peacebuilding. One could apply to these family interactions the words of *Gaudium et Spes* highlighting that peace "is more than the absence of war: it cannot be reduced to the maintenance of a balance of power between opposing forces nor does it arise out of despotic dominion."[52] Since the goal is right relationship with one another and not control or power over the other or over a family, caregivers can help calm the situation and refrain from engaging in a power struggle that involves asserting power against the child.

Anti-escalation does not mean tolerance of violence. Omer and Lebowitz recommend that caregivers offer a non-confrontational announcement that violent behavior will not be tolerated. Caregivers are encouraged to exercise vigilant care related to their children's actions. Vigilant care "emphasizes gradations of parental vigilance, from open attention, through focused attention, to active protection, with parents moving between different levels of involvement in response to danger signals they detect from the child."[53] Vigilant care responds appropriately to the situation and attempts to avoid violent escalation and invasive and controlling monitoring. The announcement and vigilant care resemble efforts among peacebuilders to institute just laws and prudent enforcement of those laws.

Omer and Lebowitz encourage caregivers to increase rather than decrease their presence to the child. They encourage caregivers to engage in a "sit-in" in which the caregiver reaffirms that violence will not be accepted and asks the child to identify alternative ways of interacting or handling situations. These practices resemble the efforts of peacebuilders to challenge injustices with marches, sit-ins, or strikes. Peacebuilding calls for political engagement rather than disengagement. Similarly, Omer and Lebowitz recommend being present to the child rather than punishing the child with parental absence.[54] Asking the child for alternative solutions also reflects peacebuilders' commitment to engage in dialogue with all relevant parties. These dialogues are likely to be difficult, and the first solution offered may not be acceptable.

52 Second Vatican Council, *Gaudium et Spes*, 78, in Flannery, *Vatican Council II*, 986.

53 Omer and Lebowitz, "Nonviolent Resistance," 689.

54 Omer and Lebowitz, 694.

Omer and Lebowitz call for communal support and transparency. They write, "By rejecting secrecy and acting in an open and public manner, NVR creates strong counter pressure to the violence, which often thrives most under a veil of secrecy."[55] If caregivers find persistent sibling violence unmanageable, they are encouraged to solicit friends and family from outside the home to support them in addressing that violence. The support group would receive training in de-escalation and would be available to help in various ways. The support group can help enforce positive motivations in the child. If the caregiver worries that a child could harm him, the communal support could accompany the caregiver when he needs to address a previous incident or to set boundaries. The caregiver also could, in a moment of calm, inform the child that he will speak with a member of the support group for help in handling the violence. Omer and Lebowitz acknowledge that involving others may trigger a negative response from the child and could raise concerns about the child's privacy. The help would need to be genuine and not another manipulative way for a caregiver to control a child. Omer and Lebowitz, however, insist that violence is never private, and they note that overcoming the secrecy of the violence often presents "immeasurable gain to both the parents and the child."[56]

The assistance of supporter groups parallels peacebuilders' efforts to document political abuses and to hold political leaders accountable by informing those who support the political leader, such as voters, political donors, business leaders, or international allies. By making the injustice known to sympathetic individuals who can influence those acting violently, one employs political motivations, in addition to moral motivations, in order to encourage justice.

Finally, the child who has acted violently is asked to make reparation for their act of violence. Omer and Lebowitz write, "This often takes the form of a clear apology and a symbolic act of compensation."[57] If the perpetrator is not willing to offer an act of reparation, the supporters can help identify an appropriate action. If the child still does not offer reparation, then the caregiver, with the supporters' help, can identify an appropriate and humane way to hold the child accountable. Omer and Lebowitz note, that over time, the child often becomes willing to engage

55 Omer and Lebowitz, 694.

56 Omer and Lebowitz, 694.

57 Omer and Lebowitz, 696.

in acts of reparation.[58] Reparation may need to go in both directions but when the violence is one-directional, right relationship requires recognition and some reparation for the harm done. This call for reparation reflects the initiative of peacebuilders toward restorative justice.

Omer and Lebowitz do not promise that nonviolent resistance will eliminate all violence, or even improve every situation. They encourage small steps over time and report that this approach has proved effective for many families. In this, their efforts reflect a realist peacebuilding approach that lives in the hope of growth but recognizes that perpetrators may continue to choose violence. Potential victims need to be protected and sometimes that protection requires that the victim or the perpetrator needs to leave or be removed from the home.

While instances of domestic violence are difficult to track for various reasons, all accounts suggest that this form of violence is quite common. Some recent studies have suggested that violence between siblings is particularly hidden and pervasive. I have suggested that the research and work of Omer and Lebowitz, while not working within an explicitly Catholic lens, offers an example of how Catholic social ethics, in this case peacebuilding practices and principles, has application to the basic social unit. Omer and Lebowitz note that when caregivers embody nonviolent practices in resistance to their children's violent acts, they often break cycles of violence and coercion, overcome parental helplessness, reduce instances of violence, and report more positive parental interactions with their children.

Peacebuilders have highlighted the need to think holistically about peacebuilding, considering economic, political, cultural, and religious dimensions but also engaging with both the international community as well more local communities at all levels of subsidiarity. The basic social unit plays a crucial role in this holistic approach to peacemaking. Omer and Lebowitz discuss more severe situations in which caregivers are seeking assistance from trained psychologists. Since peacemaking concerns efforts before, during, and after violence, one can see in family interactions many more mundane opportunities to promote peace and reduce domestic conflicts.

58 Omer and Lebowitz, 696.

God and Nonviolent Peacebuilding in the Home

How do caregivers respond when a three-year-old hits her baby brother in the head, a thirteen-year-old is repeatedly disobedient, or an older sibling employs violence to convince her siblings to do what she wants? Since the family is formative in a foundational way, political peace will depend in large part on the ability of caregivers to model peace in the home. If parents who love their children cannot relate peacefully to small children who often pose a limited threat of danger, then how will society possess the moral resources to encourage and form police officers or government leaders to act with peace when dealing with people who repeatedly commit heinous acts?

Family interactions should serve as a model of peacemaking, not violence. A familial context highlights the demand of peacemakers to love all parties involved in any conflict. In love, a parent cannot allow his or her children to cause serious harm to each other. One does not want a child to be physically harmed but neither does one want a child to suffer the moral harm or the self-identification that might result from unreconciled violence. A mother may be able to end the fighting simply by stepping into the scene or by standing between the two who are fighting, or she may need to isolate the two while they calm down, or if necessary, restrain one or both individuals. In love, a parent should avoid violence since he does not want to harm his child if he can avoid it. A parent loves both children and so seeks to protect the victim from physical harm and the violent child from moral harm.

Families also can model peacemaking in that the permanent character of family relationships can motivate individuals to move beyond conflict avoidance toward reconciliation and right relationship. A mother cannot just hope that her kids will no longer interact with one another when they live in the same house and perhaps even sleep in the same room. The permanence of the relationship motivates the mother to identify the underlying causes of the fighting and understand the cycles of coercion and violence. A mother seeking peace can help the children to identify and develop practices of de-escalation, and she can cultivate positive interactions between two children who are otherwise inclined to fight. Parents also can exercise vigilant care in which they are responsive to the situation, giving space to their children to practice peacemaking but prepared to intervene before violence occurs.

While family examples can serve as a model for the demands of love and reconciliation in peacemaking, a theology of peacemaking also offers insight into seeking peace in the home. If one sees the family as an affective, isolated refuge, one could mistakenly seek ultimate peace in family relationships. Families will inevitably disappoint this misplaced hope. If one's heart remains restless, one may blame one's parents, spouses, siblings, or children for failing to provide this hoped-for peace and become angry with any or all of them. When a family member lacks gratitude or offends us, the depth and intimacy of the familial relationship can enhance the harm and anger one may experience. Forceful intervention without violence often requires a commitment to peacemaking, which benefits from a right relationship with God. As Hildebrand highlights, ultimate peace is a gift from God and the fruit of a right relationship with God. Living in God's peace, one sees clearly that one's family cannot and need not provide ultimate peace, and that a person must be patient with oneself and one's family members. This change in expectations tends to de-escalate conflict. One cannot force family members to make good decisions or to cultivate familial relationships. One's siblings and children, for example, have a freedom that is beyond one's control. Peace is more than the absence of conflict. It is a right ordering of things and ultimately a right ordering of one's relationship with God that permeates our relationship with others. Knowing the peace that comes from God, peacemakers seek to share God's peace and love with others.

In many cases, parents do not know exactly how to handle new situations, and so they need to ask God and others for guidance and often will need to ask for forgiveness as part of the reconciliation process. Parents can reflect, after calm is restored, on alternative ways to avoid or handle similar situations. In this way, conflicts teach all parties to see the further invitation to and demands of being God's peacemakers. Beyond avoiding violence, caregivers can serve as instruments of God's peace, cultivating family relationships that prepare individuals for, even if they do not fully embody it, the peace of God's kingdom.

CONCLUSION

When one defines the family as socially detached, one misses the crucial resources that the Catholic social tradition provides to families. The social principles of that tradition are one example of those resources. These principles emerge from theological reflection and the papal encyclical tradition. They are broad enough to have wide application but provide enough content to offer guidance. Since the family is a basic social unit, these principles provide a vital resource for the internally social relations of the family. The social principles related to work and peace provide two illustrative examples of how enriching the application of social principles to family life can be.

The dignity of work highlights the meaning and value of household labor and clarifies why many parents are exhausted from moving from one kind of work to another. The Catholic social tradition's emphasis on a living wage highlights that household laborers should have access to financial resources to provide basic needs, allow for professional development, and provide opportunities for leisure. Opportunities for professional development, fellowship with other household workers, and support from the broader community are crucial resources for constructing a humane, and even fulfilling, framework for those who focus on household labor.

Principles related to peacemaking assist individuals in dealing with conflict and violence in the family. The work of Haim Omer in guiding caregivers to act nonviolently in relating to children acting violently provides examples of language for thinking about the application of these principles. Peace, however, is more than the absence of violence. Peace is an attribute of God, a gift from God, and a right relationship with God, self, and others. Consequently, these peacebuilding practices are relevant for all families. Presence, anti-escalation, communal support, accountability, reparation, and patience are practices that benefit every family in their pursuit of peace. Anchored in the peace of God, individuals can serve as instruments of peace in their interaction with others, overcoming or living nonviolently and even peacefully within the context of disagreement and struggle.

The application of Catholic social principles to family life enlightens family interactions. This application also strengthens Catholic social ethics. If individuals live out Catholic social principles in their everyday family life more fully, and especially if they have the language to see how they are living out these principles in their familial interactions, they will become formed in the practice of the principles. This formation will flow into schools, workplaces, neighborhoods, and parishes. Further, since many people can relate to family experiences, the application of social principles to family life often serves as an effective form of catechesis or pedagogy. Students can appropriate the principles more deeply when they can relate personally to the ideas, and those who frequently interact with family members will receive daily reminders and challenges for living out Catholic social principles.

Another resource in the Catholic social tradition that helps individuals to live out the internally social character of family life is the practice of the works of mercy, which especially highlights the need to care for the weakness and vulnerability of family members. In the next chapter, I explore how these works can be carried out domestically and their implications for the social life of the family, as well as for our understanding of the works of mercy themselves.

3

The Works of Mercy in Family Life

The Catholic social tradition provides rich resources for guiding the faithful in their everyday social interactions.[1] The Catholic social principles are specific enough to illuminate but broad enough to allow for prudential application. The works of mercy are another resource that focuses more explicitly on the need to care for others in their poverty and vulnerability.

I occasionally joke with my wife that in caring for our children, we live out the corporal works of mercy. We feed those who become hungry again before we can clean the table from the last meal, those who do not like the food that is prepared, those who need to be breastfed or spoon-fed, and those who struggle to stay focused enough to eat. We clothe the naked who do not understand the need for mittens in freezing weather, who grow an inch every two months, whose diaper is rancid, who are rough on their clothes, who do not like the clothes that are clean, and who like to change their clothes throughout the day. We visit those who are imprisoned in high chairs, car seats, and cribs. We welcome children to a world that is strange because they have never experienced it before. We shelter our children with a home, but also with our arms and our laps.

Are such examples just part of a quaint joke shared between spouses, or can these actions truly be works of mercy? The answer is more complicated than one might expect. As with the social principles, one encounters obstacles that prevent one from applying mercy's work to family interactions. If one reduces the works of mercy, as many do, to public actions such as food lines or clothing drives, or more dramatic actions like the forgiveness of a heinous crime, then mundane family interactions would seem to be excluded.[2] Furthermore, if the works of

1 A few sections of this chapter draw from Kevin Schemenauer, "The Works of Mercy: Francis and the Family," *Journal of Moral Theology* 6, no. 2 (June 2017): 32–47. The overlapping material is used here with permission.

2 James Keenan notes that in the early Church almsgiving was often viewed as a work of mercy. James Keenan, *The Works of Mercy: The Heart of Catholicism*, 2nd ed. (Lanham, MD: Sheed and Ward, 2008), 10.

mercy are seen as necessarily supererogatory—that is, beyond one's typical obligations—family interactions would seem to be excluded. If feeding a child or providing care for an elderly parent is required in justice, then can it be an act of mercy?

I propose that everyday family interactions can be works of mercy, and that such merciful work is crucial for the faithful's formation in mercy and for the intelligibility of the biblical witness to mercy. I develop these claims in four steps. First, I briefly analyze the nature of mercy, arguing that mercy is caring for another in a state of misery with heartfelt compassion. I propose that God alone is truly merciful, and that mercy flows from God's love. Then, I present a brief history of the works of mercy that helps clarify their object, intention, and circumstances. Third, I argue that since the family is formative in a foundational way and since key scripture passages related to mercy employ familial language, applying the works of mercy to family life is crucial for the intelligibility and credibility of a theology of mercy. And finally, fourth, I propose that family interactions can be works of mercy insofar as one acts as an instrument of God's mercy. I highlight specifically the human weakness and vulnerability present in family life, and I employ feeding the hungry and caring for the sick as examples. As with the social principles, I aim to show the fruitfulness of affirming the family's internally social character through application of the works of mercy to familial interactions. Pope Francis promoted a Year of Mercy while working on an apostolic exhortation on the family, and his writings during that time provide a specific source of wisdom on mercy in the family.

MERCY

Before reflecting on the works of mercy and the family, some cursory treatment of the meaning of mercy is necessary. Francis highlights in *Misericordiae Vultus* that mercy is a basic attribute of God: mercy "reveals the very mystery of the Most Holy Trinity."[3] Francis invites us to begin exploring the inscrutable mystery of God by seeing in Jesus Christ the *misericordiae vultus*: "the face of the Father's mercy."[4] Christ reveals the mercy that comes from God. Mercy is "the ultimate and supreme act by which God comes to meet us . . . the bridge that connects God and man,

3 Pope Francis, Bull of Indiction *Misericordiae Vultus* (April 11, 2015), 2.

4 Francis, 1.

opening our hearts to the hope of being loved forever despite our sinfulness."[5] Francis highlights that everyone needs God's mercy since our salvation depends on it.[6]

Mercy flows from God through a life of charity. Irénée Noye, who has written a detailed history of the works of mercy, notes that a distinctive feature of a Catholic theology of the works of mercy concerns the way one relates such actions to God's love.[7] Noye seems to follow Aquinas here, who clarifies that mercy "is a consequence of charity."[8] God's love is superabundant and merciful to all. After receiving God's mercy, one in turn is called to share God's love with others.

Aquinas notes that as a manifestation of charity, mercy "introduces a certain special consideration, namely the misery of the person pitied."[9] Referencing Augustine, Aquinas writes that "*mercy is heartfelt compassion for another's misery, a compassion which drives us to do what we can to help him.*"[10] Aquinas is careful to note that God's association with the weak does not express weakness. Rather, Aquinas notes that since mercy involves a working from abundance to relieve the needs of others, "mercy is something proper to God, and that it is here, above all, that he shows forth his almighty powers."[11] Although Aquinas does not reference the text, his insight echoes Wisdom 11:23: "But you have mercy on all, because you can do all things," and Wisdom 12:16: "For your might is the source of justice; your mastery over all things makes you lenient to all." In working from abundance, God is uniquely merciful. When human beings show mercy to others, they are more fundamentally sharing a gift from God's abundance. Francis writes that Jesus asks us to "be instruments of mercy, because it was we who first received mercy from God."[12] Noye notes that some medieval authors emphasize that the works of mercy encompass the whole of human life from the birth of a hungry and naked child to the burial of the body, highlighting

5 Francis, 2.

6 Francis, 2.

7 Irénée Noye, "Miséricorde (Oeuvres de)," in *Dictionnaire de Spiritualité* (Paris: Beauchesne, 1980), 10:1345.

8 Thomas Aquinas, *Summa Theologiae*, ed. and trans. R. J. Batten, OP (New York: McGraw-Hill, 1975), II.II, q. 32, a. 1, pp. 238–39.

9 Aquinas, II.II, q. 30, a. 3, ad 3, in Batten, 218–19.

10 Aquinas, II.II, q. 30, a. 1, in Batten, 208–9, italics in original.

11 Aquinas, II.II, q. 30, a. 4, in Batten, 220–21; see also Francis, *Misericordiae Vultus*, 6.

12 Francis, *Misericordiae Vultus*, 9; see also 13, 14, 25.

that nothing can be taken away from the realm of charity.[13] As a manifestation of charity, mercy knows no limits.[14]

The limitless character of mercy's concern for misery implies a willingness to encounter and engage illness and stench. James Keenan proposes that mercy is "to enter into the chaos of another."[15] Acting with mercy and receiving mercy is fraught with challenges and difficulties. In acting with mercy, one must be willing to encounter the needs of another, to prepare for the possibility of being harmed in the process of trying to help, and to receive rejection from those who do not want help or who may be suspicious of those offering help. Keenan observes that even showing mercy with those one knows can be challenging.[16]

Dorothy Day links the challenge of acting with mercy to the various forms of human poverty in need of care. She relays a story of a man who gave shelter and food to another and for those good actions had his wallet stolen. Day observes that sometimes individuals are "destitute in every way, destitute of this world's goods, destitute of honor, of gratitude, of love; they need so much that we cannot take the Works of Mercy apart and say I will do this one or that one Work of Mercy. We find they all go together."[17] One who is merciful will care for the whole person before them. Because no human person has inexhaustible strength and patience, the merciful must do so by following the example and drawing on the strength of Christ. Day often notes that Catholic Workers must pray and draw on God's grace to prevent bitterness or becoming burnt out. Appealing to leaders in the Catholic Worker Movement, Day proposes daily attendance at Mass so that "we will see Christ in each other, and we will not lose faith in those around us, no matter how stumbling their progress is."[18]

Likewise, Francis notes that the abundance of God's mercy provides consolation and hope in the face of sin and disorder:

13 Noye, "Miséricorde (Oeuvres de)," 10:1345.

14 Francis argues that mercy overcomes everything and that "wherever there are Christians everyone should find an oasis of mercy." *Misericordiae Vultus*, 12.

15 Keenan, *The Works of Mercy*, 4.

16 Reflecting on sharing mercy with one's spouse, for example, Keenan observes (143): "Mercy among equals is very difficult to negotiate because the one in chaos does not enjoy the fact of being in need and least of all wants the help of her or his most intimate partner to be a 'condescending' one."

17 Dorothy Day, *Selected Writings*, ed. Robert Ellsberg (Maryknoll, NY: Orbis Books, 1992), 100.

18 Day, 91–92.

> From the heart of the Trinity, from the depths of the mystery of God, the great river of mercy wells up and overflows unceasingly. It is a spring that will never run dry, no matter how many people draw from it. Every time someone is in need, he or she can approach it, because the mercy of God never ends. The profundity of the mystery surrounding it is as inexhaustible as the richness which springs up from it.[19]

To be an instrument of God's mercy is to receive this mercy and to recognize God as its source and strength.

Mercy is a subvirtue of charity that is specifically focused on relating well to the misery of others. Thus, mercy is not limited to public services or the forgiveness of public and heinous crimes but has the strength and reach to address every human misery, including that found in one's family. Mercy is first an attribute of God. Everyone needs God's mercy, which is extended specifically to those who are in need, weak, and entrenched in sin. Those who receive God's mercy are in turn called to draw on the great river of mercy that flows from God and to share this mercy with others, a sharing that often involves pain and sacrifice, but also leads to a deeper experience of God's mercy—"blessed are the merciful, for they will be shown mercy" (Matt. 5:7).

A BRIEF HISTORY OF THE WORKS OF MERCY

The nature of mercy and the works of mercy are intimately related but distinct. Mercy as a virtue is a disposition toward caring for the misery of another as an instrument of God's love. A work of mercy is a specific human action. In the Catholic moral tradition, the works of mercy refer to seven corporal and seven spiritual works of mercy. Knowing the basic historical contours of the works of mercy helps to clarify the nature of these actions, the role of these works in the Catholic moral life, and the mutually enriching character of the works and family life. The history that follows is largely dependent on Irénée Noye's well-researched entry on the works of mercy in the *Dictionnaire de Spiritualité*.[20]

19 Francis, *Misericordiae Vultus*, 25.

20 Noye, "Miséricorde (Oeuvres de)," 10:1327–49. As far as I can tell, a detailed history of the works of mercy does not exist in English. Keenan provides an insightful but brief history in *The Works of Mercy* (12–15). See also Federico Botana's *The Works of Mercy in Italian Medieval Art (c. 1050–c. 1400)*, Medieval Church Studies 20 (Turnhout, Belgium: Brepols, 2011). In the first chapter of his book, Botana provides a history of the works of mercy and fills out additional details in the remaining chapters.

Noye notes that while patristic authors promoted many of the actions today associated with the corporal and spiritual works of mercy, the works of mercy did not yet exist as a set list. Authors listed good actions, but these lists did not form a recognizable canon. Hermas, for example, provided a list of twenty actions. Augustine sometimes highlighted three or four.[21] Almsgiving and hospitality figured significantly in the tradition. Since the Parable of the Judgment in Matthew chapter 25 provides six of the seven corporal works of mercy, homilies and commentaries on that chapter figure prominently in the history of the works of mercy. Burying the dead would be added to the list later, although it has deep roots in the Old Covenant.

The prominence of the Parable of the Judgment highlights the central themes pervading the theological tradition concerning the works of mercy. Reflecting Christ's challenge in Matthew 25:35–36, Noye notes that sermons on almsgiving in the patristic period frequently note that in giving to the poor, one nourishes and gives to Christ.[22] Further, working within the framework of eschatological judgment contained in Matthew chapter 25, many patristic authors connect the six actions listed in the parable with the redemption of sins. Some authors are careful to clarify that one must perform the action with the proper spirit and as an expression of conversion in order to benefit from the redemptive promises of Christ.[23]

Noye observes anticipations of the spiritual works of mercy in the patristic period as well. Origen, in his commentary on Matthew chapter 25, offers an allegorical reading that speaks of a spiritual nourishing of souls, a covering with God's wisdom, and a clothing with various virtues. Augustine proposes that forgiving and giving represent two kinds of mercy, a formulation that becomes classic.[24] This memorable formulation anticipates the distinction between the corporal and spiritual character of mercy.

The canon of the works of mercy becomes largely solidified by the end of the thirteenth century. While some authors continue to list the six Matthean actions, excluding burying the dead, and one continues to see slight variations even today, the phrase "works of mercy" becomes broadly understood to refer to a specific set of actions. The impetus for this canon's solidification seems to emanate from multiple sources. First, the context of the

21 Noye, "Miséricorde (Oeuvres de)," 10:1330–31.

22 Noye, 10:1337–38.

23 Noye, 10:1335.

24 Noye, 10:1331. See, for example, Francis's use of this formulation in *Misericordiae Vultus* (14).

Investiture Conflict is relevant. A concern about the civil appointment of church leadership was that civil-minded leaders would use the patrimony of their parishes for their own purposes rather than for the care of the poor. This misuse of church wealth went side by side with new ecclesial movements that showed great care for the poor. The sacrifice of voluntary poverty present in the mendicant orders gave Saint Francis and Saint Dominic and their followers credibility with the faithful who were tired of civil and ecclesial leaders who seemed concerned only with material gain. Anticipating and following the mendicant orders, many lay associations of Christian nobles were constructed with the purpose of almsgiving, caring for the sick, housing the stranger, and burying the dead.[25] Keenan notes how these lay associations spread and develop into confraternities throughout the Middle Ages: "We cannot underestimate the relevance of these confraternities: Hundreds of them take care of prisoners and captives; others are established for the care of the mentally ill as well as those who are unable to hear and/or speak. These confraternities are only paralleled by the extraordinary number of religious orders, which themselves adopt a work of mercy to identify with their own charism."[26] The practice of pilgrimages also encouraged the practice and analysis of the works of mercy. Pilgrims performed works of mercy as an expression of their search for spiritual growth and conversion, and those who lived along the path of pilgrimages showed hospitality toward the pilgrims.[27]

The combination of the Investiture Conflict, the presence of mendicant orders and lay associations, and the prominence of pilgrimage led to an emphasis on the works of mercy and a desire to teach the faithful about them. The nobles involved in charitable confraternities often commissioned works of art and architecture in their parishes representing the works of mercy.[28] This artwork would serve as a visual instruction for all those who entered these sacred spaces. Franciscans and Dominicans preached about the works of mercy in the vernacular with a passion and simplicity that was contagious. Federico Botana points to an additional motivation for

25 Noye, 10:1339–40.

26 Keenan, *The Works of Mercy*, 13–15.

27 Noye, "Miséricorde (Oeuvres de)," 10:1341.

28 For a detailed history of such artistic works, see Botana's *The Works of Mercy in Italian Medieval Art*. For a specific example, see Terence Ward's telling of how the congregation of the Pious Mount of Mercy commissioned Caravaggio to paint his famous representation of the corporal works of mercy. Terence Ward, *The Guardian of Mercy* (New York: Arcade, 2016).

catechesis on the works of mercy—the Fourth Lateran Council. Speaking of the council's requirement for all men and women to confess and receive communion at least once a year, Botana writes, "This change forced parish priests to improve their knowledge of subjects such as the seven deadly sins, the Ten Commandments, and the works of mercy, in order to teach their flocks how to examine their consciences prior to confession."[29] Botana notes that in the confession manuals that developed, "their passages on almsgiving become extensive sections on the works of mercy."[30]

The works of mercy were also the subject of greater systematic and theological reflection in the twelfth and thirteenth centuries. Whereas past treatments of the works of mercy tended to focus on how they provide satisfaction or redemption from past sins, theologians began reflecting on them in terms of the proper use of goods. Aquinas, in his insightful and influential treatment, proposes that the works of mercy are an actualization of God's love and a fitting and compassionate response to human need.[31] Noye notes that, following Aquinas, the seven spiritual works of mercy, along with the corporal works of mercy, become a recognizable canon of works that are cited in various canonical and catechetical texts.[32]

29 Botana, *The Works of Mercy in Italian Medieval Art*, 6.

30 Botana, 7. Noye notes how in the Middle Ages the works of mercy were incorporated into easy-to-remember lists, in which the six corporal works of mercy were placed between the five senses and the seven virtues, before the eight beatitudes. Noye also notes the famous hexameter quoted in Aquinas's treatment: "*Visito, poto, cibo, redimo, tego, colligo, condo*" and "*Consule, castiga, solare, remitte, fer, ora*." Noye, "Miséricorde (Oeuvres de)," 10:1342; Aquinas, *Summa Theologiae*, II.II, q. 32, a. 2, in Batten, 240–41. To explain why the verse for the spiritual works of mercy includes only six words, Aquinas proposes that "*consule*" covers teaching and counseling.

31 Aquinas, *Summa Theologiae*, II.II, q. 32, a. 2, in Batten, 240–45; see also Noye, "Miséricorde (Oeuvres de)," 10:1344–45.

32 Noye, "Miséricorde (Oeuvres de)," 10:1343. Aquinas sees the numbering of the works of mercy as a question worthy of debate, asking whether the works of mercy are suitably listed as a double septenary. He recognizes and engages positions that would argue against his two lists of seven: Matthew chapter 25 lists six; burying the dead does not help the one who is dead; and many other human needs require the application of mercy. Responding to questions about his inclusion of burying the dead, Aquinas states that the dead man lives in the memory of men and his honor is not a matter of indifference for the man. Moreover, he points to the mercy of Tobit (see Tob. 1:17–20; 2:1–8; 12:11–15) and those who buried our Lord as scriptural testimony for the good of burying the dead. Responding to questions about other human needs, he proposes that all other human necessities can be understood in relation to the fourteen he lists. Aquinas, *Summa Theologiae*, II.II, q. 32, a. 2, in Batten, 240–45.

THE ESSENTIAL CHARACTER OF THE WORKS OF MERCY

Despite the increased uniformity of the seven corporal and seven spiritual works of mercy by the end of the thirteenth century, one continues to see slight variations in the lists depending on pressing needs. Aquinas, for example, lists ransoming captives rather than visiting the imprisoned, the formulation found in Matthew chapter 25. Welcoming the stranger, found in Matthew 25, has often given way to sheltering the homeless in the tradition. Even after Aquinas, some authors continue to list the six actions listed in Matthew 25 rather than seven corporal works of mercy. These and similar variations continue today. For example, while most contemporary lists include sheltering the homeless, Francis in *Misericordiae Vultus*, perhaps out of concern for various refugee communities, employs the Matthean language of welcoming the stranger.[33] In her list, Dorothy Day follows Aquinas in listing ransoming the captives rather than visiting the imprisoned.[34] The *Catechism of the Catholic Church* lists six spiritual and six corporal works of mercy, excluding admonishing the sinner and combining feeding the hungry and giving drink to the thirsty. The text then proposes that almsgiving presents a central manifestation of fraternal charity.[35]

Recognizing that most lists contain slight variations and that the listing and numeration of the works remains open to theological debate and analysis, it is the case that the works of mercy tend to include a list of seven corporal works and a list of seven spiritual works. The descriptions most frequently listed suggest that the standard corporal works include feeding the hungry, giving drink to the thirsty, clothing the naked, sheltering the homeless, caring for the ill, visiting the imprisoned, and burying the dead. The standard spiritual works include instructing the ignorant, counseling the doubtful, comforting the sorrowful, admonishing the sinner, bearing wrongs patiently, forgiving injuries, and praying for all people.

Clarifying the nature of mercy and understanding the history of the works of mercy helps clarify the nature of the works. As a human action, a work of mercy is more than the physical, external features of the action.

33 Francis, *Misericordiae Vultus*, 15.

34 Day, *Selected Writings*, 98.

35 *Catechism of the Catholic Church*, 2nd ed. (Washington, DC: United States Catholic Conference, 1997), § 2447; on the United States Conference of Catholic Bishops web page for the 2015–16 Year of Mercy, almsgiving replaces clothing the naked. United States Conference of Catholic Bishops website, "Works of Mercy," https://www.usccb.org/beliefs-and-teachings/how-we-teach/new-evangelization/jubilee-of-mercy/the-corporal-works-of-mercy).

Good actions must be good in their object, intention, and circumstances. The object is that one is helping another in a state of misery. One does not perform a work of mercy simply by *wanting* to help—one must truly help another in their need; for example, by providing housing for someone who lacks shelter. The circumstances vary depending on the need and the available resources and skills of the one who might help. The intention of the action must be to aid the person in their need. One does not perform a work of mercy who visits someone in prison or someone who is ill in spite and anger or who does so unwillingly. Neither does one perform an act of mercy who is motivated by selfish reasons (e.g., wanting to remove homeless people from the vicinity of one's business) or to bring glory upon oneself (see Matt. 6:2). To constitute an act of mercy, the person must knowingly, willingly, and truly help another in their misery.

From the Christian perspective, the intention to show mercy to another is always an actualization of God's mercy. God acts in a uniquely merciful manner. As the creator and redeemer, God offers humanity something that goes beyond obligation. His mercy is free and undeserved. The physical and spiritual gifts of God are superabundant. As recipients of creation and redemption, one has a responsibility to act as a steward and instrument of God's gifts to others, ensuring that everyone receives their inheritance as a person loved by God. Saint Gregory the Great writes, "When we attend to the needs of those in want, we give them what is theirs, not ours. More than performing works of mercy, we are paying a debt of justice."[36]

Since mercy is proper to God, and the one performing an act of mercy serves as an instrument of God's mercy, one does well to clarify how the moral agent's intention relates to God. Does a person performing an act of mercy need to make an explicit, conscious reference to God's mercy to serve as an instrument of that mercy? Thomas Osborne provides a helpful framework for addressing the question in an article he writes on how moral agents relate their actions to their ultimate end. He engages Aquinas and Aquinas's commentators on the topic. Osborne discerns in Aquinas "three ways in which an act can be referred to God, namely actually, virtually, or habitually."[37] I will focus on applying the first two categories to the works of

36 Quoted in Pontifical Council for Justice and Peace, *Compendium of the Social Doctrine of the Church* (Washington, DC: United States Conference of Catholic Bishops), 184. Reference cites Saint Gregory the Great, *Regula Pastoralis*, 3, 21: PL 77, 87.

37 Thomas Osborne, "The Threefold Referral of Acts to the Ultimate End in Thomas Aquinas and His Commentators," *Angelicum* 85, no. 3 (2008): 717.

mercy since the third does not imply action.[38] First, one might refer to God *actually*, that is, one's mind might be explicitly focused on God's mercy. If this were the only option, the works of mercy would seem to occupy a small range of action. Care for others often involves a certain focus, such that explicit mental reference to God's mercy would be difficult or would distract from the task at hand.

Aquinas proposes, however, that one also might refer to God *in virtute*. Insofar as one loves God as the ultimate end, virtuous acts would be ordered to God even when one does not explicitly direct one's mind to God in a specific action.[39] How does this commitment to God remain present in specific actions? Dietrich von Hildebrand offers a phenomenological analysis of "superactual" stances that helps to clarify the relationship between ultimate commitments and their role in specific actions.[40] A superactual stance is an attitude or commitment that continues even when one does not intentionally focus on the reality. The respect one has for another, for example, continues even when one does not intentionally focus on that person. One sees the enduring character of respect when one hears mention of the individual or has a chance to visit the individual again. Hildebrand proposes that some superactual stances have a profound impact on one's life. More than simply enduring, these stances color and modify one's life experience.[41] Hildebrand uses the example of spousal love and love of God. The lover continues to love even when he is not intentionally focused on the beloved. Moreover, his love, more than enduring, remains profoundly active, pervading his experience of reality. Both Osborne (drawing on Aquinas) and Hildebrand clarify that this pervading commitment requires that the moral agent make consistent and explicit reference to the relevant good.[42] The commitment needs to be explicitly cultivated in order to continue having a profound, pervading influence.

38 Aquinas proposes that individuals can, in a sense, habitually relate their actions to their ultimate end even when they are not acting with intention, as when they are sleeping. Osborne notes that Aquinas's treatment of the question largely concerns the interpretation of 1 Cor. 10:31 ("Do everything for the glory of God.") Osborne, 717.

39 Osborne, 718.

40 Dietrich von Hildebrand, *The Nature of Love*, trans. John F. Crosby and John Henry Crosby (South Bend, IN: St. Augustine's Press, 2009), 43–48.

41 Hildebrand, *The Nature of Love*, 45. Hildebrand is careful to distinguish a superactual stance from the sphere of the unconscious: "We are fully conscious of our superactual stances in the sense that we know about them and are acquainted with them" (46).

42 Osborne, "The Threefold Referral of Acts," 720; Hildebrand, *The Nature of* Love, 45.

The concepts of referring to God *in virtute* or holding God's mercy as a superactual stance help to clarify how to think about an act of mercy. Mercy is proper to God alone, since God alone offers creation and redemption as gift. Human moral agents can perform acts of mercy when they care for the needs of others as instruments of God's mercy. Individuals could explicitly focus on God's mercy while addressing another's need, or their commitment to God's mercy might color and pervade their life such that God's mercy provides a framework for engaging with and assisting others in their misery. One need not explicitly think of God in every act of mercy, but one would need to have regular and explicit focus on God's mercy in one's life for this commitment to pervade specific actions, even as one focused completely on the details of the specific task.

In charity, that is, a life operating in God's love, one can participate in the mercy of God—one can be merciful as the Father is merciful. This participation is possible only through the grace of God, which enables one to be, as Francis writes, an instrument of God's mercy to others.[43] Aquinas relays the standard definition of the works of mercy in his time as "a deed whereby something is given to the needy out of compassion and for God's sake."[44] The one performing a work of mercy, then, in addition to the intention of helping someone in need, should also remain open and attentive to how God's mercy works in and through their action. Even in mundane interactions, justice and the works of mercy can meet in the charity of God.

FAMILIAL MERCY IN THE BIBLICAL WITNESS

The works of mercy provide a language to help individuals identify needs, and to both form habits and encourage practices that help address those needs. Without the hopeful vision of mercy, individuals can so easily turn any social interaction—including one in a family—into an opportunity to compare and compete, divide and conquer, win and destroy. An ethic of mercy that cares for another in their need as an instrument of God's mercy, and therefore as an equal with those in need before God, helps keep at bay

43 Francis, *Misericordiae Vultus*, 14.

44 Aquinas, *Summa Theologiae*, II.II, q. 32, a. 1, in Batten, 236–37. R. J. Batten, OP, notes that the Latin and Greek words that Aquinas employs to discuss the works of mercy are "now usually restricted to the giving of money to the poor. As used by St. Thomas and his contemporaries, however, it includes all kinds of material as well as spiritual relief, both 'the spiritual and corporal works of mercy'" Aquinas, *Summa Theologiae*, II.II, q. 32, a. 1, in Batten, 236–37, footnote a.

that pervasive and subtle shift from self-concern to a self-serving that would prey on the weaknesses of others.

The foundation for my claim that family interactions play a specifically central, formative role in a theology of mercy comes from the fact that key scriptural texts employ familial examples and analogies to articulate the meaning of mercy and to illustrate God's mercy. The biblical witness is particularly important for the topic of mercy since mercy is first and foremost a divine attribute of God—a mystery that we can approach only through revelation and grace. In *Misericordiae Vultus*, Francis highlights the necessity of scripture for understanding and living mercy: "To be capable of mercy, therefore, we must first of all dispose ourselves to listen to the Word of God."[45] I will highlight specifically how Francis presents mercy through the language of the family, focusing on three scriptural passages that figure prominently in *Misericordiae Vultus*: Luke 6:36; Matthew 25:31–45; and Luke 15:11–32. Since I am concentrating on these passages, my emphasis will be on the familial language of father, son, and brothers.[46]

To see familial language in *Misericordiae Vultus* and its foundation in scripture one only need look as far as the motto for the Year of Mercy: "Be merciful just as your Father is merciful (Lk 6:36)."[47] This passage underscores the movement of mercy from God to us and then in turn from us to others. To be merciful as the Father is merciful, one must know the Father's mercy and share that mercy with others. In typical form, Francis highlights that the mercy that comes from God is expressed not merely as

45 Francis, *Misericordiae Vultus*, 13. See also Francis, Postsynodal Apostolic Exhortation *Amoris Laetitia* (March 19, 2016), 227, where Francis writes, repeating the words of the Synod of Bishops' *Relatio Synodi* from 2014,

> the word of God is the source of life and spirituality for the family. All pastoral work on behalf of the family must allow people to be interiorly fashioned and formed as members of the domestic church through the Church's prayerful reading of sacred Scripture. The word of God is not only good news in a person's private life but also a criterion of judgement and a light in discerning the various challenges that married couples and families encounter.

46 In drawing attention to the three passages that Francis highlights, it should be noted also that Francis draws on the language of mother and spouse that features in the Catholic tradition's theology of mercy. For references to the maternal solicitude of the Church, see Francis, *Misericordiae Vultus* (4, 22), as well as Francis, *Amoris Laetitia* (49). For a discussion of Mary as the mother of mercy, see Francis, *Misericordiae Vultus* (24). For a discussion of the need for the Church to live in mercy as the spouse of Christ, see *Misericordiae Vultus* (4, 12, 22).

47 As quoted in Francis, *Misericordiae Vultus* (13). A few paragraphs later Francis writes, "*Merciful like the Father*, therefore, is the 'motto' of this Holy Year." *Misericordiae Vultus*, 14.

a theoretical principle but is "concretely demonstrated in his many actions throughout the history of salvation."[48] Francis reflects on how these concrete actions are retold and celebrated in Psalms 103, 146, and 147.[49] Significant for the theme of mercy and the family, Francis connects this concrete expression of mercy to parental loving care: "The mercy of God is not an abstract idea, but a concrete reality with which he reveals his love as of that of a father or a mother, moved to the very depths out of love for their child. It is hardly an exaggeration to say that this is a 'visceral' love. It gushes forth from the depths naturally, full of tenderness and compassion, indulgence and mercy."[50] The name of the Father speaks both to the relationship of the divine persons and the relationship between God and the faithful. In Christ, we become the adopted sons and daughters of the merciful and loving Father. The Gospel of Luke and Francis speak not of "the" Father, but "your" Father. God's mercy is revealed and expressed concretely as a loving parent.[51]

In Matthew chapter 25, the scriptural font for the works of mercy, Christ speaks the haunting words, "Whatever you did for one of these least *brothers* of mine, you did for me" (Matt. 25:40).[52] Commenting on this pericope, Francis writes, "We cannot escape the Lord's words to us, and they will serve as the criteria upon which we will be judged: whether we have fed the hungry and given drink to the thirsty, welcomed the stranger and clothed the naked, or spent time with the sick and those in prison (cf. Matt. 25:31–45)."[53] I propose that this link between the works of mercy and eschatological judgment is not arbitrary but is wrapped into the very nature of mercy. If one rejects the flow of God's mercy through one's heart to others, then one has closed one's heart to the mercy of God, which is necessary for the

48 Francis, 6.

49 Psalm 146 speaks of how God "upholds the widow and the fatherless," quoted in Francis, *Misericordiae Vultus* (6).

50 Francis, 6.

51 See also *Misericordiae Vultus* (9, 12) where Francis speaks of mercy in the language of fatherhood.

52 Emphasis added. While not a focus in the writings of Francis, authors advocating for a list of seven corporal works of mercy often cite Tobit 12:11–15 in justification of adding burying the dead. The angel Rafael informs Tobit that he brought Tobit's concerns before God in part because Tobit risked his life to bury the dead (Tob. 12:11–15). The work of burying the dead begins and ends the book of Tobit (Tob. 1:17–20; 2:1–8; 14:12–13). Family commitments are central to the book, even as Tobit extends the responsibility to bury one's family to others as well.

53 Francis, *Misericordiae Vultus*, 15.

person's salvation and citizenship in the Kingdom of God.[54] Similarly, Francis writes, mercy is not only an action of the Father, but it becomes a criterion for ascertaining who his true children are.[55] Mercy comes to us from the Father, but it should not stop with us. If one truly lives in the merciful love of the Father, then one's life will reflect that mercy. The presence or absence of God's mercy in one's life becomes a criterion of faith.

Another parable crucial for Francis's treatment of mercy is the parable of the prodigal son, which he refers to as the parable of the merciful father or the parable of the father and two sons. In *Misericordiae Vultus*, Francis highlights how the father in the parable "runs out to meet his son despite the fact that he has squandered away his inheritance."[56] Francis sees the prodigal son's poverty as deserving a privileged focus but not to the exclusion of others: "Let us never tire of also going out to the other son who stands outside, incapable of rejoicing, in order to explain to him that his judgement is severe and unjust and meaningless in light of the father's boundless mercy."[57] Like Luke 6, Luke 15 invites us to contemplate the mercy of the Father. Francis explains that in the parable of the father and the two sons, "Jesus reveals the nature of God as that of a Father who never gives up until he has forgiven the wrong and overcome rejection with compassion and mercy."[58]

While Luke chapter 6 generally challenges us to extend the Father's mercy to others, Matthew 25 highlights the need to care for the least brothers of Christ. Luke chapter 15 seems to go even a step further. In the parable of the father and the two sons, the least brother has been disrespectful and reckless. He has greedily grasped for his father's wealth, intemperately squandered his possessions, and no doubt brought a great deal of

54 The Sermon on the Mount presents another key text concerning mercy and eschatological judgment: "Blessed are the merciful, for they will be shown mercy" (Matt. 5:7). William Mattison III argues that the relationship between the beatitude's qualifying conditions and rewards are intrinsically related. Giving mercy and receiving mercy from God are mutually constitutive. William C. Mattison III, "The Beatitudes and Moral Theology: A Virtue Ethics Approach," *Nova et Vetera* 11, no. 3 (2013): 836.

55 Francis, *Misericordiae Vultus*, 9. See also his reflection in a general audience focused on the works of mercy: "Those who have experienced in their own lives the Father's mercy cannot remain indifferent before the needs of their brothers." Francis, "Works of Mercy," Jubilee Audience, June 30, 2016, St. Peter's Square.

56 Francis, *Misericordiae Vultus*, 17.

57 Francis, 17.

58 Francis, 9. Francis continues at 9: "We know these parables well, three in particular: the lost sheep, the lost coin, and the father with two sons (cf. Lk 15:1–32)."

shame to the family. The parable of the merciful father invites one to extend and even to rejoice in the extension of mercy to those who have done harm to themselves and to their loved ones.

These three passages from scripture highlight key features of mercy. Everyone needs the Father's mercy. The flow of mercy extends from the Father and then through the one who receives mercy to others. Mercy must be extended particularly to the poor and to those who have lived in grave sin. In each passage, mercy is presented in the language of the family. God is the merciful Father. Those in need of mercy are one's brothers and sisters. One must rejoice in the extension of mercy even to a brother who has hurt one deeply. Since Christ presents mercy in familial language, living mercy in the family is a vital aid to the intelligibility and credibility of the Gospel and to a theology of mercy. By being merciful as a father or a mother, or a brother or a sister, one manifests the living character of God's Word.

FAMILIAL WORKS OF MERCY

After clarifying the nature of mercy and providing a brief history of the works of mercy, we are now positioned to address our central question: Can everyday family interactions be works of mercy? Christ provides some indication of an answer when he employs familial language to describe mercy. The biblical witness seems to suggest that family interactions can be works of mercy, and even more, that living mercy in the family is a vital aid to the intelligibility and credibility of the Gospel and of a theology of mercy. However, we need to examine the matter more closely. The challenge is twofold. First, if mercy concerns only organized almsgiving or dramatic expressions of forgiveness, then mundane family interactions would not seem to apply. Second, if mercy exceeds justice, and caring for one's family members is often a demand of justice, then family interactions are not acts of mercy. With respect to the first challenge, it is possible to see that mercy is a subvirtue of charity specifically focused on relating well to the misery of others. Charity knows no limits, and the condition for exercising mercy is human misery and someone's ability to help as an instrument of God's mercy. Since the family context includes human misery and individuals who can help, family interactions can be works of mercy. Family members can act as an instrument of God's mercy, either with explicit focus on God's mercy in their action or through a commitment to God's mercy that pervades one's action even when focusing on other details.

Concerning the second challenge, mercy does require more than fulfilling minimum obligations of justice. Beyond providing food for one's children, an act of mercy also requires two further features: the intention to help another in their misery and a commitment to act as an instrument of God's mercy. When those two features are present, one can in mercy both meet and surpass the obligations of justice toward one's family members. Justice and mercy meet in the charity of God.

To see the works of mercy in everyday family life, one does well to identify those specific family members who are vulnerable. I discussed in chapter 2 the vulnerability of those who focus on household labor. Francis also specifically highlights children, the elderly, and those who are mentally or physically ill. In *Misericordiae Vultus*, Francis highlights the poverty of children. In his commentary on Matthew chapter 25, he focuses on the need to care for "children deprived of the necessary means to free them from the bonds of poverty. . . . In each of these 'little ones,' Christ himself is present. His flesh becomes visible in the flesh of the tortured, the crushed, the scourged, the malnourished, and the exiled."[59] Recognizing that small children, those who focus on household labor, those who are mentally or physically sick, and the elderly often are uniquely vulnerable in the family, one also must note that weakness and vulnerability is an unavoidable feature of the human condition. Serving the misery of one's family member can serve as an invitation to see and accept one's own limitations.

Merciful action in families and theological reflection on the works of mercy are mutually enriching. Merciful action in the family supports social advocacy for works of mercy, since family is formative of individuals who then exercise the works of mercy in parishes, civil society, social services, and the workplace. Further, since the biblical witness often employs familial language to describe God's merciful action and the call for the faithful to participate in His mercy, works of mercy in the family can provide an evangelical function providing a concrete manifestation of mercy. In turn,

59 Francis, 15. This focus on the unique vulnerability of children is a recurring theme in Francis's ministry. He writes, for example, in his encyclical *Laudato si'*, "Since everything is interrelated, concern for the protection of nature is also incompatible with the justification of abortion. How can we genuinely teach the importance of concern for other vulnerable beings, however troublesome or inconvenient they may be, if we fail to protect a human embryo, even when its presence is uncomfortable and creates difficulties?" Francis, Encyclical Letter *Laudato si'* (May 24, 2015), 120; see also Francis, *Amoris Laetitia* (45–46, 49, 51, 241), where Francis decries the sexual exploitation of youth and the threats posed to children by migration, poverty, drug use, and divorce.

theological reflection on the works of mercy also presents an aid to individuals who struggle to minister to the misery of other family members. Beyond the formative role family members exercise in preparing individuals to live well as social beings in broader society, the family is internally social. Individuals experience misery and family members care or fail to care for those needs. The language and practice of mercy in the family helps cultivate a broader discussion of and expression of mercy.

One crucial implication of the claim that everyday family interactions can be works of mercy is that the works of mercy illuminate family interaction. Theological reflection on the works of mercy provides a language to see and respond to the needs of those with whom we live and share familial bonds. To illustrate how reflection on the works of mercy can enhance and offer guidance to family interactions, I have chosen two clear and common corporal works of mercy: feeding the hungry and caring for the sick.

Feeding the Hungry

"One does not live on bread alone"—but the Catholic tradition nevertheless admonishes Christians to ensure that every human being gets the food and water they need.[60] Because the Church teaches the universal destination of goods—that the good things of creation are given by God for the needs of each person, not simply the rich or "deserving"—it enjoins upon the faithful that these basic material goods be provided to those who cannot secure them for themselves.[61] For example, government leaders should properly distribute food to decrease starvation, and food and water should, in principle, be provided to dying patients.[62] Hunger serves as a constant reminder of one's weakness and vulnerability. Some experience the excruciating pain of extended hunger; others simply experience daily reminders of their need for food. Meeting this fundamental need is a matter of justice, but doing so with respect and attention to each individual person as an extension of God's mercy makes it truly a work of mercy.

60 Cf. Deut. 8:3, Matt. 4:4.

61 Saint Paul does say, "If anyone is unwilling to work, neither should that one eat" (2 Thess. 3:10), but this is an admonition to forestall the taking advantage of the basic Christian imperative to share that is placed on those perfectly capable of contributing.

62 Francis, *Laudato si'*, 50. See also *Ethical and Religious Directives for Catholic Health Care Services*, 6th ed. (Washington, DC: United States Conference of Catholic Bishops, 2018), part five, introduction, and section 58.

Feeding the hungry is possible first because God provides superabundantly for his creation. In the Gospel of Luke, chapter 12, Jesus encourages his listeners to trust in God's superabundance and generosity. He tells the parable of the rich man who stores food, thinking he was providing for himself a merry retirement and then dies before he can enjoy it. Jesus then states, "Do not worry about your life and what you will eat, or about your body and what you will wear. For life is more than food and the body more than clothing. Notice the ravens: they do not sow or reap; they have neither storehouse nor barn, yet God feeds them" (Luke 12:22–24; Matt. 6:25–34). Similarly, in *Amoris Laetitia*, Francis presents God as a Father who tenderly feeds His children. Francis references the prophet Hosea, who in remembrance of the manna in the desert, writes, "When Israel was a child, I loved him. . . . I took them up in my arms. . . . I led them with cords of compassion, with the bands of love, and I became to them as one who eases the yoke on their jaws, and I bent down to them and fed them."[63] These passages from Luke and Hosea manifest God's generosity and care.

I will focus specifically on feeding children. If feeding the hungry is a work of mercy, one can say with James Keenan that "parents of young children are the merciful ones par excellence."[64] Children have exceptional needs for food.[65] Infants need to be fed even when parents would like to be sleeping.[66] Toddlers can prevent their caregivers from sitting down to enjoy a meal with their requests for food and assistance. Convincing a toddler to eat vegetables, engaging an antsy child so they sit long enough to chew and swallow some food, packing a snack on a trip to the park, attempting to

63 Hosea 11:1, 3–4. Francis, *Amoris Laetitia*, 28.

64 Keenan, *The Works of Mercy*, 140.

65 Despite this unique need for food, many children disproportionately go without adequate food and water. Francis, Encyclical Letter *Fratelli Tutti* (October 3, 2020), 29. One reason for this is that children, as Francis frequently reminds us, are weak and vulnerable. Francis, *Laudato si'*, 120. They often cannot earn their bread, and they do not have the position or the words to make their voices heard.

66 Francis reflects uniquely on breastfeeding as an act of mercy, referencing Psalm 131: "I have calmed and quieted my soul, like a child quieted at its mother's breast." Francis, *Amoris Laetitia*, 28. God tenderly and intimately cares for His people like a mother breastfeeding a child. When asked about child hunger in an interview, he noted how social structures need to cultivate food conservation and create the distribution system necessary to alleviate hunger pains. He links the need for social structures to public pressure that sometimes prevents mothers from breastfeeding a hungry child in public places. He emphatically states, "Give food to those who are hungry!" Interview with Pope Francis, December 2013, *La Stampa*, https://www.lastampa.it/vatican-insider/en/2013/12/15/news/never-be-afraid-of-tenderness-1.35947042; see also, Francis, "Homily on the Feast of the Baptism of the Lord," January 11, 2015.

feed an adolescent going through a growth spurt, or preparing a meal for a picky eater are more mundane examples, but still expressions of mercy if done for the good of the other and not simply to quiet them down. In these activities, individuals seek to nourish the child so he can grow. They feed the child so that she does not become uncomfortable, irritable, or confused. The task of feeding the hungry is made even more difficult when those who are hungry do not wish to eat—they do not like the food, or they lack a desire to eat, or they are distracted by something else. Entering the chaos of another often requires patience, planning, and creativity.

The act of feeding one's family can range from the mundane to the dramatic. Some individuals heroically feed family members with mental or physical limitations, grave food allergies, or extreme dietary needs, or work multiple jobs or even go without food so that their families are properly nourished.

Others provide daily bread for family members who have not truly felt the pains of hunger. One does not perform a work of mercy, however, merely by handing one's daughter some food. She must be hungry. The food must be nourishing and presented in such a way that she actually eats and benefits from the food. One's intention must be to aid her in her misery and when possible, it should come in the context of a personal encounter, prototypically a family meal beginning with prayer and continuing with conversation. As the parable of the prodigal son shows, food is not only a means of ensuring nutrition—it is also a way to celebrate important occasions, to show recognition of another (as with a birthday party), and to build communion. Finally, recognizing that the food is first a gift of creation, one should seek to serve one's daughter as an instrument, either explicitly or by general commitment, of God's mercy.

These dispositions need not remain merely interior, but they can be made part of the family culture. Parents with multiple children can enlist an older one to help feed a younger one as a way of educating them to care for the needs of others. If there is a family pet, a child can learn this attitude by feeding the dog or cat. It will then become second nature for parents and children together to extend this care beyond the family—to take part of a batch of cookies to a neighbor, or to drop a few cans in a food drive or "blessing box" for the needy, or to make a meal for another family who has just had a new baby. Perhaps the one preparing meals can announce that this Lent, the money saved from buying less meat or fewer sweets will be given away to the poor. By approaching food as a work of mercy within and beyond the home, parents also teach their children (and themselves) to distinguish between needs and wants, between nourishment and excess, and between true festivity and self-indulgence.

Caring for the Sick

Individuals also perform works of mercy when they care for sick family members. While many praise doctors and nurses, often overlooked is the similar but hidden care that individuals provide for their family members. Francis speaks to familial care for the sick in a Wednesday audience he delivered on June 10, 2015. He affirms that illness is part of human existence and highlights that we often experience illness in the home. He proposes, "The family we can say has always been the nearest 'hospital.' Still today, in so many parts of the world, a hospital is for the privileged few and is often far away. It is the mother, the father, brothers, sisters, and grandparents who guarantee care and help one to heal."[67]

Francis notes the heart-wrenching trials of witnessing the illness of a child: "So often for a father or a mother, it is more difficult to bear a son or daughter's pain than one's own."[68] He praises those who care for their sick children or grandparents: "These are heroic deeds, the heroism of families! That hidden heroism carried out with tenderness and courage when someone at home is sick."[69] Francis also highlights daily care for those with special physical or mental needs. Quoting the Synod of Bishops' *Relatio Finalis* from 2015, Francis writes in *Amoris Laetitia*:

> Families who lovingly accept the difficult trial of a child with special needs are greatly to be admired. They render the Church and society an invaluable witness of faithfulness to the gift of life. In these situations, the family can discover, together with the Christian community, new approaches, new ways of acting, a different way of understanding and identifying with others, by welcoming and caring for the mystery of the frailty of human life.[70]

67 Francis, *On the Family*, trans. *L'Osservatore Romano* (San Francisco: Ignatius Press, 2015), 84. See also Francis, "Message for the 24th World Day of the Sick 2016," September 25, 2015, in which Francis speaks of "a mother at the bedside of her sick child, or a child caring for an elderly parent, or a grandchild concerned for a grandparent."

68 Francis, *On the Family*, 84.

69 Francis, *On the Family*, 86. Francis also speaks about care for the elderly in *Amoris Laetitia* (48).

70 Francis, *Amoris Laetitia*, 47; see also 82, 195.

Since illness is a part of human existence, Francis highlights how important it is for parents to teach children, starting from childhood, about solidarity in times of illness. "An education which protects against sensitivity for human illness withers the heart. It allows young people to be 'anaesthetized' against the suffering of others, incapable of facing suffering and of living the experience of limitation."[71] Those who recognize human weakness and vulnerability and the need for God's mercy can draw on that mercy in their service to others.

In addition to the formative role the family exercises in preparing individuals for mercy in broader society and in the intelligibility of the Gospel's familial language of mercy, the first and most fundamental motivation for exercising mercy in the family is the poverty of family members who stand before one every day in their vulnerability and weakness, crying for the face of the Father's mercy. In *Amoris Laetitia*, Francis writes about "that 'gaze' which contemplates other persons as ends in themselves, even if they are infirm, elderly or physically unattractive."[72] He continues, "A look of appreciation has enormous importance, and to begrudge it is usually hurtful. How many things do spouses and children sometimes do in order to be noticed!"[73] Often individuals hurt, and family members are the only ones who see. One has opportunities for living mercy in one's family that are available to no one else. God asks the faithful to be instruments of His mercy to their family members so that they, the faithful and the family members, can experience the joy of that mercy. This is especially true for those facing the diminishment of their capacities at the end of life. In *Amoris Laetitia*, Francis observes, "The elderly who are vulnerable and dependent are at times unfairly exploited simply for economic advantage. Many families show us that it is possible to approach the last stages of life by emphasizing the importance of a person's sense of fulfilment and participation in the Lord's paschal mystery."[74] It is in time of illness that family members can recognize their intrinsic value as persons, beyond what they can contribute.

Illness and diminished physical ability often spoil what Francis calls the "dream of an idyllic and perfect love needing no stimulus to grow." Bearing with one another through health struggles demonstrates that it is "much

71 Francis, *On the Family*, 86. Francis quotes this section again in *Amoris Laetitia* (277).

72 Francis, *Amoris Laetitia*, 128.

73 Francis, 128.

74 Francis, *Amoris Laetitia*, 48; see also 47, 82, 128, 191–93, 197.

healthier to be realistic about our limits, defects and imperfections, and to respond to the call to grow together, to bring love to maturity and to strengthen the union, come what may."[75] Families are called to image Christ's love for the Church and the communion of the Trinity. They also need guidance in their everyday struggles as they encounter one another's weaknesses and vulnerability. Every person needs God's mercy. Nothing escapes the reach of God's love. Family life is by no means the exception.

Caring for the sick involves more than just those with acute injuries or illnesses, and it rarely consists of those who are fully well caring for those who are simply incapacitated. Psychological and spiritual ailments include thoughts of inadequacy; addictions (whether to drugs, alcohol, gambling, shopping, pornography, or internet loitering); an inability to communicate or express love; tendencies toward physical, psychological, or sexual abuse; scars and self-identifications that result from such abuse; skill deficiencies; pride; jealousy; betrayal; deceit; and a lack of faith. Often in family life, those who struggle with one or more of these challenges are caring for others with their own. Mercy is proper to God. A human work of mercy never involves someone who is self-sustaining helping another who is in need, but always one person in need of mercy trying to be an instrument of God's mercy to another person in need. The intimacy and stability of family relationships surfaces and exposes wounds and vulnerabilities. Often, family members are the only ones who will see and who can respond to those needs.

CONCLUSION

The nature of mercy and the history of the works of mercy help to clarify how family interactions can be works of mercy. Mercy is a subvirtue of charity, in which one relates well to the misery of others. A work of mercy is an action in which one truly, knowingly, and willingly aids another in his need as an instrument of God's mercy. Since the thirteenth century, the phrase "works of mercy" has referred to a largely stable set of corporal and spiritual works. Since mercy addresses the misery of others, and since all individuals endure misery, individuals can perform works of mercy in their families insofar as they aid another and serve, explicitly or by general commitment,

75 Francis, 135. The reference within the quotation comes from the Chilean Bishops' Conference, *La vida y la familia: regalos de Dios para cada uno de nosotros* (July 21, 2014), https://www.iglesia.cl/4303-la-vida-y-la-familia-regalos-de-dios-para-cada-uno-de-nosotros.htm. For similar statements, see Francis, *Amoris Laetitia* (201, 221, 231–58, 269–73, 320, 325) and Francis, *Misericordiae Vultus* (6, 7, 9, 25).

as instruments of God's love. This witness of mercy in the family addresses human needs but also enhances the intelligibility of key biblical passages related to mercy that employ familial language. Finally, I offered the examples of feeding hungry children and caring for the sick. Hunger can vary from the risk of starvation to more mundane reminders of one's need for food. Accordingly, feeding one's family can range from the mundane to the heroic. Concerning care for the sick, Francis reminds us that the family is often the nearest hospital.

Answering Christ's challenge to carry out the works of mercy in family life is crucial because family members often are the only ones positioned to see and address human needs. The works of mercy, therefore, express another indication of the internally social character of the family. Family life does not exist in a private, socially isolated community with the sole purpose of providing individual satisfaction for its members. The family is a social community containing various features of social life. The family is a location for social ethics, including the application of Catholic social principles and the works of mercy. The family, however, is not a perfect, self-contained social community. In reflecting on the family's internally social character, one begins to see its social interdependence with other communities. The family, for example, forms individual members who then contribute to the broader society. Moreover, the family benefits from a theological articulation of social principles, the works of mercy, and the love of God, which animates justice and mercy. To understand how the family is a basic social unit, one needs to see both its internally social character and its social interdependence. After developing notions around the family's internally social character, I now seek to analyze in more detail the family's social interdependence.

PART II

The Social Interdependence of Families

4

The Social Interdependence of Families

Over and against conceptual models that reduce family relationships to a marriage contract aimed at individual satisfaction, I have argued that the family is internally social. However, it is important to be careful about stopping with an analysis of the family's internally social character. If one reads the internally social character of the family through the lens of isolated family models or even clan family models, one might draw the devastatingly misleading conclusion that families are self-sufficient, are not influenced by other social communities, and do not bear responsibilities toward other social communities. The family is not a complete and self-sufficient social community. In addition to being internally social, I propose that the family also is interdependent with other social communities. I develop this claim in two steps. First, I demonstrate how and why the family is dependent on other social communities. One sees the dependence of the family in the needs of the family, in the way other communities influence and provide a context for family life, and in the fulfillment of the human person, which requires love of God and love of neighbor. Second, I analyze the social interdependence of families with the Church, civil society, the state, and the economy. I propose that the family and the Church are mutually constitutive. While the Church clarifies the meaning and end of family life, families provide life and formation for the faithful. Concerning civil society, the economy, and the state, I clarify the role of civil societies and describe families as a social nucleus and as potential models, but then highlight how they are in turn molded by culture. I argue that families are dependent on and responsible to broader communities. Since families are interdependent with other communities, the question is not whether, but how, to engage with other communities.

THE FAMILY'S SOCIAL DEPENDENCE

To see the family's social interdependence, one first must recognize how families are dependent on broader social communities for meeting needs and developing friendships. Lisa Sowle Cahill challenges individualistic accounts of family and reframes the conversation: "Despite an ethos of individualism, humans rarely in fact live in isolation. Therefore, before calling for more and stronger community, we must recognize that humans typically *do* live in communities; the question is what kind of communities we create and who is accepted within them."[1] One sees the family's dependence most clearly when families struggle with basic needs and require the urgent assistance of the surrounding community.[2] Families that lack basic needs—housing, food, education, or employment—or suffer from various challenges, including addiction, abuse, physical illness, mental illness, false ideals, or an inability to communicate, will need the help of others to live out the familial mission to form members in virtue and participate in civil society.[3]

The dependence of the family on other social communities is not limited to those families with urgent needs. Every family is interdependent with other social communities and necessarily exists within a particular social and cultural context.[4] Families rely on various social structures. Lisa Cahill highlights eleven systems on which families rely: economic, political, educational, housing, health, social welfare, criminal justice, military, transportation, recreation, and communications.[5] When such structures are lacking or are riddled with injustice, families suffer. Families are harmed when their

1 Lisa Sowle Cahill, *Family: A Christian Social Perspective* (Minneapolis: Fortress, 2000), 102.

2 John Paul II, Apostolic Exhortation *Familiaris Consortio* (November 22, 1981), 6; Second Vatican Council, Pastoral Constitution in the Modern World *Gaudium et Spes* (December 7, 1965), 31, 52, 66, and 74, in *Vatican Council II: The Conciliar and Post Conciliar Documents*, ed. Austin Flannery, rev. ed. (Collegeville, MN: Liturgical Press, 1975).

3 Lisa Cahill notes that families "laboring under disadvantage" need broader support to meet their needs but also that these families "have a contribution to make in defining what family is, how families carry Christian identity, and how the church is built up in and through families." *Family*, 84.

4 Pope John Paul II, *Familiaris Consortio*, 4, 30, and 42.

5 Cahill, *Family*, 127. Cahill also emphasizes the family's need for community (98–100), and she proposes that church documents show an increasing recognition of how other practices, even international practices, impact families and how families require broader communal support (88). As evidence of this trend, see for example, Pope Paul VI, Encyclical Letter *Populorum Progressio* (March 26, 1967), 23, 26, 44, 48, and 80. See also David Matzko McCarthy's work highlighting the importance of neighbors, friends, and extended family: *Sex and Love in the Home: A Theology of the Household*, 2nd ed. (London: SCM Press, 2004). Many church documents also highlight the need for families to support other families and the role mentor couples can have in guiding those who are married toward loving relationships and productive family lives. See, e.g., John Paul II, *Familiaris Consortio*, 69; Pope Francis, Postsynodal Apostolic Exhortation *Amoris Laetitia* (March 19, 2016), 223–25, 230–32.

physical safety is threatened by war or crime, by the absence of educational or employment opportunities, when political corruption favors those in power, or when families cannot access basic healthcare.[6] Family stability and the mission of family formation require physical safety, educational support, the means for transportation and communication, and employment opportunities that pay a family wage.

Highlighting the family's need for broader social support and interaction, Pope Pius XI proposes that the family is a society that does not have "in itself all the means for its own complete development."[7] The family is not a perfect community; that is, it is not a comprehensive social community that can provide every social good necessary for its members. Neither spouses, nor kids, nor parents can fulfill on their own all of their interpersonal needs and desires.[8] The family is not an isolated, perfect community but a social, imperfect community. If one views family as a totally fulfilling affective refuge, then its members' inability to fulfill or be fulfilled by the family alone will cause frustration. Human fulfillment and a flourishing family require a broader social life. David Matzko McCarthy observes that understanding the family's broader social needs changes how one perceives its social limitations: "If we consider this lack of wholeness, not as a failure, but as part of the social character of the household, then we will be open to a network of households and friendships that enrich our marriages and cultivate the talents and skills of being loving husbands, mothers, sisters, and sons."[9] The family's social needs enable broader social relationships.

McCarthy recognizes that some social giving is asymmetrical: one gives without receiving and receives without giving. He proposes, however, that asymmetrical giving of one neighbor to another, while potentially exhausting in isolation, is sustained by a broader communal context of mutual self-giving.[10] Being the household where neighborhood kids gather can be

6 Second Vatican Council, *Gaudium et Spes*, 31, 47, 52, 66, in Flannery, *Vatican Council II*; John Paul II, *Familiaris Consortio*, 81; Francis, *Amoris Laetitia*, 23–25, 43–46; and Pope Pius XI, Encyclical Letter *Divini Illius Magistri* (December 31, 1929), 73.

7 Pius XI, *Divini Illius Magistri*, 12; see also 45, 77.

8 Francis highlights that every individual needs communion with God; one's spouse cannot fulfill all of one's needs. Francis, *Amoris Laetitia*, 320.

9 McCarthy, *Sex and Love in the Home*, 174. See also page 92 where McCarthy writes, "Spouses and children will look beyond the walls of their homes for friendship and intimacy, not when the family system breaks down, but as a matter of its good working order."

10 McCarthy, 103.

supported by other kinds of giving, like sharing garden produce or plowing snow. The social life necessary to support asymmetrical giving in a neighborhood also sheds light on the family's need for social support to sustain asymmetrical giving within the family. Family circumstances often require that individuals give without receiving, as when parents care for multiple young children or when someone in the family has temporary or permanent special needs. A supportive neighborhood or community of friends can help sustain the asymmetrical giving that family life sometimes requires.[11] One who sees the family as a perfect, isolated community will overlook the need for this broader communal support, become overwhelmed by asymmetrical giving, begin counting costs, and become resentful toward family members who seem to be draining one's life. Recognizing the dependence of the family on other social communities allows us to see that support for one's family and for broader social communities need not stand in tension. As the principle of the common good highlights, the good of the community and the good of individuals, including the poor and weak, are not competitive but harmonious goods.[12]

Even in the educational and moral formation of children, a responsibility that falls uniquely to parents, the family is interdependent with other social communities. John Paul II writes, "The family is the primary but not the only and exclusive educating community."[13] One could say that John Paul II's insight is merely a description. Whether one realizes it or not, children are "educated" and "formed" by school or daycare, friends, peer pressure, dynamic leaders, art, music, advertisements, and cultural norms. The family is not the sole educational community. Beyond this descriptive sense, the fullness of life implies that no one person or family can know all things or fully embody all skills. The broader community provides teachers and mentors who can invite family members to grow in ways that family members by themselves cannot.[14] Even parents who encourage children to

11 Francis highlights how care for the elderly can place strains on family life and that the Church therefore must support families. Francis, *Amoris Laetitia*, 48.

12 Second Vatican Council, *Gaudium et Spes*, 25, in Flannery, *Vatican Council II*, 926.

13 John Paul II, *Familiaris Consortio*, 40; see also Second Vatican Council, *Gaudium et Spes*, 31, in Flannery, *Vatican Council II*, 931; and Pius XI, *Divini Illius Magistri*, 11.

14 Pius XI, *Divini Illius Magistri*, 77. McCarthy proposes that parents "should encourage sponsorship relationships for their children, if for no other reason than to diffuse parental authority and to offer children alternative avenues of dependence. A child establishes his or her social identity not through independence, but through maintaining his or her own lines of interdependence." *Sex and Love in the Home*, 236–37.

be independent learners are dependent on social structures such as public libraries and the internet.

Further, the stability necessary for family formation requires political and economic stability. Families depend on the economic system to provide jobs and make available material goods so that individuals can provide for family needs and support family members in their pursuit of fulfillment. The workplace at its best is a community supportive of family life by providing wages, working conditions, and hours that allow parents to live out their calling to form their children and to cultivate in their family a community of love. Work also should provide individuals with opportunities to develop their talents and skills as well as meaningful relationships with their coworkers, supervisors, and customers.

Families rely on the state to enact legislation supporting the basic social role of the family. The state also promulgates laws and provides law enforcement to keep families safe. In situations of domestic abuse, keeping family members safe may require that the state intervene to protect some family members from the actions of others. Families also rely on the state to protect family rights and provide social programs for basic needs when they are not being met.[15]

When economic and political structures and support are lacking, or are plagued by injustice, families suffer. In the context of political corruption or war, families are hindered by exploitation and premature death. Similarly, in the absence of job opportunities, parents struggle to provide basic material resources for their families while also struggling with doubts about whether they have something to contribute to society.[16] Without support from just political and economic systems, the family is forced to focus on survival and struggles to develop a community of persons and to be intentional about providing a foundational formation for its members.

15 The bishops of the Second Vatican Council write in their document on religious liberty that "every family, in that it is a society with its own basic rights, has the right freely to organize its own religious life in the home under the control of the parents. These have the right to decide in accordance with their own religious beliefs the form of religious upbringing which is to be given to their children." Second Vatican Council, Declaration on Religious Liberty *Dignitatis Humanae* (December 7, 1965), 5, trans. Laurence Ryan, in Flannery, *Vatican Council II*, 803. In *Familiaris Consortio*, John Paul II calls gravely unjust aid programs that require contraception, sterilization, and procured abortion (30) and proposes that public authorities should do what they can to support families economically, socially, educationally, politically, and culturally (45).

16 John Paul II, *Familiaris Consortio*, 67.

The social dependence of the family has theological foundations as well. Everyone, and therefore every family, is radically dependent on God. At the beginning of human life, God creates a new human soul out of nothing. God's redeems humanity. The social community of the family alone cannot fulfill a person's social longing. Only union with the Trinity and membership in the Kingdom of God will bring that fulfillment. God provides His grace to strengthen and support families. One could say that the goal of life is radical dependence on and community with God.[17] Families also are dependent on the gift of creation.[18] All good things come from God. A family's possessions are first and foundationally a gift of creation. As John Paul II highlights, any work is cooperation with creation.[19] This is true also for work in one's family.

While the family is internally social, it remains dependent on other social communities. The family is dependent on other social communities because families have urgent needs, because other social communities provide the context for and influence family life, and because the fulfillment of individuals requires divine and human communion. This dependence on social communities presents both opportunities and challenges and consequently raises many questions: Should one send children to public school or private school? What kinds of volunteer or civic commitments are compatible with home and family responsibilities? What role should social media have in one's household? How should one choose a parish community? When and how should one bring work or political concerns into household conversations? Social communities provide resources for the family, but they also provide temptations to lose sight of the one thing necessary.

Interdependence is a two-way street. Families are influenced by social communities and families have responsibilities toward social communities. One sees this interdependence more clearly when one examines the relationship between the family and the Church, and the family and civil society, the economy, and the state.

17 Second Vatican Council, *Gaudium et Spes*, 19, in Flannery, *Vatican Council II*, 918–19; a section later, the bishops of the council speak of a modern form of atheism that "so insists on man's desire for autonomy as to object to any dependence on God at all." *Gaudium et Spes*, 20, in Flannery, *Vatican Council II*, 919.

18 Reflecting on Isaiah 11:6–9, Mary Doyle Roche notes "our radical interdependence with creation." Mary M. Doyle Roche, *Children, Consumerism, and the Common Good* (Lanham, MD: Lexington Books, 2009), 3.

19 John Paul II, Encyclical Letter *Laborem Exercens* (September 14, 1981), 12–13, in *Catholic Social Thought: The Documentary History*, ed. David J. O'Brien and Thomas A. Shannon, rev. ed. (Maryknoll, NY: Orbis Books, 2016).

THE FAMILY AND THE CHURCH

For many Catholic families in contemporary society, the Church is an organization whose services they receive perhaps for an hour a week, or perhaps even less frequently (as in weddings or funerals). By contrast, in describing the relationship between the family and the Church, Jana Bennett writes, "The church and the household are determinative for each other."[20] Each community is distinct but nonetheless mutually constitutive. To see the vital relationship between families and the Church, one needs to engage with attempts to collapse one community into the other, and then clarify their mutually penetrating roles and responsibilities. I will briefly describe how socially detached definitions of family and the Church often collapse the Church into the family and then engage readings of the biblical witness that reduce the family into the Church. After uncovering and showing the limits of these two reductions, I will then reflect on the distinct and determinative character of both families and the Church.

If family life and church life are merely expressions of individual rights and choices devoid of social goods and responsibilities, then both communities are a refuge from social concerns and a context in which individuals pursue self-fulfillment. The Church becomes merely a location for families to express themselves. In such a framework, the phrase "domestic church" might suggest that each family forms its own denomination, and that church is merely a physical space to gather like-minded families. The private, socially detached Church is an extension of private, socially detached families. The Church is reduced to the family, which is reduced to the pursuit of temporary self-fulfillment.

The biblical witness, however, seems to collapse family into the Church. One sees in the Gospels, especially the Gospel of Luke, the prominence of family connections in biblical times. Since family models of biblical times vary drastically from contemporary models of isolation, one does well to indicate, even if only in broad strokes, the robust social character and influence of many ancient households. Lisa Sowle Cahill explains that, for many early Christians, families extend

20 Jana Marguerite Bennett, *Water Is Thicker Than Blood: An Augustinian Theology of Marriage and Singleness* (Oxford: Oxford University Press, 2008), 46. Bennett intentionally uses the more expansive term "household" rather than family.

> both vertically to ancestors and descendants and horizontally to relatives, as well as to such unrelated persons as slaves, freedpersons with legal bonds to the family, and servants. Individual identity is defined primarily in relation to the family and its social place; it consists of the duties, responsibilities, and prerogatives one holds within one's family and by virtue of one's family role in the social network.[21]

Cahill notes that this socially robust family model helps to explain early Christianity's ambivalence toward the family—Jesus warns his disciples about specific family commitments but many of the first Christian communities gathered around households.[22]

Throughout the Gospel of Luke, Luke invites the reader to transition from commitment to one's household to the family of God.[23] Jesus tells his listeners that his family "are those who hear the word of God and act on it" (Luke 8:21) and that "from now on a household of five will be divided, three against two and two against three" (Luke 12:52). He warns, "You will even be handed over by parents, brothers, relatives, and friends, and they will put some of you to death" (Luke 21:16). Most dramatically, Jesus states: "If anyone comes to me without hating his father and mother, wife and children, brothers and sisters, and even his own life, he cannot be my disciple" (Luke 14:26).

It might be discouraging to pastoral ministers and academics who work to strengthen family bonds within a cultural context where family commitments seem weak to recall these seemingly negative statements about family life. Moral theologians might be tempted to overlook these passages or to approach them defensively; that is, to argue that Jesus is not undermining family commitments. However, one also should note the positive content of these passages. In calling for a movement from household commitments to the family of God, Luke is clarifying the interdependent relationship between family life and the Church.

21 Cahill, *Family*, 19; see also Samuel L. Adams, *Social and Economic Life in Second Temple Judea* (Louisville: Westminster John Knox Press, 2014), 8.

22 Cahill, *Family*, 18.

23 The next few pages rely significantly on Kevin Schemenauer, "Hating One's Family: Reading Luke 14:26 in the Context of Luke's Gospel," in *Human Families: Identities, Relationships, and Responsibilities*, ed. Jacob M. Kohlhaas and Mary M. Doyle Roche, College Theology Society Annual Volume 66 (Maryknoll, NY: Orbis Books, 2021), 100–11. https://orbisbooks.com/collections/series-college-theology-society/products/human-families. The author uses that material here with permission from Orbis.

First, Luke's insights highlight the family's need for the Church to frame its commitments in relation to God. Luke's strong language serves as a reminder that certain things—like self, material possessions, and family commitments, perhaps because they are such great goods—can creep into the space that ought to be reserved for God alone. Putting those things before God does not necessarily require an intentional choice; it can happen if one is not careful to avoid it. Luke's strong language can shake us out of complacency into a deeper faith that persists in reframing family commitments in relation to God and the family of God.

Second, Luke's movement from family commitments to the family of God highlights the positive role that the family can exercise in the Church. Luke shows that family commitments can provide relationships and language that enlighten Christian discipleship.[24] This movement from family to family of God is true of conceptual understandings of the faith in part because it is first true in the realm of existence and experience. John Paul II proposes that the family is the cradle of the Church.[25] Families bring life to the Church through procreation but also when they live as a communion of persons. As a social unit, the family helps to clarify that Christian love is not merely abstract, selfless love but a love ordered toward community.[26] As the basic social unit, the loving communion of family life can model for the Church what human communion entails. John Paul II writes, "Thanks to love within the family, the Church can and ought to take on a more homelike or family dimension, developing a more human and fraternal style of relationship."[27] Further, since families share mutual experiences, families often are well positioned to serve the Church in the vital mission of building up other families.[28]

The third insight from these difficult passages in the Gospel of Luke is that Christian discipleship and commitment to God contextualize family commitments: "Christian marriage is not a whole communion of two, but a particular kind of grace-filled friendship within the fellowship of the Church."[29] This

24 Schemenauer, "Hating One's Family," 109.

25 John Paul II, *Familiaris Consortio*, 15.

26 McCarthy, *Sex and Love in the Home*, 151.

27 John Paul II, *Familiaris Consortio*, 64; see also Francis, *Amoris Laetitia*, 207.

28 John Paul II, *Familiaris Consortio*, 52–54, 71; in section 52, John Paul II references Paul VI's apostolic exhortation *Evangelii Nuntiandi* (71); see also Francis, *Amoris Laetitia*, 287–89.

29 Bennett, *Water Is Thicker Than Blood*, 46; the quotation is taken from David Matzko McCarthy, "Becoming One Flesh: Marriage, Remarriage and Sex," in *The Blackwell Companion to Christian Ethics*, ed. Stanley M. Hauerwas and Samuel Wells (Oxford: Blackwell, 2004), 277.

theological context does not eliminate families but clarifies, and in some ways enhances, the role of the family. In a Christian context, the family is not limited to providing economic, social, and political support to family members. Within the family of God, one has the even greater mission of introducing family members to Christ and forming them in the way of Christ. Since family members often are connected by sacramental commitments, shared DNA, shared living spaces, and relationships that are both foundational and intimate, family members are in a unique position to share and live the Gospel with one another.

The Church also can assist families in a variety of other ways. While parents are the primary educators and formators of their children, the Church ought to provide faith formation when such formation is absent and support parents who are active in this formation. This requires, when possible, that the church community not replace the formative role of parents but empower them to provide the formation that only they can provide.[30]

The Church also provides families with faith fellowship, the Word of God, and God's life through the sacraments. John Paul II highlights the importance of the sacraments for families in *Familiaris Consortio*. He proposes that the family's mission is rooted in baptism and strengthened and made specific by the sacrament of marriage.[31] Further, he writes, "The eucharist is the very source of Christian marriage. The eucharistic sacrifice in fact represents Christ's covenant of love with the Church, sealed with his blood on the cross."[32] He also argues that "repentance and mutual pardon within the bosom of the Christian family, so much a part of daily life, receive their specific sacramental expression in Christian penance."[33] To participate in the sacraments, families need the Church to identify and support future pastors. Families enduring acute struggles also rely on the Church to form future and active ministers to support and guide families.[34]

30 Florence Caffrey Bourg invites us to imagine a shift from parish- or congregation-centered and family-supported religious education to family-centered and parish- or congregation-supported religious education. See Florence Caffrey Bourg, *Where Two or Three Are Gathered: Christian Families as Domestic Churches* (Notre Dame, IN: University of Notre Dame Press, 2004), 123, 134.

31 John Paul II, *Familiaris Consortio*, 52.

32 John Paul II, 57.

33 John Paul II, 58.

34 John Paul II, 34, 65; see also Francis, *Amoris Laetitia*, 241–42.

The family and the Church are distinct but not separate, unique communities, and they are mutually determinative. The family is not a perfect, isolated community but a social community interdependent with the Church. John Paul II writes that the Church should help families "to harmonize the intimacy of home life with the generous shared work of building up the church and society."[35] If the Church should help families, one might ask: Who makes up the Church? Surely, John Paul II is asking pastors and diocesan and parish staff to assist families. However, insofar as the Church is the people of God, then the lay faithful, as members of the body of Christ, also act on behalf of the Church when they assist families. Individuals need not wait for their pastor to ask them to help. In fact, those who have significant family commitments often are best positioned to see and respond to the needs of other families. Going a step further, in the internally social context of a family, those who identify as Catholic, for good or for ill, represent the Church to their family members. The Second Vatican Council affirms in the Decree on the Apostolate of the Laity that families are "a domestic sanctuary of the Church."[36] Here, sanctuary is a place in which the divine presence dwells rather than a refuge from external influences. A family is a location where the people of God serve, love, and experience both God's grace and the cross of discipleship.

Seeing the family as a "domestic sanctuary of the Church"—and recognizing that the Church includes more than those who are on the church's payroll—opens numerous opportunities for the Church to support families. Pope Francis writes,

> Parishes, movements, schools and other Church institutions can help in a variety of ways to support families and help them grow. These might include: meetings of couples living in the same neighbourhood, brief retreats for couples; talks by experts on concrete issues facing families, marriage counselling, home missionaries who help couples discuss their difficulties and desires, social services dealing with family problems like addiction, infidelity and domestic violence, programmes of spiritual growth, workshops for parents with troubled children and family meetings. The parish office should be prepared to deal helpfully and sensitively

35 John Paul II, *Familiaris Consortio*, 69.

36 Second Vatican Council, Decree on the Apostolate of the Laity *Apostolicam Actuositatem*, 11, in *Vatican Council II: The Conciliar and Post Conciliar Documents*, ed. Austin Flannery, OP (Collegeville, MN: The Liturgical Press, 1984), 779.

> with family needs and be able to make referrals, when necessary, to those who can help. There is also the contribution made by groups of married couples that provide assistance as part of their commitment to service, prayer, formation and mutual support. Such groups enable couples to be generous, to assist other families and to share the faith; at the same time they strengthen marriages and help them to grow.[37]

This list is by no means exhaustive. Parishes could provide, for example, full community catechesis, childcare while parents participate in parish ministries, social ministry opportunities for the whole family, guidance for family transitions, and incorporate the immobile elderly into the life of the faith community through home visits or live videos.

If both the family and the Church were perfect and isolated communities, they would share no essential connection or responsibility to one another. Instead, the family and the Church are social communities that are unique but also mutually determinative. Families are a domestic sanctuary of the Church and the Church points to the family of God. Families can provide new life, form individuals in faith, positively represent the Church, and provide a model of communion. The Church in turn helps frame family life in relation to God, and assists families through marriage preparation, marriage support, and forming a communion of believers, and by providing access to the Word of God and the sacraments.

THE FAMILY, CIVIL SOCIETY, THE ECONOMY, AND THE STATE

The family is not an isolated, private refuge from surrounding communities but interdependent with those communities. Civil society, the economy, and the state all influence families, and families in turn have responsibilities to these communities. To prepare for later discussion about how families can live social interdependence well, I present now a general analysis of the relationship between families and civil society, the economy, and the state. The family, the Church, civil society, the economy, and the state need to be distinguished because each of these communities plays a crucial role in promoting the common good. Perhaps civil society requires the most explanation. Families connected through marriage, conception, and adoption, enjoy intimate and permanent connections and thereby provide a foundational

37 Francis, *Amoris Laetitia*, 229.

formation and often enduring support. The Church is a community of faith that highlights what is most important in life: living in God's love. The Pontifical Council for Justice and Peace defines civil society as "*the sum total of relationships and resources, cultural and associative, that are relatively independent from the political sphere and the economic sphere*."[38] Whereas the political sphere forms bonds through authority and power, and individuals seek financial benefit in their economic relationships, civil society includes those bonds developed when individuals "form associations, working to develop and express their preferences, in order to meet their fundamental needs and defend their legitimate interests."[39] Civil society is the space in which individuals join various and complex voluntary communities that enrich and influence life, such as one's neighborhood, a sports league, a group of friends, a community art initiative, or a group centered around an Instagram account. Through these voluntary associations, individuals can express themselves freely and creatively, develop friendships, and develop a common public ethos. Social analysis that focuses on large social structures tends to overlook the role of civil society in socially developing and forming individuals. The voluntary associations that form civil society express the social interdependence of families.

Families, the Church, civil society, the economy, and the state are distinct but not separate. In important ways, the family and the Church are communities within civil society, even if the importance of the family and the Church requires that they be in their own categories.[40] Especially for those who are committed to their faith and to their families, most voluntary social associations occur in the family and in the Church. Moreover, family life involves economic concerns and politics, as do most voluntary associations. The state is important to economics, and economics is influenced by the state. To prepare for later discussion about how families ought to live their social interdependence well, I begin here by analyzing in more systematic and general terms the social interdependence of families. I propose that families serve civil society, the economy, and the state as a social nucleus and potentially as a model. In turn, civil society, the economy, and the state form and mold families. The dependence of families on other social

38 Pontifical Council for Justice and Peace, *Compendium of the Social Doctrine of the Church* (Washington, DC: United States Conference of Catholic Bishops, 2004), 417, italics in original.

39 Pontifical Council for Justice and Peace, 417.

40 Cahill describes the family as "an institution of civil society." *Family*, 7.

communities and the formative character of those families highlight the family's responsibility to serve the common good of those communities.

Family as Nucleus and Model

McCarthy cautions that if one trivializes the social character of the home, one risks downplaying or overlooking how ordinary practices of local interdependence form a complex system of interchange and a rich community life.[41] While civil society provides the family with a context for social interaction, the family often serves as a nucleus for such social exchange. Relationships often develop from family connections. A neighbor may become more friendly after a couple begins walking with a newborn child or a toddler. Children form friendships with the kids of their parents' friends and coworkers. Parents build relationships with others while supporting a child's sports team, band, or school. Since each member of a family has different interests and commitments, that family is a nucleus of rich social interaction.

Family relationships layer one's connections with others. One's neighbor might be a teacher to one's son, a caregiver to one's parents, or a teammate on a family member's soccer team. These relationships may begin by being focused one-dimensionally on work or fundraisers but then can develop into informal connections or bartered agreements in which there is "a local currency of skills, like welding or sewing, and informal standards of exchange, such as pies for plumbing."[42] A common task may open conversations and provide a context for sharing and meeting personal needs and wants. One family may need a neighbor to watch their kids for a few hours, or to gather mail or feed and walk a pet while they are traveling. If they are a neighbor or a classmate, they might share rides and tools and knowledge about assignments and local events and services. Families often serve as a nucleus of social interactions. In chapter 7, I develop this theme of family as social nucleus by analyzing how family responsibilities can both motivate and stand in tension with a broader social ministry.

Families also are foundational for the broader society by providing new life and forming members in social habits. One might say that society goes the way of the family. Leo XIII describes the family as the "cradle of civil society" through which "the future welfare of society will in great measure

41 McCarthy, *Sex and Love in the Home*, 86.

42 McCarthy, 92.

be guaranteed."[43] Children learn from their families to appreciate rights and freedoms and to challenge injustices. Children also learn how to engage the economic system. They learn about the relationship between justice and profit, and they grow accustomed to a particular standard of living. They are encouraged through example, education, and conversation to pursue certain occupations and to avoid others. They develop working habits.

Magisterial documents highlight ways in which families can model communal life for society. This role as model is to some extent present in the family's relationship with the Church but stands out even more when one moves from the Church—which emphasizes similar communal practices—to civil society, the economy, and the state. To say that families can provide models for broader society is not to deny the frequency and seriousness of abuse and neglect that occurs within families. The claim is not that every family is a model, or even that most families are mostly models. Rather, recognizing that the family is not immune from disorder, familial community, due to the permanent and intimate character of family relations, provides unique opportunities to model human relationships for society.[44]

Magisterial writings, true to form, offer general statements affirming the family's role and responsibility to provide a model for society. Francis speaks of the family domesticating the world and injecting a healthy dose of family spirit into society.[45] The bishops of the Second Vatican Council affirm that families show Christ's living presence in the world through "the love and generous fruitfulness of the spouses, by their unity and fidelity, and by the loving way in which all members of the family cooperate with each other."[46] John Paul II writes, "The fostering of authentic and mature communion between persons within the family is the first and irreplaceable

43 These quotations come from Cahill, *Family*, 87. Cahill cites Étienne Gilson, ed., *The Church Speaks to the Modern World: The Social Teachings of Leo XIII* (New York: Doubleday, 1954). The idea that the future of society passes through the family is often repeated in church documents. See, for example, John Paul II, *Familiaris Consortio*, 85; John Paul II, Apostolic Exhortation *Christifideles Laici* (December 30, 1988), 40; Second Vatican Council, *Apostolicam Actuositatem*, 11, in Flannery, *Vatican Council* II, 778–79; Francis, *Amoris Laetitia*, 31. McCarthy argues that twentieth-century magisterial teaching exhibits "a shift from conceiving of family as a conserving institution to identifying it as a reforming one. In theory, family moves from sustaining the social order to transforming it." He expresses concern that in asking families to transform the social order, one might be placing too much weight on them. *Sex and Love in the Home*, 112.

44 Francis writes, "Families are not a problem; they are first and foremost an opportunity." Francis, *Amoris Laetitia*, 7.

45 Francis, *Amoris Laetitia,* 183.

46 Second Vatican Council, *Gaudium et Spes*, 48, in Flannery, *Vatican Council II*, 951–52.

school of social life, an example and stimulus for the broader community of relationships."[47]

In addition to these magisterial statements, the *Compendium of the Social Doctrine of the Church* affirms that familial bonds, in addition to the responsibilities, experiences, and relatively small size of the family, invite a focus on the person that avoids both individualism and collectivism.[48] In a family, one must move beyond oneself. One participates in familial community through caring for vulnerable children and dying relatives, participating in a family meal, and sharing financial resources and material possessions. Yet, the permanent character of a family encourages its members to voice opposition to collectivism. Familial relationships are strong enough for arguments and challenges or at least permanent enough that one often is not able to just let things go.

Families also can serve as a model in the sacrifices family members make for one another. John Paul II proposes that "relationships between the members of the family community are inspired and guided by the law of 'free giving.'"[49] This gift exchange goes beyond celebrations of birthdays, anniversaries, and Christmas. Parents who give life to their children and care for them in their radical vulnerability do not demand payment for their services. Rather, "this free giving takes the form of heartfelt acceptance, encounter and dialogue, disinterested availability, generous service and deep solidarity."[50] One sees this self-gift also in the way family members share many of their possessions with one another. These natural tendencies in the family serve as a model for broader economic and social exchange, especially in those cultures in which human exchange is dominated by efficiency and supply and demand. Insofar as families follow this "law of free-giving," they invite and challenge members of the broader society to move beyond individualistic calculation to building community through self-gift.

Lastly, families model for the community the importance of intergenerational interactions. Through the connections one has with one's parents,

47 John Paul II, *Familiaris Consortio*, 43; see also 48.

48 Pontifical Council for Justice and Peace, *Compendium of the Social Doctrine of the Church*, 213.

49 John Paul II, *Familiaris Consortio*, 43. The theme of self-gift is a central theme for John Paul II. He develops the theme in *Man and Woman He Created Them*. The freedom of the gift requires that one maintains self-possession and sees the other as worthy of a gift. John Paul II, *Man and Woman He Created Them*, trans. Michael Waldstein (Boston: Pauline Books, 2006), 178–88).

50 John Paul II, *Familiaris Consortio*, 43.

aunts and uncles, grandparents, children, and grandchildren, one sees more clearly one's own generation in context and gains an awareness of what is changing and the implications of those changes. These intergenerational connections bear greater fruit when the younger generation takes responsibility for caring for their parents and grandparents and treating them with respect. Within a family, children learn from the history of their parents and grandparents and locate their family life within a broader familial and cultural context, thereby overcoming tendencies to see one's nuclear family as a perfect, isolated community. As the bishops of the Second Vatican Council write, "The family is the place where different generations come together and help one another to grow wiser and harmonize the rights of individuals with other demands of social life; as such it constitutes the basis of society."[51]

Family as Molded

Cahill highlights how "the families and households of early Christians are integral components of what today would be called 'civil society,' codependent with other important axes of social identity and agency, including economy, religion, and politics."[52] One must be careful to see how this codependence moves in both directions. McCarthy expresses concern about overly optimistic accounts encouraging families to transform society.[53] Theoretically, if families lived in isolation, they could pick and choose their moral convictions and form pure communities. However, families are neither isolated nor perfect. Since families are members of society and interdependent with it, the family is influenced by it and needs support from it. Influence goes in both directions. In recognizing the family's potential role in transforming society, one also should avoid placing too much weight on the family or fail to provide families with adequate support.

Further, since the family provides a foundational formation and often is a source of meaning and fulfillment for its members, one should ask not only how to change families in order to improve society—as if the family were merely a means to improving society—but also should reflect on how to develop society to support and improve family life. The *Compendium of the Social Doctrine of the Church* proposes that the family is "the indispensable

51 Second Vatican Council, *Gaudium et Spes*, 52, in Flannery, *Vatican Council II*, 956.

52 Cahill, *Family*, 44–45.

53 McCarthy, *Sex and Love in the Home*, 112–14.

cultural and political perspective in the consideration of persons."[54] The *Compendium* affirms that in some ways the family should maintain social priority over society itself: "neither society nor the State may absorb, substitute or reduce the social dimension of the family; rather they must honor it, recognize it, respect it and promote it according to *the principle of subsidiarity*."[55]

Families are deeply influenced by civil society, economics, and the state. The language one speaks, one's notions of a good life, the "scripts" that condition the relationship between individuals and their families, educational opportunities, and one's safety are all influenced by surrounding communities. For this reason, Francis denounces cultural and social factors "that prevent authentic family life and lead to discrimination, poverty, exclusion, and violence."[56] McCarthy notes that marriage and family itself are presented to families by society as an established social form. Couples are formed by market branding, social influencers, marriage legislation, popular TV shows and movies, and common family practices in one's local community. In institutional marriage, the structure of marriage precedes the couple, shapes their relationship and their role, and involves duties to society.[57] If one defines marriage as isolated and perfect, one will overlook or be surprised and confused by these social influences. Couples who recognize the social structures related to marriage but embrace an isolated family model might reject marriage altogether. For them, a "private marriage" means no marriage at all. They seek the impossible, a "pure relationship" for its own sake not bound to an established social form.[58] In places where society defines marriage as isolated and perfect, attempts to avoid marriage for a "pure relationship" ironically embody the established social forms even while claiming to reject social norms.

Christians need to recognize the established social forms of marriage and family life that form their understanding of love, marriage, and family life, or they risk being unwittingly influenced by those forms, or even reduc-

54 Pontifical Council for Justice and Peace, *Compendium of the Social Doctrine of the Church*, 254.

55 Pontifical Council for Justice and Peace, 252.

56 Francis, *Amoris Laetitia*, 201; he provides a reference to Synod of Bishops, Third Extraordinary General Assembly, *Relatio Synodi* (October 18, 2014), 38.

57 McCarthy, *Sex and Love in the Home*, 209. In *Family* (83), Cahill proposes that "historically, the so-called Christian family has often been co-opted by existing social structures, especially those that reproduce economic and gender inequities."

58 McCarthy, *Sex and Love in the Home*, 209.

ing the Church's account of marriage and family to those social forms.[59] Hanlon Rubio describes the story of marriage in American culture as "a stretched-out Romeo and Juliet. . . . It is about two people, irresistibly drawn to each other, in spite of their families and apart from their communities, from beginning to end."[60] Couples "fall in love" and "live happily ever after." Hanlon Rubio highlights how this romantic narrative stops at the wedding day and glosses over the realities of marriage. McCarthy notes that the implication of these romantic narratives is that the longing and desire that are part of romantic love provide a solid foundation for marriage and household practices. A household flowing from romantic longing and desire is a household that seeks to be self-sufficient through wages and income and attempts to be both autonomous and civil.[61] McCarthy argues that this pursuit of romantic autonomy and isolation lacks social variety and support and thereby provides an inadequate foundation for sustaining family life and practices. In the romantic narrative of desire and longing, marriage and its concomitant social roles are boring, something that deadens relationships.

Indirectly acknowledging the limitations of romantic ideals, other cultural narratives present family life as either a comedy or a drama. Family comedies demonstrate that family life is not always an affective refuge. However, as Hanlon Rubio notes, they "exaggerate so much in an effort to get laughs and heartwarming endings that they fail to get to the reality of familial relationships."[62] The family drama extends the desire and longing of romantic love to family life but through unremittingly sensational events and actions like a life-threatening car accident, an act of adultery, or a murder. Soap operas provide the clearest expression of this sensationalized drama.

A tempting response to the unrealistic and melodramatic idealism of romantic, comedy, or dramatic narratives is to advocate for a complacent "realism." Such realism seeks to gather facts about sexual practices, and then based on the assumption that these practices will continue, seeks to decrease collateral damage. This complacent realism, paired with private notions of sex, gives the impression that realists are not making moral claims but just

59 David Cloutier describes a narrative of romantic love and outlines biologically, psychologically, and sociologically reductive narratives of marriage in *Love, Reason, and God's Story: An Introduction to Sexual Ethics* (Winona, MN: Anselm Academic, 2008), 36–56.

60 Julie Hanlon Rubio, *Family Ethics: Practices for Christians* (Washington, DC: Georgetown University Press, 2010), 19–20.

61 McCarthy, *Sex and Love in the Home*, 1.

62 Hanlon Rubio, *Family Ethics*, 16.

being honest and practical. Teenagers will inevitably have sex, for example, and so they should be encouraged to use condoms and contraception. Stanley Hauerwas highlights, however, how the realist position "in fact presupposes an ethical recommendation."[63] Since families are interdependent with surrounding communities, those who accept as necessary current sexual practices also endorse those practices by enshrining them as normative. Moreover, the realist position risks overlooking how sexual practices are formed by surrounding communities. In a culture that emphasizes privacy and freedom, the realist position risks accepting "as morally normative the liberal assumption that sexual activity should be determined by what each individual feels is good for him or her."[64] A complacent realism, while seemingly reacting against romanticism, overlooks its influence and indirectly endorses it by accepting the practices of those formed by romantic narratives. The narratives of unfulfilled longing, comedy, drama, and realism offer families a false promise, a joke, excitement, or something to be complacently accepted.

In the face of such narratives, some moral theologians and Christian leaders ask whether Christians should withdraw from participation in civil marriage. One should be cautious not to frame such deliberations using isolated definitions of family and Church, which might suggest that Christian families are separate entities that can withdraw from social influence or engage society without being influenced in turn. Families are social communities interdependent with various other social communities. Accordingly, advocacy both for and against participation in civil marriage is social engagement, even if the engagement is oppositional, defensive, or seemingly neutral. Since families are interdependent with broader social communities, the question is not whether families and the Church should engage society but how to engage it, either through greater participation or through a public stance of opposition and separation. The unavoidability of social engagement highlights that the focus should not be merely to critique faulty narratives in order to clear the slate for private choices, but to present a family narrative that is compelling and practically illuminating. The narrative that the family is the basic social unit is one such narrative.

Because it is social, the family is not isolated and perfect but interdependent with various other social communities. While emphasizing a neighbor-

63 Stanley Hauerwas, *The Hauerwas Reader*, ed. John Berkman and Michael Cartwright (Durham: Duke University Press, 2001), 485.

64 Hauerwas, 485.

hood economy of gift exchange, McCarthy highlights three communities of support: kinfolk, friends, and neighborhood.[65] These three communities are important because they can be locations for sustained activity and therefore capable of cultivating habits. One could add here the local parish community. Familial engagement with society will look different for different families in different contexts. One should avoid simple accounts that insist that families only need intergenerational familial support or a strong neighborhood, for example. Rather, recognizing social interdependence and needs, families should turn to help and support where they can find it.

What is increasingly clear is that engagement with society will require prudence, moderation, and self-control in the use of social media and engagement with marketing. John Paul II, building on the work of Paul VI, notes the influence of social communication and advertising on families. He writes, "the means of social communication 'affect, and often profoundly, the minds of those who use them, under the affective and intellectual aspect and also under the moral and religious aspect,' especially in the case of young people."[66] John Paul II links the responsibility of parents to educate children with the task of forming children to relate well with social media.[67] The challenges of this education are many. Social media and marketing are pervasive. They impact parents and children alike. In a society of social media saturation, it becomes difficult to maintain human relationships without extensive participation in social media, and yet the frequent effect of immersion in this media environment is often more loneliness and isolation, not less.

The challenge of social media is made more difficult by isolated notions of family life. Christopher Lasch writes:

> Most of the writing on the modern family takes for granted the "isolation" of the nuclear family not only from the kinship system but from the world of work. It assumes that this isolation makes the family impervious to outside influences. In reality, the modern world intrudes at every point and obliterates its privacy. The sanctity of the home is a sham in a world dominated by giant corporations and by the apparatus of mass promotion.[68]

65 McCarthy, *Sex and Love in the Home*, 98–108.

66 John Paul II, *Familiaris Consortio*, 76; for the internal quotation, John Paul II cites Paul VI, "Message for the Third Social Communications Day," April 7, 1969.

67 John Paul II, *Familiaris Consortio*, 76.

68 Christopher Lasch, *Haven in a Heartless World: The Family Besieged* (New York: Basic Books, 1977), xvii.

Conceiving of the family as an isolated, private bubble makes families more susceptible to societal influence because they are not aware of or concerned about its presence. I will treat the question of market branding in more detail in the next chapter. For now, I want to highlight that interdependence is a two-way street. Yes, families should serve as a social nucleus and model, but we need also to recognize the limits of their capacity to transform society and an awareness of how society molds them. The family's social interdependence also highlights its responsibility to the broader society.

Family as Responsible

As the basic social unit, families should try to cultivate community. John Paul II affirms that the family should practice love of neighbor so that it does not "live closed in on itself, but remains open to the community, moved by a sense of justice and concern for others, as well as by a consciousness of its responsibility toward the whole of society."[69] McCarthy makes a distinction between closed family models that see the family as a personal refuge from a competitive world and open family models, which are permeated by surrounding communities. Building on this distinction, I propose that the family's role as a foundation for community invites families to a rich kind of openness. Families should not merely tolerate others who are perceived as a mere burden. In hospitality, families should invite and welcome others. Moreover, they should build on the relationships that naturally form through family connections and intentionally and actively cultivate community.[70] By serving as a foundation for rich social exchange, families will inevitably help and support other families and provide social opportunities for those who lack family connections.

Families that pursue a perfect, isolated family ideal will not fulfill the family's responsibility to support civil society, and communities that reduce the family to a private, affective refuge will place obstacles preventing families from serving the common good. These obstacles can include choosing isolating living situations (such as suburbs structured to discourage interactions), spending free time on non-local pursuits (whether entertainment,

69 John Paul II, *Familiaris Consortio*, 64; John Paul II is quoting from the Synod of Bishops' "Message to Christian Families" of October 24, 1980 (12); see also McCarthy's insightful reflections on closed and open families in *Sex and Love in the Home*, 93–108.

70 John Paul II writes, "With a lively sense of the common good, Christian families should become actively engaged at every level in other non-ecclesial associations as well." *Familiaris Consortio*, 72.

news, or traveling for pleasure), or emphasizing the "safety" of children to the extent that they are practically inhibited from interacting with anyone who is not a close friend or family member. In the knowledge that families are a foundation for community, family members should not work to avoid social exchange in pursuit of isolation, but to cultivate community. John Paul II writes in *Christifideles Laici* that "it is above all the lay faithful's duty in the apostolate to make the family aware of its identity as the primary social nucleus, and its basic role in society, so that it might itself become always a more *active and responsible place* for proper growth and proper participation in social life."[71]

In addition to serving as a social nucleus, families also are responsible for enriching the civil discourse that forms a foundation for political legislation and economic practices. Parents should help their children to become politically informed and engaged and form them in the prudence necessary for voting and advocating for political improvement.[72] Those who work for financial gain should consider not only the economic benefit that such work provides for their family but also how such work promotes the common good by enhancing the company's ability to provide crucial resources and services for the community.[73] Lastly, families impact the economy through every purchase made for the family.[74] The importance of consumption in the family's impact on the economy and in the economy's impact on the family is so pervasive in contemporary culture that it requires an entire chapter (the next) to discuss.

71 John Paul II, *Christifideles Laici*, 40; see also *Familiaris Consortio* (48), where John Paul II proposes that families can witness to the Kingdom of God through an "active and responsible involvement in the authentically human growth of society and its institutions." Donald Miller affirms that "the family's role as the basic foundation of and locus for the formation of civil and ecclesial community emerges clearly as social service or ministry when viewed in light of the family's baptismal call to holiness and the person's call to marital sacramentalization." Donald Miller, *Concepts of Family Life in Modern Catholic Theology: From Vatican II through "Christifideles Laici"* (San Francisco: Catholic Scholars Press, 1997), 184. Bourg cites and comments on this passage from Miller in *Where Two or Three Are Gathered*, 196n32.

72 John Paul II proposes that families should be particularly involved in those political matters that involve family life. *Familiaris Consortio*, 44.

73 Leo XIII highlights that workers and employees have mutual responsibilities to one another. Leo XIII Encyclical Letter *Rerum Novarum*, 20, in *Catholic Social Thought: The Documentary Heritage*, ed. David O'Brien and Thomas A. Shannon, rev. ed. (Maryknoll, NY: Orbis Books, 2016).

74 Benedict XVI highlights that "*every economic decision has a moral consequence*." See Benedict XVI, Encyclical Letter *Caritas in Veritate* (June 29, 2009), 37, in *Catholic Social Thought: The Documentary Heritage*, ed. David J. O'Brien and Thomas A. Shannon, rev. ed. (Maryknoll, NY: Orbis Books, 2016), 550. Italics in original.

CONCLUSION

In recognizing the internally social character of the family one might be tempted to affirm that the family is a community complete and fulfilled in isolation from other social communities. However, such conclusions are more consistent with false ideals of isolated, private family life than an analysis of the family's social roles and responsibilities. To present an image of the family as perfect in isolation is to claim that one can separate it from its broader social context, that it can remain wholly uninfluenced by other social communities. I propose that in recognizing the internally social character of the family, one sees more clearly the interdependence of the family with other social communities. The social family interacts with other communities, not in isolated opposition but through mutually penetrating roles and responsibilities.

Other social communities have responsibilities to support families because family life requires broader support. Families have basic needs and require social support that requires assistance beyond the family. Further, the social complexity of the person requires social interaction beyond family relationships.

Families are socially interdependent with the Church, civil society, the economy, and the state. The family is a domestic sanctuary of the Church, and the Church is a community that points eschatologically to the family of God. Civil society provides a necessary context for rich social interaction while families provide crucial hubs for social gathering. Family life includes work and interactions with an economy and a body politic. The shared life and identity of families with other social communities highlights the basic character of family life for these social communities but also provides a framework for understanding how these social communities influence families (and one another).

Families can serve as a social nucleus bringing together different voluntary groups. The permanent and intimate character of family life presents families with unique opportunities to model human community for society. Insofar as families overcome individualism and collectivism, follow the "law of free-giving," and live intergenerationally, they invite the broader community to deeper communal life. The social interdependence of families on other social communities implies a responsibility toward those communities. Families benefit from spiritual guidance and assistance, voluntary associations, peace in their neighborhood, economic opportunities, availability of basic material goods, and political stability. In turn, families have a responsibility to live well their role as social nucleus and model. Moreover, as a member of these broader communities, families have an invested interest in and responsibility to support the common good so that they and others may continue to benefit from the support of those communities.

By articulating the social interdependence of families in general terms, I can now reflect in more detail on elements of that interdependence. Since the family is socially interdependent, the question is not whether, but how, families should socially engage. This requires reflection on roles, responsibilities, resources, and obstacles. In the remaining three chapters, I will reflect on the influence of consumerism on family life, present a moral framework for social engagement, and then analyze specifically the relationship between family responsibilities and social ministry.

5

Consumerism and Family Life

CONSUMERISM

I introduced the idea in the last chapter that the family's interdependence with other social communities is one way that the wider culture influences families. If one defines the family as an isolated and complete social community, or if one academically separates social ethics from family ethics, one will miss the interplay between cultural ethos and family life. Consumerism serves as a fitting illustration of this influence since in developed countries (and increasingly in developing countries) it is pervasive, formatively powerful, and often contrary to the social responsibilities of families.

Most Catholics are sympathetic to forming their children in the social virtues, contributing to the common good, and developing interdependent relationships with various communities. In the context of the United States, however, individuals often struggle to find the time and resources to live this social mission. An analysis of consumerism helps to explain these challenges. In highlighting the difficulties consumerism presents for family life, one should note from the beginning that it should not be a scapegoat for all that ails the family. One should not blame all family struggles on consumerism, neglect other social influences on family life, or ignore the benefits associated with consumerism. I do not claim that eliminating consumerism will fully manifest the Kingdom of God on earth. Rather, I assume that consumerism, and specifically the consumerism that flows from capitalism, is here to stay. In recognizing that no system is perfect, and that consumerism is pervasive and formative, I seek to reflect on its negative formative tendencies in order to help ethicists and families be intentional about engaging with and responding to its often-unacknowledged influences.

I begin with two smaller sections that respectively define consumerism and highlight the pervasiveness and formative role of brand marketing. Then, the third, lengthier, and more central section reflects on how consumerism presents challenges for families trying to live their social mission. I will highlight how a consumer ethic is harmful for families who live in relative isolation from other social communities. In this third section, I reflect on how the manipulation of desires through marketing, sales, and accompanying cultural norms impact the consumer choices and desires of family members but also form the way individuals think and feel about matters related to one's family, such as sexual desire, dating, spousal love, marriage, avoiding and seeking conception, and everyday family life. While academic specialization often implies that social ethics works separately from family ethics, seeing the family as the basic social unit highlights how the profit motive leads to marketing and sales plans that join with cultural norms to form individuals as consumers rather than family members equipped to live out the social role of family life. Consumerism impacts culturally controversial topics related to sexual and medical ethics such as pornography, contraceptive acts, and abortion but also the everyday struggles and experiences of family life. I do not want to present a caricature of soulless, evil consumers, but to discuss how those who seek to respect things and people can still find themselves influenced by consumerism in ways that present obstacles to the basic social unit. Since the word "consumerism" has more than one meaning, I begin by clarifying my use of the term.

Capitalism and Competition

To understand the influence of consumer capitalism on families, one needs to recognize the various goods that a capitalist system provides for many families. In a capitalist system, those with capital have a self-interest in investing in companies that will make a profit. Business leaders compete with one another for capital investment. This competition can cultivate and reward positive habits, such as discipline, entrepreneurship, creativity, perseverance, hard work, and responsiveness to communal needs and desires.[1] When businesses provide services that are crucial to the common good, this competition ensures the availability of material goods and provides employment. Insofar as this competition encourages efficient use of time and resources, capitalism cuts down on the wastefulness that plagues a consumer ethos.

Nonetheless, the competition that fuels capitalism also encourages consumerism. My goal in highlighting the connection between capitalism and

1 See Pope John Paul II, Encyclical Letter *Centesimus Annus* (May 1, 1991), 32, 34, 42, but note the need to read those passages in whole and in relation to sections 33, 36, and 43; see also David Cloutier, *The Vice of Luxury* (Washington, DC: Georgetown University Press, 2015), 40–42, 69–71.

consumerism is to explain how consumerism makes more difficult the living out of the Church's social vision for family life. Before highlighting the negative formative influence of consumerism, one does well to acknowledge the various motivations that encourage business leaders to participate in and support a consumer ethos. In the context of market competition, especially for those who are struggling to survive or gain market share, business leaders feel pressure to game the system to maximize all available advantages. The focus for business leaders can easily become what is marketable—even if this leads to vicious habits or addictions—rather than the needs and fulfillment of society. To survive or stay ahead, business leaders feel compelled to squeeze or even oppress vulnerable workers, consume the resources of creation in an unsustainable manner, and manipulate the desires of potential customers. As Pope Francis writes, in a business system "which tends to devour everything which stands in the way of increased profits, whatever is fragile, like the environment, is defenseless before the interests of a deified market, which become the only rule."[2]

Heated competition also encourages individuals to focus on short-term gains and production. This short-term focus is present at all levels of consumer society. Corporate stockholders seek economic gain on their short-term investments. Corporate leaders lay off established workers to improve the quarterly bottom line. Employees feel pressure to demonstrate immediate productivity. Parents buy cheap to stay financially afloat while paying for debt and trying to increase consumption. Those who lack basic resources grasp for short-term resources and opportunities.[3]

The cultural emphasis on competition and short-term productivity as well as profit-dominant conceptions of business help explain why the seemingly unjust decisions of business leaders often involve more than the greed of a vicious few. Business leaders have various and complex reasons and motivations for making decisions that take advantage of vulnerable workers, harm the environment, and manipulate the desires of customers. Business leaders may not see a need to be concerned with the common good if they accept economic theories that separate market decisions from moral considerations or if they define their work as occurring in the "private" sector and therefore do not see it as coming with social responsibilities. More

2 Pope Francis, Apostolic Exhortation *Evangelii Gaudium* (November 24, 2013), 56.

3 Lisa Sowle Cahill, *Family: A Christian Social Perspective* (Minneapolis: Fortress, 2000), 115–17.

likely, they feel the pressure of industry competition, a cultural ethos that associates wealth with success and fulfillment, or a desire to develop their reputations as successful business leaders. In a discussion of capitalism and family life, one also should note how competition can join with family concerns to motivate participation in consumer practices. Business leaders may be motivated to impress parents or siblings, keep their jobs until they have funded their children's (often expensive) high school or college education, provided opportunities for their kids, or helped sustain jobs so that coworkers can provide for their families. Whatever the motivation, business decisions focused on profit and isolated from concern for the common good tend to consume what is fragile, including vulnerable workers, the environment, and the desires of potential customers. To see this consumption more clearly, a few clarifications about the meaning of consumerism is helpful.

Working Definition of Consumerism

In a 2007 article, Kenneth Himes writes about consumerism: "Sometimes the most obvious matters get the least attention from moral theologians."[4] Thanks to the work of Himes, Francis, and others, the impact of consumerism is now certainly garnering attention. Himes begins his article with some helpful terminological clarification related to the word "consumerism." He explains that it typically has three meanings today.[5] Consumerism can refer to a social movement to protect consumers (e.g., reports meant to inform consumers and online reviews). Second, some people refer to consumerism in terms of liberal economics, which focuses on freedom of choice and entrepreneurship. The idea is that business leaders and consumers should have the freedom to buy and sell what they want and that the government should not intervene. This definition of consumerism could be seen to be in conflict with the first insofar as consumer protection may require government intervention, which the second definition tends to exclude. However, if the notion of "freedom" is employed in a responsible way—to allow a reasonable autonomy for the individual as well as a structure that protects and sustains that freedom—then these two senses of consumerism can account for the many benefits consumer society has produced in terms of enhancing the material standard of living of society.

4 Kenneth R. Himes, OFM, "Consumerism and Christian Ethics," *Theological Studies* 68, no. 1 (2007): 132.

5 Himes, 133.

The word "consumerism" also can refer to a way of life. Himes writes on the first page of his article that the etymology of consumerism comes from the Latin *consumere*, meaning to devour, waste, exhaust. Following this history, the English usage of the word was popularly employed to describe tuberculosis, an illness that seemed to devour, waste, and exhaust the body. After World War II, the word "consumer" replaced the word "customer," which had implied a regular and ongoing relationship.[6] Putting these ideas together, I propose that consumerism is a way of life that tends to devour, waste, and destroy products, experiences, and sadly even people in an illusory quest for fulfillment by material means.[7]

This is the definition of consumerism that is meant by critiques of consumerism in authors like Francis, and it is the way that I will use the term for the majority of this chapter. Consumerism in this third sense involves buying things, but it also involves structures that oversimplify economic life into a quest for ever more differentiated goods and services. People are material as well as spiritual beings, and material goods can unite people and help them celebrate in addition to meeting basic survival needs. Purchases can support jobs. Consumerism is not just the act of buying something but involves buying within a system that tends to devour things in a wasteful way.[8] This kind of consumerism is not synonymous with a free market economy in which people can buy and sell whatever they want. While a free market dominated by corporate businesses might create incentives to use things in wasteful ways, one might also see such waste in command-and-control economies as well. In a socialist system, one might see devouring and wasting as social leaders attempt to maintain control and micromanage the nation's economic practices. In a distributist system, one might see waste when individual landowners lack the ability or creativity to utilize their land or the necessary economies of scale to make fuller use of livestock and produce. My focus in this chapter, however, is consumerism connected to capitalism, as this is the system found in the United States where I write and expect the most readers.

The competition that fuels capitalism encourages the consumption of vulnerable workers, the environment, and the desires of potential customers.

6 Himes, 132–33.

7 Pope Francis, Postsynodal Apostolic Exhortation *Amoris Laetitia* (March 19, 2016), 127.

8 I intentionally leave out an explanation of wastefulness at this point. My focus is to provide a working definition of consumerism rather than an airtight definition.

This competition often cultivates a contract-focused approach to wages and working conditions, which means that vulnerable workers often receive low wages and endure harsh working conditions. These injustices in the workplace have a substantial impact on family life. Parents and older siblings are compelled to work multiple jobs or work long hours. They experience the interdependence of family with the broader community as they rely on societal support for childcare, but they accept whatever childcare they can find. Their job situation prevents them from forming their children and contributing to society beyond their work, and in many cases, from celebrating their faith, especially in the absence of laws or customs limiting commerce on Sundays. Industrial pollution also impacts family life. Poor air quality and contaminated water undermine health, especially the health of a developing child and those whose health is already impaired.[9] As Francis shows, these environmental concerns are connected to life issues—pollution or poor water quality that leads to child illness and death is devastating for families and all too common.

Marketing, Sales, and Cultural Norms

One cannot understand the pervasive impact of consumerism without recognizing how market branding, sales techniques, and cultural norms form human desire. My aim with the rest of this chapter is to show how corporate marketing and sales plans pair with family isolation to cultivate dissatisfaction, busyness, and debt while spiritually forming how individuals think about family life. Advertisements are everywhere and they form us to think, feel, and act in certain ways. As William T. Cavanaugh writes,

> Consumer culture is one of the most powerful systems of formation in the contemporary world. While a Christian may spend an hour per week in church, she may spend twenty-five hours per week watching television, to say nothing of the hours spent on the internet. . . . Nearly everywhere we lay our eyes—gas pump handles, T-shirts, public restroom walls, bank receipts, church bulletins, sports uniforms, and so on—we are confronted by advertising.[10]

9 Francis, Encyclical Letter *Laudato si'* (May 24, 2015), 29.

10 William T. Cavanaugh, *Being Consumed: Economics and Christian Desire* (Grand Rapids, MI: William B. Eerdmans, 2008), 47.

One could add here how the formative character of marketing is supported by salesmen and by cultural norms of consumption.[11] The pervasiveness of advertising stands out even more when it is targeted at those in their formative years. The sociologist Juliet Schor notes how advertising in the 1920s began to focus more on mothers. The goal was to "inform" the mother about what experts thought and then link child development with their products. With cable television and child-oriented programming in the 1980s, however, marketers were able to deliver their message directly to children.[12] Marketing aimed at children increased dramatically in the 1990s. Companies spent an estimated $15 billion on direct child marketing in 2004, up from about $2 billion in 1999.[13]

Schor notes how child marketing works in tandem with an ethos that intentionally undermines parental authority. She argues that when the children's programming channel Nickelodeon "tells its advertisers that it 'owns kids aged 2–12,' the boast is closer to the mark than most realize."[14] She notes that when parents appear on screen, they are

> challenged, ridiculed, overpowered, or ignored. Nickelodeon's trademark "tude" (or defiant sassy attitude toward adults), its "sliming" campaigns (in which adults are covered with a green goo), and its relentless "kids rule" philosophy has been powerful in creating a precocious corporate-driven, substance-free rebelliousness among young kids. It stands in contrast to authentic teen rebellions rooted in political and social factors. The "anti-adult" bias that has been prominent in Nickelodeon's formula for success can be found throughout children's commercial culture.[15]

The commercials and the programming work together—the advertising forms the kids to desire the product and the programming encourages the kids to disregard guidance that parents may offer in navigating consumer

11 Cloutier discusses economic debates about whether desire for the luxury others enjoy is good or not. Both sides of the debate acknowledge that the luxury enjoyed by others forms their peers and fellow citizens. Cloutier, *The Vice of Luxury*, 40–46.

12 Juliet B. Schor, "The Viacom Generation: The Consumer Child and the Corporate Parent," in *At the Heart of Work and Family*, ed. Anita Ilta Garey and Karen V. Hansen (New Brunswick, NJ: Rutgers University Press, 2011), 208–9. She proposes that directly targeting children was likely responsible for the rising popularity of macaroni and cheese, ketchup, french fries, yogurt, Happy Meals, tacos, soft drinks, chips, chicken, and burgers.

13 Schor, 209.

14 Juliet B. Schor, *Born to Buy* (New York: Scribner, 2004), 20.

15 Schor, "The Viacom Generation," 212.

options. Schor notes that this "symbolic positioning of adults versus children" has "permeated the culture of food."[16] Schor explains how unhealthy food has been and continues to be branded as hip and rebellious, just as tobacco once was advertised to youth. The connection is no mere consequence: "Some of the largest food processing companies, Kraft and Nabisco, were owned by tobacco companies Phillip Morris and RJ Reynolds as this marketing was developed."[17]

In her 2004 book, *Born to Buy*, Schor reports that American children view an estimated forty thousand commercials annually and make approximately three thousand requests for products and services a year.[18] That's about seventy requests a week per child. Thus, parents with three children can say no two hundred times a week and still buy a handful of things every week that the family does not need. This does not count the gifts kids receive from family and friends for birthdays and holidays and the trinkets they receive from various groups and activities. Schor estimates that children in the United States accumulate "an average of seventy new toys a year."[19] The most prominent holiday celebrations in the country—Halloween and Christmas—are highlighted, respectively, by the acquisition of a multitude of store-bought, plastic-wrapped, nutritionally bankrupt candies and, if possible, a large pile of elaborately wrapped, extensively packaged, and likely plastic toys and gadgets. Families are interdependent with other social communities, and in the United States nearly every social community encourages widespread consumption.

The influence of marketing is overlooked in part because the cultural emphasis on freedom and choice suggests that individuals are more self-made than influenced by the world around them. Advertisers and salespeople appeal to this individualism when they argue that parents have the responsibility to say yes or no to their kids even while exploiting the social interdependence of family life through their intentional campaigns to undermine parental authority. Sometimes, advertisements highlight private ideals of isolation and choice in their ad campaigns. Cavanaugh offers as an example the Sprite campaign: "Image is nothing, obey your thirst."[20] If

16 Schor, 212.

17 Schor, 212.

18 Schor, *Born to Buy*, 20.

19 Schor, 19.

20 Cavanaugh, *Being Consumed*, 18.

image is nothing, and if parents have full freedom to say no to their kids, then why do companies spend billions of dollars on ad campaigns that say nothing about their products but promote a certain image by employing sports stars or other celebrities? This campaign may be self-consciously ironic, but the pervasive presence of irony and humor in advertisements is meant to convince viewers—especially young adults—that businesses providing certain goods understand their sophisticated needs better than those (parents, teachers, church leaders, and so on) who might propose a more long-term view of fulfillment. Despite their attempts to appear clever and sensitive to consumer needs, often the marketer and the salesperson hold more power to mold desires than the consumer realizes. They gather information about their customers and target advertising in a way that manipulates customer interests and desires. Moreover, advertising is nearly everywhere. One cannot turn around without encountering targeted advertisements. Mary Doyle Roche writes, "It seems nearly impossible for individual parents, and even small groups of parents, to successfully resist the efforts of a multibillion-dollar marketing industry. The 'just say no' strategy is entirely inadequate as a means to safeguard the harmful effects of advertising on young people."[21]

One of the harmful effects of marketing, sales, and cultural norms that encourage consumerism is the cultivation of dissatisfaction. Juliet Schor's 1998 research indicated that commercials and TV sitcoms suggested that the average person should try to emulate those in the top 20 percent income bracket.[22] McCarthy writes, "Consumer capitalism is less about what we have and more about desire for what we lack."[23] Similarly, Cavanaugh argues that the most important issue with consumerism is not owning and hoarding but dissatisfaction, desire, shopping, and cycles of waste. Cavanaugh argues that while cultural pressures encourage individuals to buy, the consumer is not attached to products but, rather, detached from them, as well as from the producers and the process of production.[24] The consumer does

21 Mary M. Doyle Roche, *Children, Consumerism, and the Common Good* (Lanham, MD: Lexington Books, 2009), 34; for more on the impact of advertising on children, see 32–37.

22 Himes, "Consumerism and Christian Ethics," 137; Himes is referencing the work of Juliet Schor, *The Overspent American: Upscaling, Downshifting, and the New Consumer* (New York: Basic Books, 1998).

23 David Matzko McCarthy, *Sex and Love in the Home: A Theology of the Household*, 2nd ed. (London: SCM Press, 2004), 40.

24 Cavanaugh, *Being Consumed*, 33–58.

not know how the product was made, who made it, or under what conditions and is compelled to discard products that break or replace products for new models. In New Testament terms, consumerism resembles more the prodigal son who squanders the inheritance of his father (Luke 15:13–14) than the farmer who stores grain in his bin and seeks to rest content in his possessions (Luke 12:16–21).

Cultivated dissatisfaction contributes to busyness and the accumulation of debt.[25] Consumers are busy shopping for products but also busy consuming experiences like the daily sporting event, reality TV shows and competitions, college life, or vacations. Further, they are willing to work longer hours for more pay to sustain those levels of consumption.[26] They are in debt because they are living beyond their means despite saying no to purchases hundreds of times a week. Debt accumulates not only from paying a brand premium on marketed clothes and shoes, and spending money on fine dining and vacations, but also and maybe primarily from overreaching on things that are needed for employment and everyday life, like education, phone and internet, cars, and housing.[27] University in the United States often is a full-service community that provides experiences well beyond an academic education or skills training. Cloutier describes competition between universities as a race "toward ever-more deluxe residential amenities that will impress students on their ninety minute tours."[28] Further, even after the housing bubble burst, real estate agents representing buyers continue to be paid based on the price of the house sold, and focus, as do loan officers, on the upper limit of what clients can purchase. The homeowner is not devouring and destroying the house per se (although new and expensive homes can often be made with less sustainable and durable materials so as to maximize profits), but overextended purchases, which benefit bank owners and real estate agents, consume the homeowner as they feel the

25 Himes, "Consumerism and Ethics," 148; Himes is citing Timothy Vaverek, "Christian Asceticism: Breaking Consumerism's Destructive Hold," *Houston Catholic Worker* 21, no. 1 (January 2001): 1–7.

26 Juliet B. Schor, *The Overworked American: The Unexpected Decline of Leisure* (New York: Basic Books, 1992).

27 See Cloutier, *The Vice of Luxury*, 132–38, for his discussion of paying a brand premium and his argument for instead paying a sacramental premium (use of money to do good, especially for the poor). Cloutier also describes the housing and automobile industry as consumptive markets. He notes, for example, that in the 2008–2009 economic recession, individuals postponed or avoided auto and house purchases (145–46).

28 Cloutier, 144n153.

burden of a thirty-year loan and the need to maintain and repair their home and yard. Although there are positives that come with home ownership, such as providing stability and encouraging care and concern for one's living space, the tendency toward larger and more elaborate homes also provides opportunities for cultivated dissatisfaction as the homeowner struggles to furnish and update the house according to the expectations of marketing, sales, and cultural norms.[29] Debt from house loans, college loans, car loans, and credit cards enhances dissatisfaction as significant portions of family income are lost to interest on debt.

CONSUMERISM AND FAMILY LIFE

Capitalism brings many positive goods and opportunities to family life. I am highlighting the too-often overlooked ways that the competition of capitalism can cause harm to families so that ethicists and families are aware of those influences and can respond accordingly. Specifically, families need to recognize how marketing, sales, and cultural norms place pressures on their members to increase their consumption, which leads to increased dissatisfaction. This dissatisfaction often contributes to busyness and debt but also impacts the way individuals think about family life.

I have mentioned many times already the tendency among academics to see social ethics and family ethics as separate disciplines, or even opposed parties of competing ethicists. Social ethics concerns structural and primarily political concerns, and family ethics concerns private actions, primarily questions of sexual ethics. As a result, both the social character of the family and the social context for sexual and medical ethics are overlooked. Against this tendency, I wish to explore how social concerns about consumerism collide with recognition of the family's social role. Simply put, consumerism and private, isolated notions of family life cannot eliminate the social character of the family, but they make living out that character difficult, especially for those seeking to be formed by Catholic social teaching. The profit motive separated from the common good, consumer detachment, the formative power of advertisement, and an emphasis on family privacy all impact how individuals understand sexual desire, spousal love, weddings, children, and family life.

29 Cloutier (146) notes how the decrease in house purchases in the 2008–2009 economic recession "also meant a decline in the many goods that are bought for new houses: appliances, furniture, and the like."

A consumerist framework denies the family's social role already at the conceptual level. As a consumer, one enters marriage in order to express a private choice aimed at personal satisfaction rather than to embrace a new and foundational social role. In addition to the endless consumer options surrounding the wedding (destination, cake, flowers, dress, and so on), one can choose whether one has a stable sexual partnership validated as marriage and what one wants any such marriage to mean. If marriage is merely a choice of personal identity or a form of self-expression, then the family is not necessarily responsible for a child's education, family members' psychological and medical care, or developing an economic community that draws members together in a collective life.[30] Underneath the surface, however, the family plays a crucial, even when hidden, social role in a consumerist framework. Spousal love, dating, engagement, weddings, and the bearing and raising of children all provide fuel for promoting consumptive practices. In other words, absent a robust account of the basic social unit, the family's social role in such a framework is to grease the wheels of consumption.[31] This social role is made more powerful by the façade of the isolated family ideal, which suggests that families are not influenced by others.

Recognizing the social significance of marriage and family, advertisers and salespeople use the desire for family connections to promote sales. In the process, marketing and sales consume the very things to which it appeals by defining terms and ordering desire. An advertisement that links a product with someone whose physical appearance suggests sexual appeal and availability not only misdirects a basic human desire to a possibly unrelated product but also forms consumers to detach their sexual desire from relationships and responsibility. This point deserves a more detailed exploration.

Dating, Sexual Desire, and Pornography

In a consumer culture, sexual desire and dating are defined more by consumer practices than practices of family discernment. Jason King summarizes shifts in twentieth-century dating scripts that moved from socially well-defined expectations for dating in which men call on women and the

30 Donald Miller, *Concepts of Family Life in Modern Catholic Theology: From Vatican II through 'Christifideles Laici'* (San Francisco: Catholic Scholars Press, 1997), 2.

31 In *Concepts of Family Life*, Miller highlights that the family becomes a community that coordinates social services and that consumerism maintains a major place in family life (24); see also McCarthy, *Sex and Love in the Home*, 3–4, 20, 97.

couple get to know one another in the woman's living room to "whatever people consent to is legitimate."[32] The emphasis on choice, absent social norms governing dating practices or how individuals and the community can know whether the relationship is progressing, means that couples can choose whatever they want for their relationship. Individuals can employ any means to get consent, even manipulation, and in some cases "violence becomes just another way, acceptable to some but not others, to get consent."[33] The emphasis on choice also leaves couples susceptible to consumer influences. Dating and going on a date is not an opportunity to discern marriage by getting to know the other person and their various social communities, but an opportunity to wear attractive clothing, dine at nice restaurants, attend costly events, feel "true" love, and buy expensive gifts for birthdays, Christmas, and Valentine's Day. The tagline of the jewelry store commercial, "Every kiss begins with Kay," for example, implies that developing a successful romantic life absolutely requires expensive and unnecessary purchases by the man to impress the woman. Even if consumers know that this claim is exaggerated and literally impossible, similar messages shape expectations.

The detachment from the producers, production, and products typical of consumerism impacts sexual desire. McCarthy proposes that the message of commercials that brand vehicles with sexually attractive models is less, "Get the car, get the girl," and more, "You lack both."[34] McCarthy notes how this "dominant economy of desire unsettles the self."[35] One's desire for God is disoriented and directed toward the consumption of things, experiences, and relationships. Speaking to this unsettling desire, Francis speaks of a "culture of the ephemeral" in which people move "from one affective relationship to another" believing "that love can be connected or disconnected at the whim of the consumer. . . . We treat affective relationships the way we treat material objects and the environment: everything is disposable; everyone uses and throws away, takes and breaks, exploits and squeezes to the last drop. Then, goodbye. Narcissism makes people incapable of looking

32 Jason King, "A Theology of Dating for a Culture of Abuse," in *Leaving and Coming Home: New Wineskins for Catholic Sexual Ethics*, ed. David Cloutier (Eugene, OR: Cascade Books, 2010), 30–35. King notes that he is outlining dating scripts and not necessarily dating practices. He also notes that each dating script presents risks of injustice.

33 King, 36.

34 McCarthy, *Sex and Love in the Home*, 33.

35 McCarthy, 41.

beyond themselves, beyond their own desires and needs."[36] One sees this disposable approach to sexual desire and relationships most acutely in the practices of pornography.

The pornography industry embodies various aspects of consumerism. First, pornography presents a motivation toward profit.[37] Blaise Cronin, who writes on pornography from a business perspective, notes that while identifying exact revenue figures for pornography is difficult for several reasons, it is clearly a billion-dollar-per-year industry, with higher estimates running into the tens of billions.[38] Sex sells. The revenue provided by pornographic services and the prevalence of pornography have made it mainstream. Companies whose primary work is to provide pornography have stock traded on NASDAQ. Pornography is pervasive and hard to avoid. Cronin estimated in 2008 that ten to fifteen thousand pornographic movies are made annually in the US.[39] With the new capacity of artificial intelligence to create lifelike simulated pornographic images and videos, the production of such material no longer has a conceivable limit. Less extreme variants of pornography have become a media and advertising staple for various products.[40]

Due to its prevalence, minors who go on the internet—which is virtually all of them—are likely to be exposed to pornography and are at a growing risk of inadvertent exposure to pornography.[41] Profit and prevalence also give pornography industry leaders power over technological developments. While Cronin offered caution about claims that over half of internet use is for pornographic purposes, he argued that the pornography industry clearly has impacted mainstream technological developments:

> [Pornographers] have been, and continue to be, either directly or indirectly responsible for major technical innovations, or at the very least, for taking such developments to the next level of sophistication (e.g. subscription services, exit consoles/pop-up windows, streaming video, and affiliate

36 Francis, *Amoris Laetitia*, 39.

37 I am focusing on pornography producers and distributors that charge fees rather than those who provide free content.

38 Blaise Cronin, "Eros Unbound: Pornography and the Internet," in *The Internet and American Business*, ed. William Aspray and Paul E. Ceruzzi (Cambridge, MA: MIT Press, 2008), 508–33.

39 Cronin, 497.

40 Cronin, 518.

41 Cronin's research focused on chat rooms and peer-to-peer networks, which were the primary vehicles for such exposure in 2008. Cronin, 497, 519.

> marketing schemes). As the futurist Paul Saffo put it: "the simple fact is porn is an early adopter of new media. If you're trying to get something established . . . you're going to privately and secretly hope and pray that the porn industry likes your medium."[42]

Pornography is pervasive, socially powerful, and in many cases mainstream. The industry thrives on socially detached definitions of business and sexual expression and the detached character of consumerism. Those who produce, market, and sell pornography "prefer a culture of anonymity or pseudonymity, striving to stay out of the limelight and away from the unwelcome attention of the Internal Revenue Service, the Immigration and Naturalization Service, or [the] Department of Justice."[43] The industry also benefits from socially isolated notions of sexual desire and expression. Cronin, reflecting on changes to the pornography industry that occurred with video production and the internet argues that the "shift in locus of consumption from public to private spaces was crucial to the industry's subsequent growth trajectory."[44] Pornography also typifies the detached character of consumption. Cronin writes, "Continuous product refreshing is a *conditio* sine qua non for a business whose paying customer base has a notoriously short attention span. . . . Customer loyalty is extremely fickle when it comes to representations of sex. . . . This is a market propelled by an insatiable appetite for freshness and novelty."[45] Typical of consumerism, the focus is not acquisition but desire for more. W. Bradford Littlejohn reflects on this detached desire for more from the perspective of the viewer and argues that porn use is more reflective of the vice of curiosity than lust. Referencing the work of Gary Wilson, who compiled and synthesized thousands of testimonials from recovering porn addicts, Littlejohn writes, "It's not uncommon for porn users to move from genre to genre, often arriving at places they find personally disturbing and confusing."[46] Bradford argues that porn use

42 Cronin, 495, quoting Dawn C. Chmielewski and Claire Hoffman, "Porn Industry Again at the Tech Forefront," *Los Angeles Times*, April 20, 2006, available at http://www.latimes.com/business/la-fi-porn19apr19,1,5662527.story?coll=la-headlines-business.

43 Cronin, "Eros Unbound," 509.

44 Cronin, 500.

45 Cronin, 499.

46 W. Bradford Littlejohn, "Addicted to Novelty: The Vice of Curiosity in a Digital Age," *Journal of the Society of Christian Ethics* 37, no. 1 (Spring/Summer 2017): 189–90. Littlejohn is citing Gary Wilson, *Your Brain on Porn: Internet Pornography and the Emerging Science of Addiction* (Margate, UK: Commonwealth, 2014), 46.

is "driven primarily by that trademark of curiosity, the thirst for novelty in which the gaze objectifies and devours its object almost immediately and must move restlessly on to the next, never satisfied."[47]

The competition of the market, private notions of business, and a sense of detachment in pornography also encourage the mistreatment of workers. Cronin notes that due to an oversupply of both pornography and of willing, desperate labor, producers feel compelled and enabled to push industry boundaries for working conditions. As a result, porn workers "burn out more rapidly, both physically and psychologically, become overexposed, and" in Cronin's words, "gradually lose their market appeal."[48] Porn workers, for the most part, "are commodified bodies for hire, paid off the books."[49] They are used temporarily for the sake of profit and then discarded. Cronin notes that legislation requiring documentation showing that models are over the age of eighteen caused some companies to pull materials from the market or withdraw from the market altogether.[50] These practices suggest, as John Paul II argues, that the issue with pornography is not that the images show too much but that they do not show enough.[51] Pornography reduces the person to his or her physical sex appeal. Hidden from view is the person's personal history, social context, family obligations, hopes and dreams. Francis describes pornography as the "commercialization of the body."[52] Marketing for pornography involves exposure to the product, which hooks people and leaves them seeking more.

If one separates sexual ethics from social ethics, one will miss the social context and consumptive dimensions of pornography. While seemingly a socially detached action, those who view and purchase pornography do so in part because strategic marketing campaigns get them hooked at a young age and keep them desiring more. Pornography provides revenue for companies and embodies the social detachment typical of consumerism. The

47 Littlejohn, "Addicted to Novelty," 190. Littlejohn further explains that while opioids give us pleasure, dopamine leaves us wanting more. He argues that the digital age provides "a feedback loop of perpetual seeking and self-satisfaction in the privatized possession of novelty." Littlejohn, 191.

48 Cronin, "Eros Unbound," 506–7.

49 Cronin, 505.

50 Cronin, 503.

51 John Paul II, *Man and Woman He Created Them: A Theology of the Body*, trans. Michael Waldstein (Boston: Pauline Books, 2006), 372–78.

52 Francis, *Amoris Laetitia*, 41.

high revenues for the pornography industry do not occur without paying customers who waste time and resources on pornographic services. W. Bradford Littlejohn reports that "63 percent of eighteen- to thirty-year-old males report viewing [pornography] at least several times per week."[53] In summarizing the trend, Cronin notes that more people are spending more of their disposable income on pornographic goods and services.[54] Pornography also forms the desires of consumers to restlessly seek more and associates sexual desire with private, erotic pleasure rather than a spousal love committed to the social responsibilities of marriage. Littlejohn, while acknowledging that only a minority of porn users develop addictions, highlights that for those who are addicted, "the effects are devastating—not just the obvious breakdowns of marriages and relationships but inability to form loving relationships, depression, anxiety, suicidal thoughts, sexual dysfunction, ADHD, poor academic and work performance, and—the hallmark of any addiction—the inability to quit."[55] Some of these patterns of consumption (the profit motive, power and vulnerability, private notions of sexuality, and detachment from people) become only more pronounced in illegal practices, such as human trafficking, prostitution, and child pornography.

Spousal Love

Competition and the profit motive also impact cultural notions of spousal love. If the goal is to link desire with one's product, then the human desire for sexual union and the inclination to have and raise children serve as excellent fuel for the fire. Advertisements manipulate the natural human desire to improve one's relationship with one's spouse and children and to raise one's children well. The pervasiveness of marketing and the manipulation of family connections to sell products not only intentionally misdirects desire to the relevant products but also indirectly links spousal love with dissatisfaction and fleeting feelings and experiences.[56] In a culture of consumerism, love and sexual desire are consumed. Spousal love is reduced to romanticism, in which one has intense but ultimately fleeting feelings of sexual attraction for another. The romantic quest becomes a quest for personal fulfillment in which the other is ultimately disposable when he or she no longer serves one's ostensible needs.

53 Littlejohn, "Addicted to Novelty," 181.

54 Cronin, "Eros Unbound," 532.

55 Littlejohn, "Addicted to Novelty," 188.

56 Francis, *Amoris Laetitia*, 89.

Consider for example the most successful commercial film of the 1990s, *Titanic.* While the movie devotes ample time to the tragic sinking of the *Titanic,* it is primarily a Hollywood romance, in which the repressed heroine Rose finds personal liberation through a romance with an American artist, Jack, who represents "being true to oneself, of giving free expression to one's individuality, of valuing creativity, personal integrity, and passion above all."[57] Their forbidden romance ends with Jack perishing to save Rose from the disaster, denying the usual expectation of a Hollywood "happily ever after." As film critic Steven Greydanus points out, this would be a deeply sad story if the goal of the romance was a communion of life and love including the raising and educating of children, but the film presents the story as a triumph because the romance is merely the means of the heroine's self-discovery and self-expression.[58] While this highly successful commercial film presents itself as having nobler motives than crass consumerism, the result is the same—the lover is enjoyed, even admired, but is also expendable.

The reduction of spousal love to temporary erotic feelings undermines twentieth-century developments in Catholic sexual ethics, which highlight spousal love as foundational for marriage and propose that this love images the love of God for humanity and the love of Christ for the Church. In a consumer culture, this rich theology risks being reduced to a Hollywood romance. If spousal love is based on temporary erotic feelings, then marriage seems to promise perpetual feelings of romantic love.[59] McCarthy observes, however, that for many, the movement from romantic love to sharing and developing the skills and practices necessary for family life can be difficult.[60] Private feelings of love do not necessarily give way to the common household tasks of marriage and family life.[61] McCarthy proposes that romantic love understood as temporary affection is ill fitted to be a foundation for the skills and practices necessary for a fulfilled marriage "because it hopes to stabilize marriage through what is known to be a fragile bond."[62] Moreover, the private character of romantic love leaves the couple

57 Steven Greydanus, review of *Titanic*, directed by John Cameron, http://decentfilms.com/reviews/titanic1997.

58 Greydanus, review of *Titanic*.

59 And moreover, faithfulness to God promises perpetual feelings of joy.

60 McCarthy, *Sex and Love in the Home*, 9.

61 McCarthy, 9; see also 51.

62 McCarthy, 153.

without the support and wisdom of surrounding communities to discern what is needed to sustain marriage or to work through challenges that occur when their love changes. If marriage promises perpetual romantic love and one spouse does not feel that love, then he or she will wonder what has gone wrong: they might blame themselves or become detached from their spouse, their kids, or the social institution of marriage, or they might look for spousal love elsewhere. Many realize at some level that spousal love and marriage involve more than temporary erotic feelings, but such a conclusion reflects more a personal choice than socially supported wisdom.[63] Certainly, few Hollywood films show romance transitioning into a stable and durable marriage, even if unlike *Titanic* they end with a "happily ever after."

One sees more clearly the impact of consumerism on spousal love when one recognizes that spousal love can be more than a mere erotic, and ultimately temporary, feeling. When the bishops write in *Gaudium et Spes* that love serves as a foundation for marriage, they recognize the need to distinguish spousal love as foundation for marriage from spousal love understood as mere erotic attraction.[64] Paul VI writes that it is of supreme importance to have an exact idea of the characteristic marks and demands of conjugal love.[65] John Paul II and Francis follow this tradition, arguing that spousal love is indeed a foundation for marriage even while critiquing false or shallow forms of spousal love.[66] Francis, for example, clarifies that spousal love is not foundational in the sense that it provides a perfect and unchanging support for marriage:

> It is not helpful to dream of an idyllic and perfect love needing no stimulus to grow. A celestial notion of earthly love forgets that the best is yet to come, that fine wine matures with age. As the Bishops of Chile have

63 McCarthy works from culturally prevalent notions of romantic love and notes how these notions serve as a poor foundation for marriage. He describes romantic love as "obsessive, possessive, and anxious." McCarthy, 58. McCarthy seems to suggest that one must choose between a personalist and a social foundation for marriage; with respect to this dichotomy, he favors a social foundation and seems to imply that utilitarian calculation or social status are adequate motivations for entering into marriage. McCarthy, 26–27.

64 Second Vatican Council, Pastoral Constitution on the Church in the Modern World *Gaudium et Spes*, 49, in *Vatican Council II: The Conciliar and Post Conciliar Documents*, ed. Austin Flannery, rev. ed. (Collegeville, MN: Liturgical Press, 1975), 952.

65 Paul VI, Encyclical Letter *Humanae Vitae* (July 25, 1968), 8–9.

66 Francis calls for a deeper understanding of conjugal love and argues that love sustains married couples through marital struggles and challenges in raising children. *Amoris Laetitia*, 162. See also John Paul II, Apostolic Exhortation *Familiaris Consortio* (November 22, 1981), 18.

> pointed out, "the perfect families proposed by deceptive consumerist propaganda do not exist. In those families, no one grows old, there is no sickness, sorrow or death. . . . Consumerist propaganda presents a fantasy that has nothing to do with the reality which must daily be faced by the heads of families." It is much healthier to be realistic about our limits, defects and imperfections, and to respond to the call to grow together, to bring love to maturity and to strengthen the union, come what may.[67]

Spousal love is not a perfect, perpetual, private, isolated, temporary feeling, but combines an erotic desire for unity with the beloved with respect for the beloved, a desire for and commitment to permanence in the relationship, and the conviction that the couple can run a household together. While spousal love, like virtue, should be accompanied by ordered desire and cultivated affections, desire and affections will inevitably ebb and flow.

Spousal love is foundational in that spouses should not merely use one another as instruments for personal satisfaction or social gain. The strength of their respect for each other and of their relationship significantly impacts their ability to manage a household and raise children together. Thus, spousal love is not a love that opposes the practical skills of family life but a love that invites lovers to reflect on those skills and practices, as well as on the social support necessary for a fulfilling life together. Spousal love is a necessary but not sufficient foundation for marriage. Spousal love is foundational in that it serves as a motivation for marriage; the spouses, in committing to marriage, commit to cultivating their love for one another. In order to form a solid marriage, however, further support from the other social foundations for marriage is needed, including social commitments to spousal fidelity and to the sacrifices vital for bearing and raising children.

It is tempting to think that if families were isolated and uninfluenced by market branding and cultural notions of romantic love, moral theologians and church leaders could simply clarify the nature of spousal love and the faithful would live accordingly. Families, however, are social institutions interdependent with various other social institutions. The Church does not want families who live in isolation, but families who actively participate in building a robust Christian culture in the midst of countervailing forces. In seeking this authentic culture of family life, a key component of what John Paul II calls "a civilization of love," it does no good to pretend that Christians are separate from the wider cultural trends toward roman-

67 Francis, *Amoris Laetitia*, 135.

ticized erotic love. Christians, after all, made up much of the audience of *Titanic*. McCarthy helps to remind us that shallow notions of romantic love are not merely found in the culture but are also found in the hearts and minds of the faithful. Failure to recognize how consumerism and other formative influences distort notions of spousal love will either lead to shallow accounts of spousal love or confusion about why the faithful do not understand the permanent orientation of spousal love.

Socially Isolated Marriage, Cohabitation, and Same-Sex Attraction

Those who experience a spousal love that is ordered toward commitment and a shared life together often struggle to make the commitment of marriage in the context of consumerism. Many are discouraged from marriage by the expectations of an excessive standard of living.[68] If advertisements cultivate dissatisfaction that inclines people to live beyond their means, then they will be motivated to postpone marriage until they have attained a rare form of economic stability. The median age of those getting married for the first time has increased by about one year per decade since 1960, and while the Church does not necessarily encourage marriage as early as possible, this trend seems to reflect a reluctance to commit oneself to the task of building a permanent family.[69]

Definitions of marriage that see it as something socially isolated also encourage couples to avoid marriage.[70] Francis notes that "many countries are witnessing a legal deconstruction of the family, tending to adopt models based almost exclusively on the autonomy of the individual will."[71] If marriage is merely an expression of an autonomous will, then we cannot be surprised if many couples, even those in long-term sexual relationships, conclude that they do not need a public wedding ceremony or a legal document validating their self-defined relationship. Indeed, many are making that decision.

68 Francis, 40.

69 United States Census Bureau, "Table MS-2: Estimated Median Age at First Marriage, by Sex: 1890 to Present," availabale at https://www.census.gov/data/tables/time-series/demo/families/marital.html. The estimated median age for first marriage for men moved from 22.8 years in 1960 to 29.5 years in 2017. During that same time, the estimated median age for first marriage for women moved from 20.3 years to 27.4 years.

70 See John Paul II, *Familiaris Consortio* (81) and Francis, *Amoris Laetitia* (40), for various reasons why couples avoid marriage.

71 Francis, *Amoris Laetitia*, 53.

In a focused study on premarital cohabitation among women in the United States, Esther O. Lamidi reports that the "share of American women aged 30–34 who had cohabited at least once nearly doubled, from 40% in 1987 to 75% in 2013."[72] A 2019 Pew Research Center report observed that while growth in cohabitation rates has slowed in the last decade, "cohabitation rates have increased across all age groups since 1995."[73] The Pew Research report also affirms that while "the share who are currently cohabiting remains far smaller than the share who are married, the share of adults ages 18 to 44 who have ever lived with an unmarried partner (59%) has surpassed the share who has ever been married (50%)."[74] The number engaging in serial casual sexual relationships instead of serious or long-term ones has also skyrocketed, especially among those in their teens and twenties, although these numbers are more difficult to determine.[75]

Amidst the ubiquity of sexually "intimate" casual dating and the "hookup culture," cohabitation comes to be seen as close to marriage and contrasted with singleness; older family members are often relieved to see young people settling into a more domestic lifestyle with a steady partner. McCarthy proposes, however, that living together should be sharply contrasted with marriage, since couples are sharing all the benefits of a marriage-like relationship while attempting to avoid the institutional roles (viewed as constraints) of marriage.[76] McCarthy observed that for those in the 1990s, "cohabitation [was] not a state of life as much as a transitional stage."[77] Lamidi, however, compares a cohort of women who began cohabiting in the 1980s with a group that began cohabiting between 2006 and 2013.

72 Esther O. Lamidi, Wendy D. Manning, and Susan L. Brown, "Change in the Stability of First Premarital Cohabitation among Women in the United States, 1983–2013," *Demography* 56 (2019): 428; see also Jane Anderson, "The Impact of Family Structure on the Health of Children: Effects of Divorce," *The Linacre Quarterly* 81, no. 4 (November 2014): 378–79.

73 Juliana Horowitz, Nikki Graf, and Gretchen Livingston, "Marriage and Cohabitation in the U.S.," Pew Research Center, November 6, 2019, https://www.pewresearch.org/social-trends/2019/11/06/marriage-and-cohabitation-in-the-u-s/.

74 Horowitz, Graf, and Livingston, "Marriage and Cohabitation in the U.S."

75 See Jason King's research on and analysis of hookup culture on Catholic campuses in *Faith with Benefits: Hookup Culture on Catholic Campuses* (Oxford: Oxford University Press, 2016).

76 McCarthy, *Sex and Love in the Home*, 209.

77 McCarthy, *Sex and Love in the Home*, 209–10; McCarthy notes that according to one study, "forty percent of all cohabiting couples either marry or stop living together within a year, and only one-third are still cohabiting after two years." The study McCarthy references is Lee A. Lillard, Michael J. Brien, and Linda J. Waite, "Premarital Cohabitation and Subsequent Marital Dissolution: A Matter of Self-Selection?," *Demography* 32, no. 3 (August 1995): 438.

She finds that as cohabitation has become more common, fewer cohabiting couples have transitioned to marriage, and more such couples have had children while cohabiting. For the 1980s cohort, 30 percent of women in cohabiting relationships transitioned to marriage before the end of one year, whereas for the 2006–13 cohort, only 13 percent of women in such relationships transitioned to marriage within a year.[78] Lamidi also reports that "the share of births to unmarried women in the United States has doubled since the 1980s, and nearly all the increase in nonmarital childbearing over the past few decades was due to increasing births among cohabiting women."[79] The trends suggest that cohabitation has increasingly come to replace marriage rather than serve as a transition to it, even while cohabitation remains a relatively unstable relationship in which to have and raise children. Lamidi reports that even when children are born in cohabiting relationships, 27 percent of those relationships dissolve within three years.[80]

In addition to encouraging cohabitation, consumer accounts of marriage suggest that individuals can choose what marriage means for them. While conflict over the definition of marriage has appeared most prominently in cultural debates about whether same-sex couples qualify for marriage, McCarthy argues that "homosexuality is not a decisive issue that will determine the viability of marriage as an institution. The idea of marriage as socially detached and contractual is already firmly in place. To this degree, practices of cohabitation among heterosexuals present a far greater challenge to marriage as a set of social and sexual habits."[81] To the extent marriage is socially isolated and contractual, the same-sex marriage discussion led to both a meaningless debate and a foregone conclusion. If the meaning of marriage is defined by the whims of the individual spouses, then the state and civil society can have no reason to exclude same-sex relationships from this essentially vacuous legal partnership. At the same time, however, if marriage is merely a private contract between two consenting adults, then the state and civil society have no need or responsibility to oversee or support marriage commitments at all. While marriage and family law in the United States, for instance, has traditionally been overwhelmingly focused on the welfare of children, more recent approaches to

78 Lamidi, Manning, and Brown, 437.

79 Lamidi, Manning, and Brown, 430.

80 Lamidi, Manning, and Brown, 438.

81 McCarthy, *Sex and Love in the Home*, 214.

redefine marriage have focused far more on the free choice of the spouses to do whatever they desire.[82]

Before the Supreme Court decided *Obergefell v. Hodges*, McCarthy argued that "each side of the [same-sex marriage] debate, particularly in theology, puts forward its arguments with little recognition that we, in the West, live in an age that is already post-marital."[83] I cannot exactly agree with this statement. While McCarthy is right to highlight how socially detached accounts of marriage undermine the need for public discourse about marriage, *public* debates about and emotionally charged calls for *public* recognition of same-sex unions also indicate that the West is not completely post-marital, but still implicitly recognizes the social character of marriage and the family, at least in terms of rights and privileges, if not always in terms of responsibilities and social roles. Even most cohabiting couples recognize the social role of marriage and family life, and imitate it insofar as they participate in extended family gatherings, create stationery with both people's names, and/or coparent any children they conceive or bring from prior relationships. Some cohabiting couples see themselves as on their way to marriage while others are reacting against specific accounts of marriage, rather than denying altogether that their sexual partnership leads to social roles. and above all child-rearing. Even if some seek to reduce the social role of family life, they cannot, even if they so desired, eliminate or avoid altogether the social roles and responsibilities that living as though married entail.

Any meaningful argument related to the public definition or recognition of marriage must provide some account of the social roles of marriage. Underneath debates about legal recognition of private rights are disagreements about the social role and responsibility of families. Cohabitation challenges the significance that social commitments, social support, and permanence have for marriage and raising children. Same-sex marriage

82 Helen Alvaré, *Putting Children's Interests First in U.S. Family Law and Policy: With Power Comes Responsibility* (Cambridge: Cambridge University Press, 2018).

83 McCarthy, *Sex and Love in the Home*, 213. McCarthy also highlights that advocacy of same-sex unions is not free from the pervasive reach of consumerism. He writes, "Public recognition of homosexual unions is emerging in a time that is also post-sexual-orientation. Market desire has freed us for a multitude of sexualities, including homosexuality. . . . Same-sex desire has become a commodity or style that is . . . freed for a market of heterosexual consumption" (213). He describes the metrosexual and the heteroflexible as examples of consumers in a homosexual market. Moreover, he proposes that the portrayal of same-sex couples in movies and TV series seems to provide acceptance of same-sex desire but often "allows representations of homosexuality to be consumed and enjoyed while being belittled" (215).

challenges the social role that natural marriage plays in promoting the conception of children within a stable community of love.[84]

Sexual Union and Procreation

Consumptive practices and accounts of family life that isolate the family also distort the concepts related to and the practices of sexual union and the procreation and raising of children. Certainly, sexual union is private in that it should not be presented for public consumption. However, the privacy of sexual acts does not mean that sexual union lacks social significance.[85] Problems occur when one moves from seeing sexual union as private in the sense of protecting intimacy to private in the sense of acting with self-concern to the neglect of the beloved or to the neglect of the orientation of sexual union toward procreation. The reduction of sexual expression to pleasure parallels the commodification of sexual desire for profit found in the advertising principle that "sex sells."[86] Francis writes that sex often "'becomes the occasion and instrument for self-assertion and the selfish satisfaction of personal desires and instincts.' In our own day, sexuality risks being poisoned by the mentality of 'use and discard.' The body of the other is often viewed as an object to be used as long as it offers satisfaction, and rejected once it is no longer appealing."[87]

84 McCarthy argues that the Catholic position overcomes some of the challenges to private definitions of marriage and consumptive practices by highlighting the two ends of marriage, and thereby recognizing the procreative end as necessary to the unity between husband and wife. Within a generative framework, same-sex relationships are not equivalent to heterosexual relationships. McCarthy, *Sex and Love in the Home*, 220. Francis, often cast as a supporter of typical LGBTQ political goals, makes an even stronger statement about the dissimilarity between Christian marriage and homosexual relationships. After affirming that "every person, regardless of sexual orientation, ought to be respected in his or her dignity," Francis writes: "There are absolutely no grounds for considering homosexual unions to be in any way similar or even remotely analogous to God's plan for marriage and family" *Amoris Laetitia*, 250–51. Here, Francis does not describe the Catholic vision of sexuality and marriage that grounds the distinction between marriage and same-sex unions but critiques international bodies that pressure local churches by tying financial aid to legal support for marriage between persons of the same sex.

85 Stanley Hauerwas writes, "Any discussion of sex must begin with an understanding of how a sexual ethics is rooted in a community's basic political commitments." Stanley Hauerwas, "Sex in Public: How Adventurous Christians Do It," in *The Hauerwas Reader*, ed. John Berkman and Michael Cartwright (Durham: Duke University Press, 2001), 489.

86 John Paul II expresses concern about a culture that reduces sexuality to the body and selfish pleasure in *Familiaris Consortio* (37).

87 Francis, *Amoris Laetitia*, 153; the internal citation is from John Paul II, Encyclical Letter *Evangelium Vitae* (March 25, 1995), 23.

Contemporary culture is often described as "sex-positive" and continues to be contrasted with the supposed frigidity and repressiveness associated with traditional sexual ethics, and above all, with Catholicism. Rose and Jack in *Titanic* are just one example of how eliminating all sexual restrictions (besides the rule of consent) has supposedly liberated Western individuals to find true fulfillment. However, the rise of the Me Too movement has shown that all is not well in this supposed paradise of sexualized consumption and consumptive sexuality. Even when the rule of consent is respected, the possibility for manipulation and emotionally and physically damaging sexual encounters and relationships remains high. Sexuality is not simply dangerous because we might enjoy it too much—although moderation is also a virtue not sufficiently appreciated by consumer culture—but rather because it involves a deeply personal and vulnerable part of the psyche as well as the body. In this sense, the Church is not "sex-negative," but "sex-cautious," and such caution is profoundly realistic.

Recognizing risks associated with sexual desire and sexual union, the Catholic tradition speaks of marriage as a *remedia concupiscentia.* Marriage provides a remedy because the commitment of marriage, the love shared between spouses, and the grace of the sacrament provide the strength and appropriate context to direct and purify sexual desire. John Paul II and Francis both warn that even in marriage, spouses can use one another for sexual pleasure.[88] Their affirmations clarify the nature of the *remedia concupiscentia.* It does not mean that because spouses legally "own" one another's bodies, they can selfishly or even abusively make use of their spouse for their own pleasure.[89] Rather, marriage serves as a remedy by helping to focus sexual desire toward a stable, exclusive, and procreative relationship. The commitment of marriage does not thereby give license for lust or manipulation. Francis writes that "a conjugal act imposed on one's spouse without regard to his or her condition, or personal and reasonable wishes in the matter, is no true act of love, and therefore offends the moral order in its particular application to the intimate relationship of husband and wife."[90] To apply Cavanaugh's language of detachment to sexual ethics, one could say that the use of one's spouse for mere sexual pleasure is a consumptive practice that, despite the intimate union of sexual union, involves a detachment from the beloved.

88 Francis, *Amoris Laetitia*, 153–54; John Paul II, *Man and Woman He Created Them*, 297.

89 Michael Waldstein, introduction to John Paul II, *Man and Woman He Created Them*, 56.

90 Francis, *Amoris Laetitia*, 154.

If sexual expression is merely a tool for financial gain or private pleasure, then pornography, masturbation, prostitution, adultery, and—despite attempts to maintain the rule of consent—even rape are logical implications. Moreover, if marriage and sexual union are merely opportunities for self-expression, then where can those who are harmed by these practices turn for help? All too often, abuse and violence are handled privately in the family without social accountability. An apology is made without a genuine resolution to care for those who continue to be harmed or a plan for the offending family member to receive the treatment, formation, and legal boundaries necessary to avoid future abuse and violence.

An individualistic, consumptive approach to sexual union risks harming not only one's spouse but also overlooking the connection between sexual union and procreation.[91] McCarthy writes, "Sex in the dominant market must be detached not only from marriage and home, but also from procreation."[92] If the meaning of marriage is something one can self-define, then children become an optional and expensive accessory to marriage. This "choice" for or against children, however, is situated within a broader cultural and political context. For some, economic and political instability or danger makes procreation unsafe. In cultures of consumption, spouses are influenced by cultural expectations of career success, the need to maintain certain standards of living, and aggressive marketing from the big business of child prevention. McCarthy writes, "Any aspiring middle-class couple knows that children are a liability."[93] In a consumer culture, children are career obstacles and financial burdens and limit one's choices as a consumer. John Paul II proposes that for those of wealthier means, "excessive prosperity and the consumer mentality . . . deprive married couples of the generosity and courage needed for raising up new human life: thus life is often perceived not as a blessing, but as a danger from which to defend oneself."[94] Similarly, Francis writes, "Consumerism may also deter people from having children, simply so they can maintain a certain freedom and lifestyle."[95] While few people would say that they do not want children so they

91 McCarthy writes that "the dominant contractual economy is inhospitable to children." *Sex and Love in the Home*, 228.

92 McCarthy, 231.

93 McCarthy, 232.

94 John Paul II, *Familiaris Consortio*, 6.

95 Francis, *Amoris Laetitia*, 42; Francis in turn is quoting from Synod of Bishops, Fourteenth Extraordinary General Assembly, *Relatio Finalis* (October 24, 2015), 7.

can have a nice house, car, and retirement, some are willing to express what others tacitly endorse by their actions.[96] More troubling, however, are the ways in which consumerism impacts those who wish to be generous toward children but struggle to do so because of financial and social pressure.[97]

In addition to financial influences, the false ideal of a private, isolated family also challenges the place of children in marriage, since a private and isolated family must bear a substantial burden in raising children on their own. If having and raising children is merely a choice, then child-rearing is the sole responsibility of the parents (or even just the mother), and the community bears no responsibility to help.

Since sexual union leads to children, however, those who do not want children are faced with the challenge of preventing sexual union from resulting in pregnancy. This challenge is seemingly overcome by scientific developments that allow the spouses to exercise control over their fertility, often the woman's fertility. McCarthy writes, "In light of what science can do, procreation has the aura of always being a choice."[98] However, just as the choice to prevent children is culturally conditioned, so also the choice of family practices is influenced by consumer patterns. The responsible parenthood promoted by the Church through the use of fertility monitoring ("natural family planning") does not fit the prevailing consumer model. This is not to deny that the use of fertility monitoring to postpone pregnancies is especially challenging for some couples—for example, those who deal with inconsistent cycles and those spouses who struggle with abstaining from sexual union. But one also needs to recognize how consumer tendencies impact spouses' choice of contraception over fertility monitoring. Fertility monitoring does not sufficiently free spouses to have sex when they so choose; it requires discipline and sacrifice rather than purchasing a product.[99]

Contraceptive marketing promises that couples who act contraceptively will passionately express their love for one another without having to repress sexual desire and without the risk of children; they will live happily ever after, or at least, enjoy their time together until they move on to other lovers

96 Nadia Taha, "Opting Out of Parenthood, with Finances in Mind," *New York Times*, November 13, 2012.

97 Claire Cain Miller, "Americans Are Having Fewer Babies: They Told Us Why," *New York Times*, July 5, 2018.

98 McCarthy, *Sex and Love in the Home*, 235; see also Francis, *Amoris Laetitia*, 42.

99 McCarthy, *Sex and Love in the Home*, 231.

and interests. If this sounds like a misleading pharmaceutical advertisement, it should. Contraception is a big business. Developing a drug takes time and financial investments, and those managing the research want to recuperate their costs. Bernard Lonergan prophetically observed in 1942, during World War II, that "governments dare not venture, even in the present rubber shortage, to interfere with the big business—over $250,000,000 a year in the U.S. alone—of supplying inefficacious contraceptive devices."[100] Eighty years later, the contraceptive industry is business that is bigger than Lonergan may have imagined. Bayer's YAZ earned over a billion dollars annually, even while Bayer was being charged with deceptive marketing and fighting in the courts to postpone health regulations due to blood clotting issues until after the YAZ patent was gone.[101] A year later, the contraception industry reached the gold standard for pharmaceutical companies by successfully lobbying for a Health and Human Resources mandate requiring all health insurance policies to include free coverage of contraception. Contraception is now considered by many to be a basic human right akin to food, water, and education.

However, contraception is just as likely to provide a fulfilling family life as are heart and cholesterol drugs. Contraception marketing promises that couples can have sex whenever they want. The reality is that the sexual desire of husband and wife will not always correspond (and some contraceptives can even interfere with sexual desire). Contraception marketing promises a healthy marriage that frees spouses to cultivate their romantic love without the burden of children. The reality is that a fulfilling family life will develop only over time, after passing through challenges, encountering limitations, and drawing on the communal support of other social communities.[102] Further, despite the promise of avoiding children, the human body and human error cannot be avoided. While perfect-use effectiveness for hormonal contraceptives is typically in the 99 percent range,

100 Bernard Lonergan, review of *Marriage*, by Dietrich von Hildebrand, in *Collected Works of Bernard Lonergan*, ed. Frederick Crowe and Robert Doran, vol. 20, *Shorter Papers* (Toronto: University of Toronto Press, 2007), 154.

101 Jim Edwards, "FDA Issues Blood-Clot Warning for Bayer Birth Control Pills . . . and Bayer Cheers," CBS News website, updated June 1, 2011, https://www.cbsnews.com/news/fda-issues-blood-clot-warning-for-bayer-birth-control-pills-and-bayer-cheers/; Natasha Singer, "Health Concerns over Popular Contraceptives," *New York Times*, September 25, 2009.

102 The bishops of Vatican II argue in *Gaudium et Spes* (47) that spousal love has been "dishonoured by selfishness, hedonism, and unlawful contraceptive practices," in Flannery, *Vatican Council II* (949).

practical-use effectiveness is closer to 92 percent. This means that, practically speaking, couples using contraception will have a child on average once every twelve to thirteen years. Like most pharmaceutical advertisements, the promises do not correspond to the reality.[103] Also like most pharmaceutical advertisements, this one quietly and quickly ends with a list of potential negative side effects.

While the wider cultural institutions and indeed most Catholics in the West have largely accepted this exalted role of contraception as a fait accompli, the Church's unchanged prohibition of its use has kept the debate over its moral status alive, at least among Catholic theologians. Often missing in the fifty-year debate about whether contraceptive acts are intrinsically evil is the impact of consumerism on the practice. Those who support the teaching of *Humanae Vitae* present theological arguments endorsing natural family planning but fail to acknowledge how the mom-and-pop store of fertility monitoring stands no chance against the big business of contraception. Those who argue in support of contraceptive practices often overlook how their theological arguments are received through the lens of consumerism, million-dollar marketing campaigns, and effective political lobbying efforts. While Catholic moral theologians continue to debate whether contraceptive acts are intrinsically evil in all cases, often overlooked is what should be a consensus that in most cases fertility monitoring presents a better alternative to contraceptive acts. With fertility monitoring, spouses learn about the wife's body and how to work with it rather than rendering healthy sexual organs infertile. With good instruction, fertility monitoring is comparable with hormonal contraceptive acts in terms of perfect- and practical-use effectiveness. Moreover, fertility monitoring does not thin the uterine wall and thereby avoids the risk of preventing the implantation of an embryo. Why then do so few Catholics know about fertility monitoring and so many Catholics contracept? One needs to include in one's answer that, among other reasons, contraception comes with a profit motive that influences advertising campaigns and supports a cultural structure of sexual expression in which individuals can consume one another for sexual pleasure. Consideration of financial profit and structures of commodification need to be part of the

103 While fertility monitoring has not yet provided the profit potential seen in contraceptive practices, those who advocate for it sometimes fall into similar patterns of using misleading advertisements when they highlight perfect-use effectiveness to the neglect of practical-use effectiveness and when they overlook challenges that often result from fertility monitoring, such as challenges relating to communication and abstention from sex.

broader conversation. Without such an account, some will advocate for fertility monitoring without realizing why no one seems to listen, while the words of others who have genuine concern for unique circumstances that seem to them to require the intervention of artificial contraception risk becoming a free advertisement for large pharmaceutical companies.

While debate in Catholic moral theology has long focused on hormonal contraception, statistics show that the growing trend is toward longer-term contraception. The 2017–19 National Survey of Family Growth shows that among women ages 15–49 who are using some method to postpone pregnancy, 21.4 percent use the pill while 36.3 percent employed either female (27.7 percent) or male (8.6 percent) sterilization and another 15.9 percent used a long-acting reversible contraception.[104] The largest changes in use from the 2002 survey to the 2017–2019 survey were the increase in long-acting reversible contraception and the decrease in the pill and condoms.[105] The survey shows that sterilization is a more common method of preventing pregnancy than the pill and that this has been the case for at least twenty years. The preference for longer-lasting forms of contraception stands out even more for those who are married. Among married women aged 15–44 who are employing some method to postpone pregnancy, 44.5 percent employ either female (28.8 percent) or male (15.7 percent) sterilization, while 17.9 percent employ the pill and 12.8 percent (compared to 3.1 percent in 2002) employ long-term reversible contraception.[106]

Those seeking sterilization tend to be married, in the older range of female fertility, less educated, and have two or more children. The increased incidence of long-term contraception for those who have children suggests that the intentions for long-term contraception are not antichild or an expression of the culture of death. Rather, in addition to concerns about pregnancy complications

104 Kimberly Daniels and Joyce C. Abma, "Current Contraceptive Status among Women Aged 15–49: United States, 2017–2019," NCHS Data Brief No. 388 (October 2020), https://www.cdc.gov/nchs/data/databriefs/db388-H.pdf. The percentage of those who employ sterilization dramatically increases as women enter the later years of fertility.

105 While these trends reflect changes that occurred between the 2002 survey and the 2011–13 survey, the 2017–19 survey expanded the age range from 15–44 to 15–49.

106 These statistics come from the 2011–13 survey. The 2017–19 survey did not differentiate with respect to marriage status. The numbers are even higher (58% female sterilization) for those who are employing some form of contraception, were formerly married, and are not now married or cohabiting. The 2011–13 survey studies the 15–44 age range, which was expanded to 15–49 for the 2017–19 study. Kimberly Daniels et al., "Current Contraceptive Use and Variation by Selected Characteristics Among Women Aged 15–44: United States, 2011–13," National Health Statistics Report no. 86, November 10, 2015, https://www.cdc.gov/nchs/data/nhsr/nhsr086.pdf.

as they approach their late thirties and early forties, these women may already feel the burden of raising children in an isolated family; it is also possible that their employer does not provide support for pregnancy and child-rearing, or that they feel pressured to provide the children they already have with the experiences and material goods expected in their cultural context.

Consumption and the ideals of an isolated family seem to impact the practice of sterilization, not so much as a moneymaker for hospitals and doctors or as an explicit choice made by parents to pursue a nicer car over more children, but rather, it appears that consumerism impacts cultural trends, which in turn impact family decisions. Families are overwhelmed by the lack of communal support and the burden of trying to live according to expected levels of consumption. Social communities and resources are set up to accommodate families with one, two, or at most three children. Delivery doctors routinely ask mothers if they would like tubal ligation following a C-section delivery. Tax breaks stop after three children. Hotel search engines cannot compute families with more than three kids. Society pressures couples to seek a long-term solution. As a result, the fertility of one or both spouses is consumed.

Abortion and In Vitro Fertilization

One sees a similar dynamic in the practice of abortion. Julie Hanlon Rubio reports that those who seek abortions often are willing to give birth to children they did not intend to conceive.[107] They are not opposed to having children, but they are motivated by their responsibility to other individuals, financial concerns, fear that having a baby would interfere with work or school, and a lack of support from a partner or family and friends.[108] Those who seek abortion tend to be unmarried, in their twenties, and living near or below the poverty line.[109] The statistics highlight the importance of relationship stability for having and raising children and the economic pressure that comes with doing so in a consumer culture that embraces socially detached family ideals.

107 Julie Hanlon Rubio, *Hope for Common Ground: Mediating the Personal and the Political in a Divided Church* (Washington, DC: Georgetown University Press, 2016), 159.

108 Hanlon Rubio, 159–82.

109 Guttmacher Institute, "Induced Abortion in the United States," January 2019, https://www.guttmacher.org/fact-sheet/induced-abortion-united-states; Tara C. Jatlaoui et al., "Abortion Surveillance—United States, 2013," Centers for Disease Control and Prevention, Morbidity and Mortality Weekly Report, November 25, 2016, https://www.cdc.gov/mmwr/volumes/65/ss/ss6512a1.htm.

Especially as scientific developments continue to demonstrate the complexity of development in early life, abortion practices reflect cultural pressures more than convictions about when life begins. Stanley Hauerwas argues that a Christian approach to abortion supports the least of God's people, and this includes both the pregnant mother in need and the preborn child.[110] Consumerism and the ideals of an isolated family life appear to pit the pregnant mother against the preborn child but in reality they encourage people to be detached from both. The consumer is detached, for example, from the pregnant factory worker who feels compelled to have an abortion to keep her job. The community is detached from the preborn child who is vulnerable and remains unseen.

Private ideals of isolation and the practices of consumption are crucial here. One sees the language of privacy in the legal and cultural support for abortion, which argues that abortion is a private, socially detached choice that others need to tolerate. This language of privacy masks the interdependence of the human person with respect to various social communities and the impact that abortion has on the surrounding community. Most who choose abortion do so not because they are making a personally determined choice but because of social influences. The language of a personal private choice masks public pressures that encourage parents to avoid and eliminate pregnancy. A cultural emphasis on private choice, while providing the appearance of being morally neutral, risks isolating pregnant mothers in need and therefore overwhelming those making their "private" decisions. Abortion is often more a statement about the community's ability or lack of ability to support and sustain new, vulnerable life.[111] Many who ask doctors to abort their child, like many who risk the dangerous path of undocumented immigration, do not see any options available and act in desperation.

One clear indication of how consumerism impacts family planning is how various consumer options for avoiding children coexist with various consumer options for attaining pregnancy. Often the desire for children is most intense when spouses are struggling to have children or when a couple

110 Stanley Hauerwas, "Abortion: Theologically Understood," in Berkman and Cartwright, *The Hauerwas Reader*, 603–22.

111 Hanlon Rubio speaks of community adoption as a way of highlighting the importance of communal support for raising children. *Hope for Common Ground*, 182. McCarthy proposes that neighborhood reciprocity gives every adult a parenting role. *Sex and Love in the Home*, 236. He also writes in *Sex and Love in the Home*, "If single-parent households cannot be sustained, then something is wrong with a community's practices of marriage and home" (204).

has postponed child-rearing because of career goals and/or a late marriage. Childbearing deferred gives way to extreme efforts to attain a child before fertility has gone completely. While child-rearing is foundational to the social role of the family, children are not a right or a consumer option. As Francis cautions, "[The child] is not an accessory or a solution to some personal need."[112] Children are not a consumer choice that serve merely as a means of entertainment or experience for the parents, but a gift that is full of challenging surprises and persons exercising their freedom.

Perhaps the most dramatic example of making children into a consumer option is the increasingly common practice of in vitro fertilization (IVF). After fertilizing numerous eggs, couples can choose to implant the embryos who are "genetically promising" and then freeze the remainder just in case.[113] In order to increase the chance of implantation, numerous embryos are inserted into the woman. If too many embryos implant, one can get a "pregnancy reduction." In the name of helping a couple "choose" life, seven or eight embryos die in the process. McCarthy writes, "Growth capitalism simply cultivates its markets by drawing attention to what we lack. . . . It is particularly troublesome when children are conceptualized as a kind of self-possession."[114] A 2014 article in *Time Magazine* noted that "the infertility services market, from infertility clinics and sperm banks to fertility drugs and surrogacy programs, now tops $3.5 billion, up four-fold from 25 years ago."[115] A research team in England found that "desperate couples are being sold costly yet unproven add-ons, such as endometrial scratches, embryo glue, immune therapy, and intralipid infusions in a bid to increase their chances of having a baby."[116] English IVF doctor Mohamed Taranissi made 25 million pounds in one year.[117] Bourg discusses

112 Francis, *Amoris Laetitia*, 170. Similarly, Stanley Hauerwas writes, "I can think of no greater burden than having to be a wanted child." Hauerwas, "Abortion: Theologically Understood," 618.

113 Francis argues that to know the color of a child's hair or possible future illness is not to know the child. *Amoris Laetitia*, 170.

114 McCarthy, *Sex and Love in the Home*, 235.

115 Donna Rosato, "How High-Tech Baby Making Fuels the Infertility Market Boom," *Time*, July 8, 2014.

116 Maria Lally, "Fertility Exploitation: The Couples Paying a High Price for Wanting a Baby," *Telegraph*, June 26, 2017; http://www.telegraph.co.uk/women/family/fertility-exploitation-couples-paying-high-price-wanting-baby/.

117 Neil Sears, "The £25m IVF Doctor: Clinic's Profits Fuel Criticism of the 'Human Life Industry.'" *Daily Mail*, May 13, 2012; http://www.dailymail.co.uk/news/article-2143934/The-25m-IVF-doctor-Clinics-profits-fuel-criticism-human-life-industry.html.

> advertisements that have become increasingly common in Ivy League campus newspapers, seeking "generous" female students (with stipulated heights, ethnicities, and SAT scores) to provide eggs for "loving" infertile couples (in exchange for tens of thousands of dollars). The desire to parent a child of one's own at any cost, which at first glance seems an expression of pride in one's heritage, self-sacrifice, or altruism, can become distorted when infertility therapy becomes a lucrative commodity, but the distortion is shrouded by romantic language of love and generosity.[118]

The practitioners who commodify every step of the IVF process in order to maximize their profits, or calculating parents who seek through this process to maximize the genetic potential of their children, should not be seen as isolated villains. Those examples reflect a broader and deeper tendency so pervasive that those who recognize the great good of children and family life unknowingly participate in the objectification and destruction of human life, and they do so while seeking a child or helping others have one. Moreover, IVF is promoted as the preferred option, even while less morally problematic, less expensive, and perhaps equally effective methods remain available.[119] One witnesses similar dynamics of commodification and profit in the pursuit of children through adoption.[120]

Permanence and Divorce

Cultural emphasis on competition and short-term productivity also challenges spouses' ability to build a stable context for cultivating spousal love and raising children. Socially detached notions of marriage and family and consumptive patterns encourage couples to enter and exit marriage without due consideration for the social role of marriage and family and the importance that family stability has for those roles. Andrew Chervin highlights that, compared even to other developed nations, individuals in the United States enter and exit marriage at a faster rate, a reality he describes as the Marriage-Go-Round.[121] If marriage is merely a private, autonomous decision,

118 Florence Caffrey Bourg, *Where Two or Three Are Gathered: Christian Families as Domestic Churches* (Notre Dame, IN: University of Notre Dame Press, 2004), 92.

119 Thomas W. Hilgers, *The Naprotechnology Revolution: Unleashing the Power in a Woman's Cycle* (New York: Beaufort Books, 2010).

120 Anne Moody, *The Children Money Can Buy: Stories from the Frontlines of Foster Care and Adoption* (Lanham, MD: Rowman and Littlefield, 2018).

121 Andrew J. Cherlin, *The Marriage-Go-Round: The State of Marriage and the Family in America Today* (New York: Alfred A. Knopf, 2009).

then, as Francis writes, "Marriage, marked by a commitment to exclusivity and stability, is swept aside whenever it proves inconvenient or tiresome."[122] An ethos of consumerism encourages individuals to see marriage merely as a social contract chosen by two people for the sake of their mutual satisfaction. While few people fully embody this framework, marriage and family life are demanding, and the habits cultivated by consumerism can make working through challenges more difficult. Endorsement of an isolated marriage model overlooks how communities, and especially children, are impacted by the separation of spouses.

Even the often-painful process of divorce and separation is not protected from consumptive practices. Around 2010, the city of Indianapolis, Indiana, in an attempt to fund a more adequate public transportation system, started to sell advertisements on the sides of the city's buses. One of the first advertisements I saw was for a group of divorce lawyers. The tagline was "call us before your spouse does." The implication seemed to be that if a person is struggling in their marriage, it is not necessary to work through the difficulties because divorce is easy and a team of divorce lawyers is ready to help stick it to the spouse. Also, just in case someone is not motivated enough to look up a phone number in order to get the divorce process started, they can dial their easy-to-remember number (1-800-Divorce). The growing world of social communication and online dating also provides extra incentive and opportunities for those who see marriage as an autonomous choice to change their hidden, private lives. Francis warns against the negative consequences of divorce and invites couples to be discerning rather than hasty in dealing with marital problems.[123] Counteracting social narratives that encourage couples to enter and leave relationships as they see fit, Francis raises a series of questions highlighting the social implications of marriage and divorce. He asks couples to reflect on their responsibilities to children, spouses, extended families, the broader community, and those preparing for marriage.[124]

Families can serve as a witness to their communities of the love and sacrifices necessary to build a communion of persons. While difficult to document, divorce and separation mean that marriages are not modeling love

122 Francis, *Amoris Laetitia*, 34.

123 Francis, *Amoris Laetitia*, 41; the internal quotations reference Synod of Bishops, Third Extraordinary General Assembly of the Synod of Bishops, *Relatio Synodi* (October 18, 2014), 10.

124 Francis, *Amoris Laetitia*, 300.

for broader society in this way. More obvious is the impact that divorce and separation have on children.[125] Francis expresses concern about "'the consequences of separation or divorce on children, in every case the innocent victims of the situation.' Apart from every other consideration, the good of children should be the primary concern, and not overshadowed by any ulterior interest or objective."[126] Children whose formation benefits from stable family relations struggle with the disruption of parental separation.

Catholic ethicists may respond by simply reaffirming church teaching about marital indissolubility, or else justifying divorce and remarriage because abuse is present in many marriages, but both of these responses are insufficient. The former overlooks how consumerism and notions of family life based on isolation undermine the significance of permanent marriage. Merely reaffirming rules also overlooks abusive situations that demand physical and perhaps legal separation. On the other hand, highlighting unique circumstances that require separation becomes problematic in the absence of some account of the social role of families. If family is merely a socially isolated choice, then all spouses can choose to enter and exit a marriage, as has become the norm in the United States. Those who need to separate because of abuse or other serious issues may have a legal and cultural pathway for separation but when family and friends identify marital separation with a personal choice, they will overlook the support that they should provide to those who suffer from the trauma of abuse and the challenges of managing a one-parent household.

Family Life

In addition to impacting dating, sex, procreation, and divorce, consumerism also impacts the everyday interactions that occur in family life. Spouses feel compelled to work long hours or multiple jobs either because they are viewed by their employers as a cost of production and are not provided a living wage, or because they are working overtime to sustain cultural expectations for consumption. Francis writes, "Parents come home exhausted, not wanting to talk, and many families no longer even share a common meal."[127]

125 See, for example, Julie Hanlon Rubio, *Family Ethics: Practices for Christians* (Washington, DC: Georgetown University Press, 2010), 32nn7–9.

126 Francis, *Amoris Laetitia*, 245; the internal quotation references Synod of Bishops, *Relatio Synodi*, 47.

127 Francis, *Amoris Laetitia*, 50.

Time that is potentially available is easily lost to practices of consumption. For families with children, the experiences, purchases, and challenges change as the children age, but the consumption and struggle against false ideals remain constant. While caring for young children presents opportunities to wonder about creation, to slow down, and to grow in virtue, it also involves the physically demanding job of holding kids and the ever-present need to change diapers, provide meals and snacks, clean up messes and toys, moderate sibling fights, deal with emotional meltdowns, and console kids through the night. Both the joys and struggles of parenting young children provide opportunities for consumption. McCarthy notes, "The very economic environment that structures childhood as an economic drain conceives of raising children in terms of consumption and entertainment."[128] Since children are so precious, innocent, and formative, they are seen as deserving nothing but the best diapers, food, toys, car seats, clothes, TV stations, cribs, memberships to children's museums, educational apps. As kids move toward and through adolescence, parents deal with emerging independence and difficult attitudes. Kids yearn to fit in with their peers. Parents feel compelled to buy trendy clothes and shoes and smartphones and other new gadgets, and they are expected to chauffeur their children from one cultural experience and sporting practice to another and to organize yearly vacation getaways.

The temptation is to say that those spouses and parents—who work long hours, are distracted by social media and practices of consumption, and do not find time to interact with their families—are selfish or are failing to prioritize family life. However, spouses and parents who decide to work long hours and participate in cultural norms of consumption often do so not because they are self-seeking consumers who intentionally put their job and their purchases ahead of their families. Many adults spend most of their time caring for their kids and if asked would say that their family is the top priority. However, their understanding of family is filtered through the lens of consumerism and socially detached ideals of family life. Family-first in a consumer society does not mean building a formative community of persons that participates in the life of society and the Church and grows through the challenges and joys of everyday life. Rather, family-first means developing the financial security necessary for a broad-ranging independence and providing family members with products and experiences. The

128 McCarthy, *Sex and Love in the Home*, 232.

horizon of family life can become not the Kingdom of God but the "magical kingdom" of Disney.

At some point, often when children begin to prioritize peers over family, most parents realize that family-first really ought to mean developing family life as a community of persons. Hanlon Rubio writes,

> One can hear in the conversations of middle-class adults a certain dissatisfaction with this way of life, a yearning for a slower pace, deeper friendships, and more time to simply be with their spouses and their children. They are conscious of their relative privilege and of the waste of resources that middle-class life entails. They know their children do not really need more things and more activities. They wish they had more time to do something for the poor. They would like to spend more time in prayer or meditation.[129]

This desire to slow things down, spend time with family, serve the poor, and grow in faith often is not enough in the face of the formative power of consumerism. In a culture of competition, private isolation, and romantic ideals, spouses, parents, and kids lack the language, skills, and time to do these things.

A cultural emphasis on competition, which is a hallmark of consumerism, can present obstacles to family communion. Parents who are vulnerable workers need to work multiple jobs in a competitive, consent-focused wage system to put food on the table. Often, children who come from families lacking financial resources are forced to work for gainful employment or are encouraged to focus on and competitively grasp for the limited resources available in contexts lacking in mentors and safety.[130] On the other hand, children who come from families with financial means are overloaded with activities that emphasize competition and performance results.[131] They need to make the travel team and score well on standardized tests at school. In both cases, practices are more focused on productive competition than on the development of children's character and virtue.

Marketing that manipulates family commitments within a market focused on productive competition encourages spouses, parents, and kids to compare their family lives with those of other individuals, parents, and

129 Hanlon Rubio, *Family Ethics*, 191.

130 Cahill, *Family*, 114–19.

131 Roche, *Children, Consumerism, and the Common Good*, 42.

children. They compare their situations to the apparent joy in other spousal relationships, the wages earned in their jobs, the amount of family flexibility provided by their jobs, how many kids they have, the quality of their house and landscaping, the success of their kids. Emphasis on competitive productivity isolates families that care for individuals with mental and physical disabilities or who struggle with addictions and therefore cannot keep up. Emphasis on competition also can make sharing joys with other families difficult. Sharing successes in conversation or through social media can become an invitation for others to assert superior successes or to cultivate dissatisfaction that their family has not experienced similar kinds of successes. Marketing and family comparisons lead spouses, parents, and kids to focus on the best and worst of what others have and to become either disappointed or prideful.

An emphasis on competition that flows from a capitalist-oriented consumerism often pervades the dynamics of family interactions. In a culture of competition, spouses and siblings compete for the favor of children and parents in skills and intelligence, fight for control of the household, and compete to get out of doing household chores and childcare responsibilities. Despite the potential benefits of competition in families—the possibility of innocent fun and the opportunity to grow and cultivate community—when it is not contextualized by respect for individuals and concern for the common good, competition can become antithetical to human community. Francis highlights how competition can undermine one's ability to see the dignity of others and destroy love.[132] Competition, absent an account of the common good, leads to jealousy and envy within the family, so that family members even rejoice in the failures of those they love.[133]

Competition and pursuit of an isolated family separate families from the broader community, but these same notions of individualism, paired with dissatisfaction and busyness, also isolate family members from one another. One sees this isolation when a teenager does not feel welcome at home and decides to hole himself up in his bedroom, or when a working parent cannot discuss work successes and struggles because no one seems to care or understand, or when an aging parent has no visitors. Sometimes isolation within a community is even more painful than isolation from community. Social media presents potential for connecting family across dis-

132 Francis, *Amoris Laetitia*, 98, 109.

133 Francis, 109.

tances, but it also introduces temptations to substitute for personal dialogue and thereby further cultivate isolation.[134]

Even those spouses and parents who realize that family is about more than increasing consumption struggle: "Deepening communion is hard work and, in the rush of contemporary family life, easy to avoid."[135] Intentional steps taken to develop family community can easily become consumerized. Family game night turns into competitive arguments about rules and a trip to the playground becomes a reminder to kids that their parents need to do work on their phones and do not have time for them. After years of busy consumption, one cannot simply flip the community-building switch. Francis writes, "Once a couple no longer knows how to spend time together, one or both of them will end up taking refuge in gadgets, finding other commitments, seeking the embrace of another, or simply looking for ways to flee what has become an uncomfortable closeness."[136]

This challenge to move from consumer to community-builder is made more difficult by marketing. Knowing that spouses, parents, and children long for deeper family community, marketing manipulates those desires to promote family events that provide for more consumption rather than community-building. McCarthy writes, "I cannot help but be suspicious that Father's Day sustains a construction of fatherhood that is more useful to the market than to my life at home."[137] One could say similar things about Mother's Day, baby showers, Valentine's Day, birthdays, and anniversaries. These special days that could help foster the family as a community of persons instead so often foster family as consumer. Religious events are no exception. Easter, All Hallow's Eve, Christmas, and marriages are culturally hard to understand without the consumptive practices associated with them.

Vacations perhaps serve as the prototype for consumption masked as family building. Marketed vacations offer a chance to get away from a busy life of consumption by falsely promising fulfillment through a busier week of greater consumption. While vacations often produce lasting memories and broadening learning experiences, they often do not provide the romantic

134 Francis, 278; see also Francis, 84, 278; John Paul II, *Familiaris Consortio*, 76, referencing Paul VI, "Message for the Third Social Communications Day" (April 7, 1969).

135 Hanlon Rubio, *Family Ethics*, 77.

136 Francis, *Amoris Laetitia*, 225.

137 McCarthy, *Sex and Love in the Home*, 66.

experience of family harmony that marketing promises.[138] They often are busy, stressful, exhausting, and expensive. They are packaged as an opportunity to get away from life (production-focused work and dissatisfaction) by placing families in tourist traps that often enhance dissatisfaction and busyness. Vacations promise to develop family community by getting families away from their struggles, rather than helping them better understand their life and community together.[139]

CONCLUSION

While the family is the basic social unit, the interdependence of the family with other communities means that one's ability to live out the family's social roles is influenced by these other communities, including the market competition and cultural consumerism that is part of them. Consumerism is a way of life that devours and wastes material creation, experiences, and people. In a capitalist economy, this way of life is fueled by human desire formed by profit-driven marketing and cultural norms. Consumer capitalism, like all systems, includes aspects that prevent individuals from living a life of holiness.

Consumerism impacts families in a variety of ways. While market competition can provide broad availability of material goods and employment opportunities, consumer capitalism also leads to dissatisfaction and busyness. Families are dissatisfied with what they have, and parents work extra jobs to expand the family's opportunities for consumption. As kids age, the consumption of diapers and educational toys gives way to the consumption of experiences, as parents drive adolescents from event to event and as they begin to feel the pressure to obtain the best education for the sake of the future higher earnings needed to sustain the same standards of consumption. Parents are committed to family first, but they frequently are too busy serving and providing resources to the members of their families to spend time with them.

Marketing often manipulates the human desire for family relationships, ordering that desire toward products and experiences. This marketing not only directly forms individuals to desire products but also indirectly forms them to think about sexual desire, spousal love, marriage, children, and

138 McCarthy, 81.

139 William T. Cavanaugh, "Migrant, Tourist, Pilgrim, Monk: Mobility and Identity in a Global Age," *Theological Studies* 69, no. 2 (2008): 340–56.

everyday family life in ways that focus on competitive productivity and short-term satisfaction.[140] The pervasiveness of consumerism means that few if any family issues are left untouched by the marketing and cultural norms that support consumer practices. Consumerism impacts culturally controversial topics like the definition of marriage, contraception, abortion, IVF, and assisted suicide. We miss the connection between family ethics and consumerism if we define family as isolated and separate social ethics from family ethics. Even beyond these often-debated issues, however, consumerism impacts the everyday lives of families. It cultivates dissatisfaction about the family's possessions and relationships and encourages busyness and social isolation, which undermine communication. Consumerism also places the burden of maintaining family relationships and raising children on isolated spouses. An emphasis on competitive productivity encourages individuals to neglect or even do harm to the vulnerable. Those with limited job skills, if they can find employment, work long hours for little pay. Families who care for vulnerable groups, such as the preborn, newborns, those with addictions, family members with physical and mental disabilities, and the aging and dying, are pushed to the periphery and forced to care for these needs in isolation.

Certainly, various other factors impact family life even in contexts dominated by consumerism, and the influence of consumerism varies from place to place. Consumerism, however, has a pervasive influence and provides a lot of explanatory power for why families struggle to live their social role. While individuals may be sympathetic to living out the social role of the family, most families will struggle to do so without a direct recognition of and response to the ways that consumerism makes living that social role difficult. The vocation to marriage and the responsibility to care for one's family is necessarily complicated and perhaps therefore specifically susceptible to consumer marketing. Against these negative influences, one must ask: How does one resist? How does one care for the various needs of a family and live the social interdependence of a family without losing sight of Christ, the one thing necessary? The infused virtue of simplicity helps to frame a thoughtful response to these questions, as I discuss in the next chapter.

140 One also could add reflections on the impact of consumerism on various other dimensions of marriage and family life, such as the celebration of marriage or care for the elderly.

6

Simplicity: A Framework for Social Engagement

If consumerism has such negative implications for family life, then one might presume that the proper response is for families to embrace a simple life that involves a withdrawal from society: allow no television or "smart" devices in the home and build a homestead in the country. Complete withdrawal from society, however, is not the solution. The social interdependence of the family and other social communities means that complete social withdrawal is neither practical nor ideal. Families need political order, job opportunities, and robust social outlets for individual family members to express and fulfill their social desires and inclinations. Families have a responsibility to participate in the life of the Church and of civil society. Individual family members find their fulfillment in union with God, and participation in the Kingdom of God and love of God implies love of neighbor.

The moral approach to family life, then, is to discern when and how families should interact with or withdraw from broader social communities. This moral analysis is demanding, although no more so than the physical and emotional demands of child-rearing or the spiritual demands of following Christ. Questions about social engagement feature prominently in the concerns of those who have responsibility for family groups. Should one financially support one's family by working in a certain profession; for example, at a nuclear arms factory?[1] Should a family cultivate friendships with other families in which the parents seem overly authoritarian in disciplining their children? Is sending a child to a particular summer camp an enriching experience or one that introduces bad influences? Decisions about social involvement include the neighborhood in which to live, the extent of involvement in a particular parish church or ministry, the school family members will attend, the extracurriculars in which they will participate, the friends

1 M. Cathleen Kaveny poses a similar question. See M. Cathleen Kaveny, "Appropriation of Evil: Cooperation's Mirror Image," *Theological Studies* 61, no. 2 (2000): 286.

or strangers who are welcome in the car or at the house, the TV programs they watch, the balance between work and the home, the extent to which family members will engage with social media, the decision whether or not to visit friends when someone in the group is sick or immunocompromised, the social issues one's family discusses over supper, and the strategies to choose for protecting family members from violence, addiction, harassment, or abuse. While not often the focus of moral theology, these questions about social engagement keep many parents awake at night.

Absent an ethical framework for working through these questions, parents often rely on moral intuitions or the path of least resistance. They can easily look back on years of family life and ask, "Where did the time go, and what was I thinking?" The temptation is to assert one's responsibility to one's family or, alternatively, one's responsibility to the common good, without doing the difficult work of discerning how these commitments stand in tension and converge. This is especially true if personal responsibility to one's family is highlighted in a context where an isolated nuclear family model dominates thinking. Focusing on a primary responsibility to one's family can easily encourage a family member to overlook family interdependence with other social communities and the need to serve the common good and those in need. On the other hand, a family busy with social activities and commitments may miss important responsibilities specific to being parents, children, or siblings.

I propose in this chapter that Catholic social ethics provides crucial resources to help individuals discern how and when their families should engage society. First, I frame the conversation using the neglected virtue of simplicity, proposing that Christian simplicity is a way of life that is united in the love of God. Simplicity provides the lens of analysis for the pressing daily decisions that families face: Do specific forms of social interdependence enhance one's love of God or present obstacles for living in God's love? To help apply this framework to concrete questions facing families, I draw on other resources in the Catholic social tradition: material cooperation, moral appropriation, the virtue of justice, and the common good. The goal of intentional simplicity is, in part, to mitigate the negative social influence of consumerism discussed in the last chapter, but more broadly, I wish to demonstrate how Catholic social principles clarify and guide families in living their social interdependence. I work from categories that help families avoid cooperation with sin and reflect on cooperation with the good actions of others, and about actions and dispositions that help families integrate their social lives in God's love. I am concerned to show how Catholic social principles apply to questions crucial for family life. Since my emphasis is on the social interdependence of the family, my focus in this chapter is decisions about social engagement with broader social communities that explicitly impact a family community.

SIMPLICITY

If consumerism presents obstacles to families trying to live out the social roles of family life, as I established in the last chapter, then the response would seem to be a simplicity that reacts against consumerism. The risk, however, in a culture dominated by consumerism is that the pursuit of simplicity becomes just another consumer product line. One can buy a stack of books that proclaim "the joy of tidying up," or subscribe to magazines that focus on simple living, or simple cooking, or simple home décor, or one can buy simple clothing, read about simple parenting, or go on simple vacations. Of course, I don't mean to say that one should not avail oneself of the reasonable or prudent advice of others. Rather, the danger can be that "simplicity" becomes just another instance of trying to purchase products that come with the same false promise of complete control over one's needs and problems, instead of opening a family up to reliance on God. To guard against the self-assertion inherent in market accounts of simplicity, one does well to clarify theologically the meaning of simplicity.

Saint Francis de Sales and Dietrich von Hildebrand, two authors who were prophetic in their concern for the holiness of spouses and parents, make excellent guides on the topic of simplicity.[2] Both authors offer extended and insightful treatment of Christian simplicity. Hildebrand dedicates a chapter of his modern spiritual classic, *Transformation in Christ*, to simplicity.[3] De Sales focuses on simplicity in talks he gave to the Sisters of the Visitation.[4] Their works bear even greater fruit when read in conversation with one

2 While substantially altered, some material from this chapter derives from Kevin Schemenauer, "The Infused Virtue of Simplicity: Saint Francis de Sales and Dietrich von Hildebrand," *Logos* 20, no. 3 (2017): 95–121. The earlier article provides more details on why Hildebrand and de Sales are specifically well suited to speak on the topic of simplicity to those who live in the world. The material is used here with permission.

3 Dietrich von Hildebrand, *Transformation in Christ* (San Francisco: Ignatius Press, 2001).

4 Saint Francis de Sales, "On Simplicity and Religious Prudence," in *The Spiritual Conferences*, trans. Abbot Gasquet and Canon Mackey, OSB (Westminster, MD: The Newman Bookshop, 1943), 212–33. De Sales also discusses related themes throughout his corpus.

another. Hildebrand, the philosopher, clarifies the nature of simplicity, offers insightful distinctions between harmful and necessary forms of complexity, and diagnoses false forms of simplicity. De Sales, the pastor, encourages humble recognition of one's limitations and directs questions related to the complexity of life to the love of God from which Christian simplicity flows and to which Christian simplicity is ordered.

Embracing the virtue of simplicity might seem to tip the discussion of family priorities in favor of withdrawing from other social communities. In common parlance, simplicity often means a withdrawal from complexity, and "getting involved" with others usually means more complexity. Christian simplicity, however, is, like all virtues, a mean between extremes. One of Hildebrand's central insights in his treatment of simplicity is that it is a unity of life. Hildebrand begins his treatment in the original German by clarifying that he is speaking of "*Einfachheit*" (simplicity) in the sense of an "*inneren Einheit des Lebens*" (inner unity of life).[5] The unitive character of simplicity as implied by the German *Einfachheit* is illuminating to English speakers because it distinguishes the virtue of simplicity from other uses of the word that imply a mere lack of complexity. Simplicity is not merely the avoidance of too many things or activities. As a mean between extremes, simplicity avoids both too much complexity and too little, both a lack of unity and a forced or cramped unity.

Hildebrand roots the connection between simplicity and complexity in a metaphysical principle: "The higher a thing is, the simpler it is."[6] He illustrates this metaphysical principle by working his way through different levels of being. He explains that different objects exhibit different kinds of inner unity. Whereas inanimate objects possess a mere "combination of things rather than creative interpenetration," the various parts of living things are "subordinated to *one* principle" and are characterized by a greater "mutual interpenetration."[7] Of the human person, Hildebrand writes, "the principle of interpenetration is far more predominant even than in the [ordinary] living organism."[8] By virtue of its spiritual character, the human person has "far more substantiality and depth than has the living organ-

5 Dietrich von Hildebrand, *Die Umgestaltung in Christus: Über die christliche Grundhaltung* (Einsiedeln: Benziger, 1950), 57; the work was first published in 1940.

6 Hildebrand, *Transformation in Christ*, 72, 75.

7 Hildebrand, 74–75

8 Hildebrand, 75.

ism. . . . By the same token it also possesses much more simplicity."[9] As one moves to greater beings, one witnesses a greater unifying principle of life and interpenetration of parts. The higher a thing is the simpler it can be. This character of simplicity grows, Hildebrand writes, "along the ascending hierarchy of the cosmos until it culminates in the *one eternal Word of God, in quo est omnis plenitudo* ('in whom is all plenitude of divinity')."[10] God, while providing for the diversity of all things, is Simple and One.

De Sales also articulates how unity and diversity coincide in God when he writes in his *Treatise on the Love of God*, "God's supreme unity diversifies all things and his permanent eternity gives change to all things, because the perfection of his unity is above all difference and variety and must therefore have both means to furnish all diverse created perfections with their being and contain power to produce them."[11] God's simplicity is not a unity that denies difference but one, to use de Sales's language, that is "above all difference." In the simple unity of God, one finds the integration of all complexity.

Simplicity is fundamentally an attribute of God. God has no parts. And yet, God also accounts for the diversity of all things. The oneness and plurality of the Trinity stand as a foundation for the unity and diversity of all things. Unless one finds unity in God, and ultimately in the Kingdom of God, then one's unity of life, and therefore, one's practice of simplicity will be limited. Only in Christ can one integrate all things into one's life. Francis de Sales, always with his compass set on God's love, proposes that "simplicity . . . seeks nothing but the pure love of God."[12] Only from the stance of God's love does one see not only the character but the telos—the ordering principle and destiny—of all things. This infused virtue of simplicity has God as source and goal. Infused simplicity is possible because of God's grace and implies Christian conviction and an openness and willingness to allow God's love to operate in one's life. Combining the insights of Hildebrand and de Sales, I propose that simplicity is a way of life united in the love of God that is available to families despite the complexity and brokenness of human society.

In his philosophical genius, Hildebrand cautions against various false forms of unity, and therefore, false forms of simplicity. I will summarize his

9 Hildebrand, 75.

10 Hildebrand, 76, italics in original; see also Hildebrand, 84. L

11 Francis de Sales, *Treatise on the Love of God*, trans. Henry Benedict Mackey, OSB (Westminster, MD: The Newman Bookshop, 1945), 68.

12 De Sales, "On Simplicity and Religious Prudence," 219.

categories and apply them to the question of familial social engagement. Hildebrand notes that one way a person's life can lack unity is to move from activity to activity without stopping long enough to bring intentionality and unity to life. Hildebrand writes how various aspects of one's life can be "controlled by diverse and mutually contradictory currents . . . without being coordinated or confronted with one another."[13] How true this is of modern family life! Preparing meals, cleaning laundry, producing or purchasing goods, mediating conflicts, chauffeuring adolescents between events, and working to sustain the family financially are inevitably a part of the contemporary experience of family life. Different activities will feature more prominently depending on one's circumstances and the ages of one's children. One can easily separate one's life into separate compartments, failing to integrate them intentionally into a unified way of life. Even more, family members can become isolated from one another, living in their own separate worlds of separate interests and media consumption, without meaningful conversation with or support from parents, siblings, children, or other relatives.

Other families have a clear unity of life, but their focal point is not Christ. These families may organize their lives around music, or basketball, or books, or travel, or even social ministry. Such commitments provide family members with something to discuss and enjoy together, strengthening the bond of their family community. The simplicity of such "purpose-driven" families can serve as a model for other families whose lives lack integration. Their simplicity, however, is only an analogy to the simplicity that families can find in Christ. Hildebrand notes that while many goods "can stand the test before the face of Christ, we must never abandon ourselves unqualifiedly to their immanent logic."[14] God alone can illuminate, and therefore bring unity to, all aspects of one's life. For this reason, Hildebrand proposes that while a high vocation or a great love can unite one's life to some extent, only God can serve as the ultimate principle:

> Within the limits of the purely natural sphere, we cannot—and must not—aspire to an all-pervasive inward simplicity. Only to God, only to the living God who manifests Himself in Revelation, may we so deliver our whole life as to keep our regard fixed on one thing exclusively: the *unum necessarium*. He alone . . . may impart to our whole life that ultimate unity

13 De Sales, 71.

14 Hildebrand, *Transformation in Christ*, 93.

> and simplicity which, far from diminishing its wealth of substance, permeates it with a new and incomparable abundance of being.[15]

When one gives oneself completely to something other than God, this alternate unifying principle can only end up obscuring reality in some way. One is unable to respond appropriately to things that do not fit into the picture suggested by this truncated unity of life. A father yells at a referee because the athletic success of his son is the ultimate good for his family. A wife ignores the needs of others in the community in order to save money for the next vacation. True simplicity, on the other hand, "is a state of mind entirely different from the obsession of blind zeal which compels one to talk always about the one thing one is absorbed in, without regard to the situation and without applying the necessary discretion."[16] Simplicity, then, is not merely a way of life united under one principle, but a unity of life that integrates and illuminates all things. This unity is found in God alone, who alone is able to order all creation rightly. In the next section, I will consider specifically how to unite in God's love one's responsibilities to family relationships with a family's broader social interdependence.

AVOIDING UNJUST ENGAGEMENT WITH SOCIETY

Christian simplicity provides a helpful framework for discerning how and when families should interact with broader society. The goal is not merely withdrawal from society but to unite one's life in God's love, a love that implies the fulfillment of family responsibilities and love of neighbor. Since the lens of analysis is a way of life united in God's love, then one can begin by seeking to avoid taking unjust actions against others.[17] A way of life united in God's love is incompatible with sin against others. Bernard of Clairvaux puts this strongly to his Cistercian community:

> I am amazed at the impudence of some monks among us, who, after they have upset the entire community with their singularities, have irritated us

15 Hildebrand, 82.

16 Hildebrand, 89.

17 One should be clear that moral evil and corruption exist within the family just as they do outside the family. Radical withdrawal from society into the family to avoid contact with sin can only be a false utopia, a turning away from the sin of others only to be confronted with it in one's own family. Even if the avoidance of sin were possible, Christian simplicity reminds one that the goal of life is union with God, not the mere avoidance of sin, which otherwise always becomes the avoidance of certain well-defined sins and the allowance of other vices and distortions.

> with their impatience, condemned us with their rebelliousness and their bad tempers, nevertheless dare to aspire, with the most fervent prayers, to mystical union with the Lord of all purity. . . . The centurion begged the Lord not to enter under his roof, because of his own unworthiness: and yet the fame of his faith went out through all Israel: and these men would compel him to enter into their dwelling, vile with the filth of such great vices? What would you have me do, such a one will ask? I would have you first of all cleanse your conscience of every stain of anger and hasten to drive out of your heart whatever goes against peace with your brethren or obedience to your superiors. Then to adorn and prepare yourself with good works, with praiseworthy thoughts, with the sweet odor of virtues.[18]

Bernard highlights the constitutive relationship between love of God and love of neighbor. Unrepented sin toward one's community harms both the community and one's ability to approach God. To live in God's love is to love others. Acting unjustly toward others manifests a failure to live in God's love.

Sometimes individuals harm their neighbor in an attempt to unite their lives around family relationships. A father, for example, cheats and manipulates customers as a salesman to fund the best possible opportunities for his daughter. An aunt bribes an admission committee member to accept her nephew into a prestigious college so he can receive a quality education. A grandmother cooks more food than her family can eat for special occasions while her neighbors go without. A way of life united in God's love, by contrast, does not entail treating those outside one's family unjustly but instead disposes one to stand in right relationship with others.

While family commitments can motivate individuals to treat others unjustly, this does not mean that tension between family commitments and service to civil society necessarily leads to unjust results. Sometimes individuals worry that they disturb the social peace by their families' very presence in public spaces. Parents with young children worry that their loud, active, and unruly children will disturb passengers taking public transportation or prevent fellow parishioners from participating in Mass. A father may worry that if he attends a public event with his daughter who needs a wheelchair they might inconvenience others at the gathering. If one expects

18 Jean-Baptiste Chautard, OCSO, *The Spirit of Simplicity*, trans. and annot. Thomas Merton (Notre Dame, IN: Ave Maria Press, 2017), 102. The second half of this work is a series of quotations from Bernard of Clairvaux gathered by Thomas Merton, who also provides commentary on the passages. This quotation makes reference to Bernard of Clairvaux, Sermon 46 on the Canticle of Canticles, ¶ 6.

the family to be isolated, then individuals may think they should hide family imperfections from being seen in public places and that a family's presence in public places is necessarily a pollution to civil society, which is thought of as the sphere of rational, well-behaved adults. By contrast, if families are the basic social unit, and children are a gift to parents and to society, and if individuals are to give preferential care for the poor and serve the common good, then families should not fear stepping into the public sphere, even in their imperfections. This is not to say that families should have no concern about becoming a public nuisance, but it does challenge the logic that families and their imperfections need to stay hidden in socially detached homes. Infused simplicity is a way of life united in God's love, not the mere avoidance of tension with others.

MORAL COOPERATION

Injustice can move from a family to society but also from society to a family. Families need to reflect on the ways that their good actions cooperate in the evil actions of others. Can one support one's family by working at a nuclear arms factory? Can one watch a football game on TV knowing that corporations will be marketing their products to one's family by, at some point, using sexualized imagery? The categories of moral cooperation provide a helpful resource for assessing these and similar questions. They help one to assess whether certain actions can be united in God's love. The distinction between formal and material cooperation is foundational. Formal cooperation is participating in the sin of another while sharing the intention of the sin. For example, a grandmother wants low prices at the store so that she can buy more gifts for her grandchildren at Christmas, and she therefore shares in the indifference of those who lead transnational corporations toward their employees, who are overworked and provided with inadequate wages. Or a father signs a petition to give one's neighborhood a historic designation, knowing and hoping such designation will increase taxes and maintenance costs and thereby push low-income minorities out of the neighborhood. Formal cooperation in sin is always sinful.

Material cooperation in the evil of others is more common and more complicated ethically. Material cooperation occurs when one has reason to think that one's good action will be used by another for evil purposes. One cannot avoid all forms of material cooperation in the evil of another, but one must avoid certain forms. One should not, for example, hand a gun to someone breathing murderous threats, but one need not worry about how each penny of a ten-dollar purchase will be subsequently used by a corporation. Most every purchase will cooperate in some form of evil, often unseen: unethical worker practices, inordinate pollution, or wages that employees will use to support drug or gambling addictions. However, this complexity does not mean that one should simply throw up one's hands and say that, as long as the cooperation is not formal, it must be okay. Since one cannot avoid all forms of material cooperation in evil, one needs to discern when to materially cooperate and when not to materially cooperate in the evil actions of others.

These questions have long been a focus of moral theology. Moral theologians developed the categories of material cooperation in great detail in the modern moral manuals. These manuals emerged from the desire to provide guidelines for confessors. Since the task was to determine which forms of cooperation were sinful and which were not, the advice tended to focus on the limits of moral laws and therefore on minimum moral obligations.[19] The moral manual tradition highlights various questions and categories for the purpose of analyzing questions of cooperation. One does well to synthesize them into a manageable set of questions. I propose that the following five categories provide vital clarification for analyzing questions of cooperation: gravity, reason for cooperating, individual difference, proximity, and scandal.[20] Gravity refers to the kind of evil performed by the primary agent. How significantly does the evil impact one's ability to live a life united in God's love? Reason for cooperating refers to the reason the secondary agent is cooperating in the evil action. How is one positively seeking to live in God's love through the action? Individual difference refers to the influence that the cooperator has in encouraging or preventing the primary agent from performing the evil action. Proximity refers to how closely connected the secondary agent is to the primary agent's evil action. Scandal concerns how one's cooperation might cause confusion about good and evil or encourage others to perform similar evils in the future.

How does one apply these categories to concrete moral scenarios? First, one should note what these categories do not provide. They are not part of a

19 Hanlon Rubio argues that while the manuals are generally rigid in their moral analysis, overlooking the uniqueness of individual persons and individual circumstances, their discussion of cooperation tends to be more flexible. Julie Hanlon Rubio, "Cooperation with Evil Reconsidered: The Moral Duty of Resistance," *Theological Studies* 78, no. 1 (2017): 102–4.

20 Kaveny provides a similar list. See Kaveny, "Appropriation of Evil," 284–86.

computerized formula that provides easy answers to every dilemma. The five questions pertaining to cooperation draw attention to central moral considerations. They serve as instruments of prudence, which is the capacity to reason well about concrete actions, in two ways. First, they highlight essential details and thereby help to develop the capacity to practically reason. Second, these questions often are insufficient for deriving concrete moral decisions. The moral agent will have to examine the information and then decide how he will apply this information to specific situations. One person may be inspired to act as a prophetic witness by forgoing an expected benefit, and another may not. After asking the questions, individuals will still need to discern whether personally, for example, they will invest in retirement plans that finance companies engaging in unjust working conditions, pollution, and problematic political advocacy. The answer will vary depending on the individual's circumstances, personal calling, and capacity for and habits of practical reasoning. Considering prudence also highlights that the ethos of communal life influences the way one reasons practically. The basic social unit and other interdependent communities form one's practical reasoning. Looking at some examples of moral cooperation may be helpful.

Should one provide alcohol at a neighborhood party, knowing that some neighbors struggle with alcoholism and others may use the opportunity to become excessively drunk? The categories of material cooperation are helpful. What is the **gravity** of the relevant evil? Alcoholism is a serious concern that can have devastating implications for living in God's love; drunkenness, while considered socially acceptable in some contexts, temporarily destroys one's reason and can lead to deleterious social interactions and even car accidents that endanger property and life. Therefore, it seems fair to say that the moral concern is sufficiently grave to merit further analysis. However, this is not the only consideration. Is there **sufficient reason** to risk such an evil? It is well-known that alcohol eases social engagement and improves camaraderie, which is the reason that the neighborhood party is being held in the first place. It helps individuals relax and be free with their speech. One neighbor might brew his own beer and enjoy sharing it with others, and others may enjoy trying and discussing different flavors. Having good beer may encourage people to attend the party who might otherwise remain in social isolation, where irresponsible drinkers are free to drink excessively. Even though it is certainly possible to hold a party without beer, in many American neighborhoods, it seems that there could be sufficient reason to make it available. In fact, the neighbors who struggle with the abuse of alcohol might benefit from a social gathering in which beer is used responsibly. On the other hand, it could cause **scandal** to hold an event whose atmosphere suggested that only by drinking could one have a good time. By contrast, the host making a point of abstaining—even if one would like to partake—may help the alcoholic (as well as nondrinkers) feel more at ease.

These considerations lead to the question of how likely the gathering is to encourage responsible consumption. **Individual difference** suggests that the prudence of providing or allowing alcohol may have to do with the influence the party-thrower could have on individual behavior. One may not know, however, how likely this event would be to encourage the alcoholic to relapse or the drunkard to have too much, but these concerns could be mitigated if the alcohol is monitored by a server rather than simply floating freely available in a cooler. The evil would obviously be of greater **proximity** if one handed the alcoholic a drink or gave another beverage to someone obviously reaching serious inebriation. Buying fewer but more expensive and better-made beer might encourage appreciation for the craft rather than excessive consumption. And so on. In short, these categories do not provide a clear answer without knowing all of the circumstances. One might make different decisions based on the many unknown details of the case. Nevertheless, the categories do highlight central, clarifying questions aiding the prudential discernment of situations often faced by those entrusted with the care of families, helping them to unite their lives in God's love, a love that implies love of neighbor.

The categories of material cooperation help families discern their cooperation in the sinful actions of others. Familial interactions with broader society, however, is not limited to cooperation in sin. To account for other kinds of interactions, one must expand the framework of the categories of cooperation in four ways. First, one should frame the categories of moral cooperation in relation to the virtue of justice; that is, with the end of relating well with others.[21] If the goal is to relate well with others, then the task is something greater than avoiding sin. One wants to decrease one's cooperation in the evil (not just sin) of others while increasing one's cooperation in their good actions. Second, one must move beyond questions of cooperation and include consideration of formation and appropriation.

21 William C. Mattison III, *Introducing Moral Theology: True Happiness and the Virtues* (Grand Rapids, MI: Brazos Press, 2008), 139

Third, one must consider good forms of social cooperation and appropriation. Fourth, situated theologically in simplicity and dependence on God, one sees that cooperating in and appropriating the grace of God is central to Christian discipleship. These four expansions of the analysis of moral cooperation will allow families to draw more fully on the categories of cooperation in their discernment of social engagement.

Cathleen Kaveny makes an insightful, and underappreciated, distinction between moral cooperation and moral appropriation.[22] Whereas moral cooperation involves assisting an evil action yet to be performed, moral appropriation is benefitting from an evil action already completed. Examples of moral appropriation include buying clothing produced in a sweatshop, receiving a vaccine developed using cells derived from an aborted fetus, or accepting gifts and support for one's family from a friend who is persistent and vocal in being anti-Christian. Kaveny highlights the formative character of moral appropriation.[23] Even if one's appropriation does not contribute to future evils, one still risks the moral formation or moral seepage that can result from the identification with an evil action that results from benefitting either as an individual or family. One might intentionally or unintentionally associate the good of one's action or benefit with the evil of the past action and thereby become morally insensitive to the evil action.

In distinguishing between material cooperation and moral appropriation, one should note that the two categories can overlap; they are distinct but not always separate. Moral appropriation also may encourage future evils, and cooperation with future evils may cause moral rationalization or appropriation. However, one or the other is often more thematic in a particular situation, and as Kaveny notes, analyzing cases of appropriation as if they were cases of material cooperation often leads to a contorted and confusing ethical analysis.[24] The moral analysis for moral appropriation is similar to but slightly different from that for material cooperation. Whereas with material cooperation, one is concerned with how one encourages another's evil, in moral appropriation one is concerned with how one identifies with and is formed by association with a past evil.

The concept of moral appropriation has direct application to many aspects of consumer society, such as engagement with market branding. In

22 Kaveny, "Appropriation of Evil," 282–89.

23 Kaveny, 281, 289.

24 Kaveny, 289–97.

the context of infused simplicity, however, I will focus on an example that relates more directly to our relationship with God: should one allow one's children to accept gifts and support from a college friend who is vehemently anti-Christian? The friend's negative presentation of the Christian faith could be a **grave matter** for those, like small children, whose faith commitments are developing and flexible. One, however, might have **sufficient reason** to receive the gifts and support she provides. Perhaps, the friend is willing to watch the kids, models joy and kindness, invites your family to join her for a vacation, or contributes to your children's college savings. This support, especially for families generally lacking communal support, could be crucial for the family's vitality. On the other hand, the children's **identification** with the friend and her antifaith convictions could become significant if they spend lots of time with her, and she is giving them gifts that they enjoy. If children were to appropriate the friend's religious sentiments, those who allowed the children to benefit and receive support from the friend would be closely connected to the formation of their distorted views. The children might be confused into thinking that their parents are indifferent to the friend's antifaith convictions since they so often facilitate interaction with the friend. In assessing application of the categories, one sees once again that there is no clear answer that would apply to all of the unknown circumstances. In reflecting on the question of identification, one would need to discern how often the family benefits from or interacts with the friend. How influential and persuasive is the friend in expressing her antifaith convictions? Is she open to conversation about her convictions or willing to hold her tongue with the children? How articulate are the parents in expressing their faith and responding to questions and challenges to the faith that might emerge? Does the family also have social outlets that would cultivate identification with a mature faith in their family members? Parents can use these questions of identification to aid in their practical reasoning about living in God's love. No doubt, the relationships between family members and the friend and the issue of religious formation will be dynamic and require ongoing discernment.

While the categories of cooperation and appropriation do not always provide clear answers to complicated questions, they do provide a framework that serves as an instrument for prudence. Beyond these categories, the Church is a formative community that can help individuals and families to practically reason well in the light of God's love and revelation. Without such questions and support, one risks blindly following moral intuitions or a false simplicity that reduces morally complex situations to basic motifs, such as one's primary responsibility is to one's family, or families have an obligation to contribute to the common good and serve the poor. If one defines the family as merely an isolated group that seeks to separate from other social communities, one may overlook questions of social engagement altogether.

COOPERATION AND THE COMMON GOOD

While the material cooperation tradition of the moral manuals tends to focus on avoiding sinful cooperation with evil, the Catholic social tradition also provides resources for thinking about positive social contributions and cooperating in the good actions of others. Expanding moral cooperation to cooperation in goodness is crucial if families are to attain a way of life that is united in God's love. Framed by simplicity, one sees the purpose of avoiding cooperation in sin. By avoiding cooperation in sin, one removes obstacles to God in order to cooperate more fully in His life and love. Infused simplicity reframes moral cooperation. To reflect on cooperation with God is to connect the categories of moral cooperation to the center and telos of the moral life—cooperating in God's love.

One will miss the invitation of grace if one is overly focused on fortifying one's family against negative extrafamilial influences. If one's family is seen as an isolated refuge, then one avoids the influence of others. Taken to the extreme, this would exclude the influence of God. Families are not radically autonomous; they are radically dependent on God, who creates human souls out of nothing and offers redemption and grace. Infused simplicity is possible only with God's assistance. Moral cooperation in God's work highlights that God is the primary moral agent of family life, even while recognizing human and personal responsibility for freely accepting and participating as a cooperator with God.

Cooperation with God's love provides a framework for thinking about cooperation with the goodness of others. The Christian faith entails social complexity because love of God implies love of neighbor and love of Christ implies participation in the social community of the Church. De Sales writes, "Your neighbor is there, in the Heart of the Saviour, there, as so beloved and so lovable that the divine Lover dies of love for him!"[25] Rooted

25 De Sales, "On Simplicity and Religious Prudence," 230.

in the love of God, infused simplicity requires that one not ignore, but love, one's neighbor. A complete denial of social complexity would send one running away from the needs of one's human brothers and sisters. The Catholic social tradition instead speaks of one's contribution to the good of the community with the principle of the common good.

The definition of the common good often repeated in the papal social encyclical tradition states that the common good is "the sum total of social conditions which allow people, either as groups or as individuals, to reach their fulfillment more fully and more easily."[26] The common good is comprehensive (the "sum total of social conditions"). The common good promotes the good of the broadest community while also promoting the good of smaller groups and individuals. Families benefit from social structures and social services, and they in turn have a responsibility to contribute to the common good for the sake of other groups and individuals. They should contribute to the common good without thereby undermining their own fulfillment.

Direct service to the common good, as well as cooperation with or appropriation of the good actions of others, sheds new light on our earlier examples. The goal is not merely to avoid negatively harming others or to avoid the negative formation resulting from the other's evil. One also can offer positive contributions to society, and benefit from the public ethos of civil laws and cultural norms. The second category of material cooperation—the reason for one's cooperation or appropriation—alludes to this positive consideration. However, the way one frames the broader question can significantly impact one's moral analysis. To place greater emphasis on contributing to the good, one could switch the role evil and good play in the moral calculation and begin with the question of cooperating in goodness. What is the **gravity** of the good that one can assist? What **reasons** does one have to avoid contributing to that good? What kind of **individual difference** could one make in supporting that good activity? How closely connected is one to the proposed good (**proximity**)? How would one's support encourage others to offer similar support (**witness**, as the opposite of scandal)? A family often recognizes and has the resources to respond to social needs that no one else recognizes. The categories of cooperation and appropriation can help clarify situations of positive contribution to society by

26 Pontifical Council for Justice and Peace, *Compendium of the Social Doctrine of the Church* (Washington, DC: United States Conference of Catholic Bishops, 2006), 164. This definition, or something closely related, is reproduced in various papal social encyclicals.

asking, for example, How should one support a neighborhood party? Other questions might be: How much money should one tithe to the parish or contribute to the diocesan appeal? How many hours of work should one contribute to one's job? How active should one be in forming and disciplining neighbors' kids?

Framing the questions in terms of the common good and cooperation in goodness can enhance the moral analysis. For example, if a pastor tells parishioners that they should tithe because God should be the most important commitment in their lives, and they therefore have an obligation to be generous, parishioners may give money, but they likely will not know how their giving relates to their commitment to God and the local church.[27] If, on the other hand, the pastor explains the good and necessary things that tithing enables the parish and diocese to accomplish, then parishioners not only understand more clearly why giving generously is a good thing to do, but they also can identify with those ministries as they occur throughout the year, even if they are not able to personally participate. One can place the gravity or the significance of the good things that the parish and diocese are doing in relation to the reasons one might have for using money for other purposes. How much difference will one's tithing make in parish and diocesan programs? What if a significant percentage of people gave a similar amount?[28] How closely connected is one to the intended ministries? How might one's contributions encourage others to contribute?

The way one frames the moral question also impacts the moral analysis. For example, there was a concern raised in recent years about the organization Catholic Relief Services, because it once provided mosquito nets to an organization that provides contraceptive services. Instead of focusing entirely on whether the organization is cooperating with evils according to church teaching, one can look more comprehensively at the good that the organization does. In the case of Catholic Relief Services, this means their

27 Hanlon Rubio writes, "Typically, theological justifications for tithing advanced in contemporary tithing churches center on recognition of God's sovereignty and links between believers' tithing and their salvation; concern for the poor and discussion of the effects of the excesses of consumerist lifestyles on believers are rare." Hanlon Rubio, *Family Ethics: Practices for Christians* (Washington, DC: Georgetown University Press, 2010), 178.

28 Albino Barrera highlights the need to consider accumulative harms in one's analysis of moral cooperation: "Accumulative harms have a peculiar feature in that activities pursued at the individual level are harmless but become injurious at the aggregate level when lumped together with other similar acts." Albino Barrera, *Market Complicity and Christian Ethics* (New York: Cambridge University Press, 2011), 39.

global, innovative, and life-changing ministry to the radical poor, refugees, and those suffering from natural disasters. Similarly, asking whether one should go to Mass since one's kids will misbehave and distract others is different than asking why would one refrain from participating in Mass in light of the opportunity to gather with the community of faith, hear the Word of God, and receive and be united to the body of Christ.

The category of moral appropriation also can apply positively. One's family can **appropriate** good things from other social communities, thereby identifying with the good that those communities do. Families can receive meals from a parish organization supporting the birth of a child or benefit from marriage preparation classes. One can attend Mass and benefit from those who serve as greeters, ushers, musicians, and readers, or from the work that the deacon or priest put into preparing the homily. One's family can benefit from public library events, local parks, or parades. More basic to everyday needs, families benefit from access to water, roads, internet, and other social services. This reliance on the community is usually taken for granted, but families can find ways to appreciate the goodwill and hard work of others and to show that appreciation.

If the family were an isolated community that stands against others, then families should grasp for and utilize every resource they can. They should fight other customers to buy Christmas gifts on Black Friday and cut off people on the road to get a better seat at the basketball game. However, since the family is interdependent with other social communities and therefore responsible for the common good, families should consider how their appropriation of communal resources relates to the needs and wants of others. For example, should one draw from welfare resources if one can survive without them, or how long should one wait before insisting that one's child share the park swing with another child?

Let me give an example from my personal experience. During the COVID-19 pandemic, when food transportation was breaking down, local farmers in rural southern Indiana received a grant to provide dairy and vegetables for free to the local community. The food was distributed through a Catholic parish. Program organizers were concerned that food would go to waste and so they informed the public that everyone was welcome to receive the food. My wife and I struggled to discern whether we should pick up some of this food for our family. We were not starving, but we did have four children to feed, and we knew we would use the food. The categories of appropriation were helpful. In receiving the food, we benefitted from it and supported local farmers. We were glad to cultivate an identification of our kids with local farmers and the parish community, especially since we could not go to Mass at the time. Rather than simply take what we could get, we drew closer in proximity to this good work—we live next door to the parish and I helped distribute the food. Knowing the circumstances of the food distribution allowed us to make informed decisions—we made different decisions on different distribution days based on whether I had helped that day, how much food we had in the fridge, and how much food was left when the line was empty.

FRUGALITY AND ASCETICISM

In discerning how to avoid cooperation with or appropriation of evil or to increase cooperation with or appropriation of goodness, one quickly realizes that a commitment to one good will inevitably involve a withdrawal or sacrifice of other goods. The commitment to serve as a cooperator in the grace of God or in the good actions of others implies withdrawing from and sacrificing other social engagements, even positive ones. Simplicity as a way of life united in God's love requires more than avoiding sin, decreasing cooperation with evil, and increasing cooperation with good. Simplicity also means that families will withdraw even from some instances of positive social engagement for the sake of God and their other commitments. Since the family is internally social and socially interdependent, discernment about cooperation with or appropriation of goods will inevitably involve tension between different kinds of internal interactions, as well as tension between different kinds of interactions outside of the family. The goal is not to eliminate the tension between the internally social and socially interdependent dimensions of family life but to live in memory both of one's commitment to one's family and of the desire to cultivate friendship, taking seriously the responsibility to love one's neighbor in service of the common good.

Sometimes, an individual's involvement in a social activity also benefits other family members. If the mother and wife of a family enjoys participating in a recreational volleyball team, her volleyball games could be a location for a broader social gathering in which her husband and children can enjoy fellowship with the families of the other players. Other times, decisions to socially engage seem to stand in more direct tension with family commitments or other social commitments. One only has so much time, energy, and resources. One may decide to donate generously to the parish, but then is not able to fund a family vacation to Europe, or one might contribute to a niece's band fundraiser but then is not able to contribute to a neighbor's Boy Scout fundraiser. One may miss one's grandma's funeral to be with one's wife as she prepares for the birth of a child. One may travel for a work conference rather than be home for a family birthday. One may support music lessons for one's kids rather than participation in a travel sports club. One may choose to play ball in the yard or board games with one's kids rather than go out with friends.

Because simplicity is a way of life united in God's love, moral discernment requires more than seeking to increase one's time with or away from family. There is a certain natural necessity for children to have the time and attention of their parents, so the kinds of activity that draw one away from the family must be scrutinized, but the kinds of activities engaged in by the family must also be considered. Hildebrand and de Sales warn that focusing on superficial activity distracts from God. Hildebrand, writing in the context of modern society, warns against concentration on illustrated magazines, many cinema pictures, gambling, thrilling novels, and social gatherings dominated by idle talk (one can imagine what he might say about social media). He notes that certain activities are not opposed to God but draw us to the periphery and make unity in God more difficult.[29] De Sales, offering a parallel caution, writes, "Sports, banquets, parties, fine clothes, and stage comedies are all things that, considered in themselves, are by no means evil. They are indifferent acts and therefore they can be either good or bad."[30] Some social engagements may be good, but due to the focus of the social engagement or the character or habits of individual family members, the engagement may lead family members away from their commitment to God and their response to God's call in their lives. If one focuses one's moral analysis on individual actions and on the avoidance of sin, then the lists that de Sales and Hildebrand provide may appear scrupulous. However, if the framework is a way of life united in God's love, then one's engagement with these activities and the way that engagement moves one toward or away from God's love becomes worthy of discernment. Being a

29 Hildebrand, *Transformation in Christ*, 92–93.

30 Francis de Sales, *Introduction to the Devout Life*, trans. John K. Ryan (New York: Image Books, 1966), 77. In one of his letters, de Sales cautions a man preparing to leave for court to avoid gaming. De Sales writes to the young man of his fears that gaming will "make all the flowers of your good desires wither." De Sales, *Letters to Persons in the World*, trans. Henry Benedict Mackey, OSB (New York: Benziger Brothers, 1900), 180.

sports fan or learning facts through Google searches, for example, can be good, but these activities become an obstacle to simplicity when a family's ethos dedicates significant time and energy to these activities. Does the time spent watching or reading about sports allow enough time for family prayer? Does the internet intrude into family meals or take away from time talking, playing, or working together? Moreover, both of these examples are caught up in a consumerist society, insofar as the incentive for the companies behind these activities (the team, Google) is to increase engagement endlessly, so that they can become an addiction. These kinds of activities can also form family members to expect immediate gratification rather than take on the longer task of promoting the kingdom of God.

Simplicity as a way of life united in God's love thus requires the sacrifice of goods or the alteration of one's pursuit of certain goods. We will not see the need for this sacrifice if we limit our moral analysis to individual actions. Is it evil to conduct a Google search to find out what is the deepest part of the ocean? Is it evil to watch a Premier League soccer game? When focused on whether an individual action is a sin, one misses the broader picture provided by the virtue of simplicity. The default position is that everything is acceptable unless one sees that something is gravely wrong. In the framework of simplicity, one asks a different question. Does picking up the phone to do a Google search in bed instead of talking to one's spouse cultivate the love of God? Does spending two hours watching a soccer game on Sunday morning cultivate God's love and respond to His call in my life and for my family? How is God inviting me to live in His love in this situation? How might the framework of God's love unite or transform this activity in relation to other activities or commitments?

Perhaps the greatest challenge of Christian living is making choices between goods, especially when the choice means sacrificing goods that are personally appealing. Sometimes certain goods attract one to the periphery, and one sacrifices them in service to something greater. At other times, a good or responsibility related to one's vocation, occupation, or life circumstances requires attention, which implies less attention for other goods less connected to those commitments. These sacrifices can be great or small. One might miss a few minutes of a TV show to change a soiled diaper. One might sacrifice family privacy and family time in order to pursue political office for the common good. One might deliver a conference paper and miss a call from one's college-aged son. One might turn down a desirable job or promotion to protect time with one's spouse and children. The goal of thinking through these choices is not to become morally paralyzed over all of the possible ramifications, but to make the choices thoughtfully and to patiently assess the fruits of those choices. Choosing to pursue goods is best understood as an iterative process, in which large decisions and commitments that cost significant sacrifices are rooted in the experience of how small actions in the same direction affect oneself, one's family, and one's community.

This discernment of the fruits of a family's activity happens in the presence of God's providential care. Hildebrand notes that one temptation that is opposed to simplicity is to give oneself to something good in itself, such as a noble friendship or scholarly pursuit, but in a manner that ought to be reserved for God alone. Hildebrand writes that while these good things "can stand the test before the face of Christ, we must never abandon ourselves unqualifiedly to their immanent logic."[31] The temptation to give oneself unreservedly to something other than God is particularly strong when one is dealing with great goods, such as one's occupation, friendships, or even one's family.

The person acting out of infused simplicity is focused on Christ with a single-minded devotion. This devotion leads to a withdrawal of one's heart or at minimum a reservation of one's love for all goods that are not God. Both de Sales and Hildebrand reinforce the point near the end of their accounts of simplicity. De Sales concludes his conference on simplicity by reflecting on a verse from the Gospel of Matthew: "Behold, I am sending you like sheep in the midst of wolves; so be shrewd as serpents and simple as doves" (Matt. 10:16). After reflecting on being "simple as doves," de Sales turns his attention to Christ's invitation to be "shrewd as serpents." He argues that serpents, "when they are attacked, expose their whole bodies in order to preserve their heads. So too ought we to do, exposing ourselves and all that we have to danger when necessary, in order to preserve within us, untouched, Our Lord and His love; for He is our *Head*, and we are His *members*."[32] Everything is exposed for the sake of Christ. In the third to last paragraph of his chapter on simplicity, Hildebrand similarly speaks of a heroism that flows from Christian simplicity: "We are ready to sacrifice, without reserve, all lower goods to a higher one; that we gladly sell all we possess in order to buy the land where the treasure is buried."[33] Christ is

31 Hildebrand, *Transformation in Christ*, 93.

32 De Sales, "On Simplicity and Religious Prudence," 232.

33 Hildebrand, *Transformation in Christ*, 104.

the treasure and one should be prepared to dispense with all else to attain it. This is not to say that one generally should forego one's basic needs, but rather that one should be honest in evaluating the ways one is accustomed to trying to meet those needs. If one finds that a particular activity has become a greater object of one's love and attention than Christ, then whatever justifications could be given for continuing its pursuit, one may be called to give it up or change one's relationship to it.

De Sales and Hildebrand insist that withdrawal and reservation toward various goods of creation are necessary for Christian simplicity—one can fall into sin and away from God, become busy or distracted with the goods of the world, and even give oneself to great goods in ways that ought to be reserved for God alone. This does not entail, however, that family members should withdraw their hands and feet from all activities that are not spiritual in nature. Hildebrand warns that "the advantage derived from the avoidance of complexity is outweighed by a grave defect or aberration."[34] The goal of familial simplicity is not a denial or ignorance of social complexity, which could easily lead to a boredom flowing from a lack of complexity. Due to the goodness of creation, the necessities of human life, the social complexity of life and social fulfillment, and the call to love one's neighbor, true simplicity cannot be merely a withdrawal from, but also must be an integration of, all things in Christ.

INTEGRATION

To say that all things must be integrated in Christ may seem well and good, but how can it be done? De Sales and Hildebrand maintain that active participation in grace provides hope that one can live in the world without being of the world. De Sales writes, "A strong, resolute soul can live in the world without being infected by any of its moods, find sweet spring of piety amid its salty waves. . . . True, this is a difficult task, and therefore I wish that many souls would strive to accomplish it with greater ardor than has hitherto been shown."[35] One can deal with a variety of responsibilities without being distracted from Christ, but only with hard work, the willingness to fail and try again, and the assistance of grace.

Not only can they avoid being overwhelmed by the world, but in Christian simplicity families also can progressively integrate their lives in Christ.

34 Hildebrand, 81.

35 De Sales, preface to *Introduction to the Devout Life*, 34.

Hildebrand provides a framework for thinking about this integration, and de Sales provides pastoral guidance and application. In his treatment of simplicity, Hildebrand highlights three ways to integrate all things in Christ: sacrificing to Christ through one's work, gratitude, and by analogy. Underlying this threefold framework is a foundation emphasized in the writings of both Hildebrand and de Sales: prayer.

Prayer

Hildebrand and de Sales highlight how an encounter with God in prayer enables us to unite our lives in God. While recognizing that one must take care of the necessities of life, Hildebrand affirms that in order to "baptize all these things . . . we must dominate them by reason of our conscious, direct, and permanent contact with Christ."[36] De Sales beautifully illustrates the transforming and unifying character of prayer: "Since prayer places our intellect in the brilliance of God's light and exposes our will to the warmth of his heavenly love, nothing else so effectively purifies our intellect of ignorance and our will of depraved affections. It is a stream of holy water that flows forth and makes the plants of our good desires grow green and flourish and quenches the passions within our hearts."[37] Since God provides the source, sustenance, meaning, and end of all things, one will not be surprised that prayer unifies one's life.

Many families, however, struggle to find time to pray—even families in which the parents are deeply committed to the faith. Julie Hanlon Rubio highlights how parents often become so busy or exhausted that family time for prayer is sacrificed, and she observes that many parents are also not on the same page in terms of faith commitment, whether they share the same faith tradition or not. Individual family members might prefer different forms of prayer, and some family members may not be interested in praying

36 Hildebrand, *Transformation in Christ*, 94.

37 De Sales, *Introduction to the Devout Life*, 81. See also Hildebrand's discussion of prayer in his chapter on recollection and contemplation, which he links with simplicity; this discussion follows immediately after his discussion of simplicity:

> We must guard from performing the inner prayer as though we were dispatching a business among others. . . . Whatever I am wont to carry and to hold in my arms I will let fall before Jesus. It will not fall into the void. . . . I am not abandoning them as I would abandon them in seeking diversion: I know that in Jesus they are truly in a safe harbor. When at His call I relinquish and abandon all things, I am not casting them away; on the contrary, I am assigning everything to its proper place. (Hildebrand, *Transformation in Christ*, 139–40).

in the way the family prays, or in praying at all. Young children usually struggle to stay focused, sit still, be quiet, or share conversation with a God whom they cannot visibly see. The cultivation of family prayer may require a willingness to try different ways of praying and to adjust as family members mature and as their commitment to and interest in prayer ebbs and flows. A diversity and complexity of approaches to family prayer may be necessary to help family members stay united in God.

Family prayer can be difficult to establish as a habit, but it is a necessary one—families can hardly live a life united in God's love if they are not praying. Hanlon Rubio writes, "Though the practice of prayer is no doubt difficult to sustain in the context of modern living, it is crucial if parents and children want to see the rest of life through the eyes of faith and practice resistance to more typical forms of middle-class family life."[38] Hanlon Rubio's observation that prayer can be an action of resistance is important in the context of cultivating simplicity in the midst of a consumerist culture. Echoing Saint Augustine, William Cavanaugh writes, "The solution to the restlessness of desire is to cultivate a desire for God, the Eternal, in whom our hearts will find rest."[39]

De Sales warns, however, against praising the formative character of prayer while neglecting the need to change one's life. After a rich discussion of mental prayer, he insists that one should end mental prayer with a resolution for concrete action. He even proposes that mental prayer can be harmful without such a concrete resolution: "Virtues meditated on but not practiced sometimes inflate our minds and courage and we think that we are really such as we have thought and resolved to be."[40] While de Sales offers this qualification in his discussion of mental prayer, the insight about concrete action applies regardless of the prayer form. Family prayer will do no good, and may even be harmful, if individuals despise doing it or think they are holy simply because they externally completed the prayer. This is not to say that parents or children will always experience family prayer as life-changing, or that the concrete fruit will be immediately clear, but over time, one should expect family prayer to illuminate aspects of family life. In fact, if it does not do so, families might consider alternative forms of prayer. It

38 Hanlon Rubio, *Family Ethics*, 215.

39 William T. Cavanaugh, *Being Consumed: Economics and Christian Desire* (Grand Rapids, MI: William B. Eerdmans, 2008), 90.

40 De Sales, *Introduction to the Devout Life*, 90.

can be hard for parents to set aside their image of what family prayer should look like (e.g., the family praying five decades of the rosary), but attentiveness to what works to draw in their children's hearts and minds will likely bear much greater fruit than enforcing a particular regimen no matter what.

While authentic prayer is transformative of life, families should not make prayer, and therefore God, into a mere instrument for family improvement. With Stanley Hauerwas, Hanlon Rubio notes that when people say, "the family that prays together stays together," some might be tempted to think "that prayer is good simply because it strengthens family ties."[41] Hildebrand clarifies that God ought to be the primary focus of prayer: "We must actually throw ourselves open to the radiance of the *lumen Christi*, without attempting to adapt it to our own nature or to falsify it by our natural categories. We must not humanize and interpret in an easy oversimplified manner the One in whom is all plenitude of divinity (*in quo est omnis plenitude divinitatis*), lest we succumb to the pitfall of false simplicity."[42] All forms of family prayer should seek God's glory and cultivate relationship with God. Prayer purifies and unifies one's thoughts and one's life but only if one's focus is on God and only if one's prayer regularly manifests itself in concrete action.

Making One's Work a Sacrifice

One means of integrating all things in Christ is to offer one's work as a sacrifice to God.[43] While Hildebrand and de Sales do not give significant space to this theme, the process of sacrificing one's work is crucial for the integration of social complexity since most people spend a large portion of their lives working. If simplicity is a way of life united in God's love, then one's ability to live a united life will be largely dependent on one's ability to see one's work in God. By offering our works as a sacrifice to God, before, during, and after work, we place our work into God's hands and thereby reorient our work as coming from and going toward God.[44] One sees in one's work, both

41 Hanlon Rubio, *Family Ethics*, 214; here Hanlon Rubio is engaging the work of Stanley Hauerwas in Stanley Hauerwas, "The Family as a School for Character," in *Perspectives on Marriage: A Reader*, ed. Kieran Scott and Michael Warren (Oxford: Oxford University Press, 1993), 148.

42 Hildebrand, *Transformation in Christ*, 85.

43 Hildebrand, 95–96.

44 De Sales in "On Simplicity and Religious Prudence" (227) writes, "Not only in prayer, but in the conduct of their whole life, they ought to walk invariably in a spirit of simplicity." See also Saint John Paul II's rich spirituality of work in sections 24–27 of his 1981 encyclical on work, *Laborem Exercens*.

within and outside of the household, an opportunity to cooperate with God's activity. Offering one's work to God is particularly important for individuals struggling with balancing family and work commitments. These two activities often stand in tension, but they can find unity in God's love. Offering one's work to God also can help those who struggle to see meaning in their household work, or those who work only to receive a paycheck. Their work involves something greater than its monetary value when it contains sparks of divine love. Work is an essential part of human life. A life united in Christ requires that one see one's work in the light of Christ.

Practically speaking, this can involve finding small ways to integrate prayer into work. Particularly in modern office work, computer technology can engage one so thoroughly that the day slips by, often without the accomplishment of the most important tasks, due to the incessant arrival of emails and the distractions of internet browsing. Making a plan for occasional short prayers—either before opening one's email inbox, or at set times during the day—can interrupt this busyness of business and bring needed perspective. A traditional prayer for the intercession of Saint Joseph asks for the grace to work in "orderliness, peace, moderation, and patience, without shrinking from weariness and difficulties."

The way one treats one's bodily needs in the course of the workday is not tangential to the offering of one's work as a sacrifice to Christ. Saint Paul urges Christians "to present your bodies as a living sacrifice to God" (Rom. 12:1), and this does not cease to apply during the workday. Excessive coffee drinking, unhealthy eating, and long periods of sitting without interruption are not conducive to the spiritual value of work. Unhealthy eating can include skipping meals because one is too busy; while fasting is a good spiritual practice and can be a good complement to the sacrifice of labor, it should be done with intentionality and in moderation. De Sales cautions against excessive fasting, especially among laborers, advising, "Both fasting and labor mortify and subdue the flesh. If your work is necessary for you to contribute to God's glory, I much prefer that you endure the pains of work rather than of fasting."[45] Of course, some labor is not necessary, especially when an office culture demands attention to emails at all hours of the day or night. Part of offering one's work as a sacrifice is preparing one's body to be able to work by getting adequate rest, nutrition, and exercise, and refusing as much as possible modes of work that undermine these conditions.

45 De Sales, *Introduction to the Devout Life*, 185–86.

Gratitude

A third means of integrating all things in Christ is gratitude. Hildebrand argues that gratitude presents a "profound connection between the genuine goods of the world and God."[46] He goes on to note that "by all gifts we are reminded of the Giver: 'In all things give thanks' (1 Thess. 5:18)."[47] For his part, de Sales begins his *Introduction to the Devout Life* with four meditations that highlight gratitude.[48] He also provides an excellent illustration of the importance of gratitude in his analysis of wealth and possessions. He proposes that since all possessions ultimately belong to God, one should care for one's possessions with the same attentive care as a gardener would care for the garden of a prince or king. In turn, these possessions, which ultimately belong to God, should be shared generously with the poor.[49] In gratitude, one sees one's family and one's possessions in their proper light; namely, as coming from God and as being ordered by and to God.

There are many books, even from secular authors, highlighting the positive benefits of gratitude and proposing ways of enacting this virtue. Some advise keeping a journal where one daily writes down things for which one is grateful; others suggest reaching out to people for whom one is grateful. A ritual of asking each person at the dinner table for one thing for which they are grateful is one way to incorporate this practice into family life. Expressing gratitude for one another is especially important in marriage and in parent-child interactions. It seems generally agreed that interactions of praise and positive affirmation should strongly outnumber criticism and negative feedback, even when the latter are necessary. I am not aware of anyone outside of a psychological study actually counting instances of these, but expressing gratitude for one another's care and help, however small the acts, is an important way to amass those positive interactions.

46 Hildebrand, *Transformation in Christ*, 96.

47 Hildebrand, 96. See also p. 100, where Hildebrand writes, "Only if we receive every good (by the methods just described) in mindfulness of God and *qua* gifts and tokens of God—if in all values we are anxious to discern and to meet God—then the formal simplifying power of every value as such will become operative and conducive to true simplicity."

48 De Sales, *Introduction to the Devout Life*, 52–59.

49 De Sales, 164–65.

Analogy

Finally, one can integrate all things in Christ by analogy. One sees not only that God is the source of all things but that all things in one way or another represent their creator. Hildebrand writes that for those who see the analogy of God, "the cleansing effect of water will evoke in our minds the redemptive power of Baptism."[50] The warmth and light of the sun are signs of the all-sustaining love of God. The tools of work are not exempt from being the subject of this viewpoint. The solidity of a workbench brings to mind the stability of God on which we rely for all our efforts; a hammer and chisel is a rough analogy for how God forms us through the circumstances of life. Hildebrand clarifies that to see things as an analogy of God is not a subtle way of withdrawing from or misrepresenting the goods of the world. Rather, "If we consider all things *in conspectu Dei*, every genuine good finds its right place in the cosmic order and discloses its specific value more splendidly than if we attend to it in arbitrary isolation."[51] Analogy allows us to see the true nature of the good and to see that good properly in relation to a vast hierarchy of goods. The products we make and the services we provide form a part—sometimes a hugely important part—of God's providential care for the human race.

The analogy of God stands out more profoundly for higher spheres of being. Hildebrand proposes that a genuine encounter with great goods, like the human person, or the beauty of Beethoven's Ninth Symphony, or the manifestation of a generous soul, has a particular potential to elevate one to God.[52] Marriage and family is a particularly profound analogy. "The deep union of two human beings in marriage will acquire a new meaning in the light of the bond between Christ and His Church, and of the mysterious union, transcending all conceptual understanding, of the three Divine Persons in one Substance."[53] The movement toward God presented in the analogy of such goods contains "a faculty of coordination and unification, both

50 Hildebrand, *Transformation in Christ*, 98.

51 Hildebrand, 85. See also p. 98, where von Hildebrand affirms that seeing the world's goods in reference to God "leads us through its innermost core to God." See also Jame Schaefer's work, especially her chapter titled "Reverencing the Sacramental Universe," in Jame Schaefer, *Theological Foundations for Environmental Ethics: Reconstructing Patristic and Medieval Concepts* (Washington, DC: Georgetown University Press, 2009), 65–102.

52 Hildebrand proposes that the human person as *imago Dei* serves as the most profound analogy of God. *Transformation in Christ*, 96.

53 Hildebrand, 98.

in an interpersonal and intrapersonal sense."[54] While one should not give oneself completely to these values, Hildebrand argues that one also cannot merely encounter such goods. One must actively cooperate in this invitation from God to be raised to Him and to recognize the mission of these goods "to liberate one from lower attachments."[55] One learns from the love of one's spouse or parents or the trust of one's children how to stand in relationship to God. Similarly, one sees the face of Christ in the needs of one's neighbor and in the beauty of God in nature. One sees in these great goods an invitation to grow in simplicity as a way of life united in Christ.

PASTORAL APPLICATION

The possibility of integrating all things in Christ does not imply that everyone or every family, in their current state, can quickly bring things to perfection. In his pastoral guidance, de Sales reminds us that one's ability to integrate complexity into one's life will depend on the magnitude of a person's faith and fortitude. One sees examples of this pastoral application in his *Letters to Persons in the World*. Despite a general concern about the risks of complexity, in one of his letters he discerns in his conversation partner a high potential for integration in Christ. He praises the man for maintaining his faith within the complexities of legal and political work: "My dearest son, though you may change place, occupations and society, you will never, I trust, change your heart, nor your heart its love. . . . The variety of the faces of court and world will make no change in yours. Your eyes will ever regard heaven, to which you aspire, and your mouth will ever demand the sovereign good which you hope to have there."[56] For another man in a similar situation, however, de Sales is more concerned. He concludes that while the man's faith is strong enough to engage in legal and political work, he should be cautious to avoid vanity and ambition, bad books, fond loves, gaming, and delicacies.[57] The pursuit of integration in Christ requires an honest assessment of those things that might easily derail one's focus or the focus of family members from what is most important.

De Sales reminds us that a comprehensive integration in one's life will not occur on earth. The pursuit of Christian simplicity requires a humble

54 Hildebrand, 101.

55 Hildebrand, 103.

56 De Sales, *Letters to Persons in the World*, 187.

57 De Sales, 176–83.

awareness of one's weaknesses and limitations. Accordingly, de Sales proposes that perfection on earth is not having all things integrated in Christ, but knowing how to deal with one's imperfections.[58] He writes that "*this* is the height of virtue, to correct immoderation moderately."[59] In one letter, de Sales provides a vivid analogy cautioning against a rash and self-asserting eradication of imperfection: "Huntsmen push into the brambles, and often return more injured than the animal they intended to injure."[60] This insight is all the more true when one is bringing one's family into the brambles, so to speak. The one who impetuously pursues a sweeping program of simplification will likely find himself overwhelmed by the complexity of the world and his own vain pursuits, just as a parent who tries to implement ideal practices of house organization will soon find those joyful ideas ruined by messy and time-consuming children. The gradual development of Christian simplicity requires grace and time: "The soul that rises from sin to devotion has been compared to the dawning day, which at its approach does not drive out the darkness instantaneously but only little by little."[61] Only through humility, self-awareness, and an eye toward gradual growth, all rooted in the hope of eternal life, will one help one's family grow into the simplicity of God.

CONCLUSION

Because families are interdependent with other social communities, those entrusted with care for a family must discern when and how to engage other social communities. Social engagement between families and other communities involves good and evil influences, and the influences go in both directions. Families face questions about when and how they should interact with other social communities. Infused simplicity provides a rich theological framework for analyzing these questions. Simplicity is not an avoidance of complexity but a way of life united in God's love. God is the source of this simplicity. God is One and Three. God is creator. God is unity and the source of diversity. To live a life united in God's love is to love those God loves. Within this framework of simplicity, the Catholic social tradition

58 De Sales, *Introduction to the Devout Life*, 47–48.

59 De Sales, *Letters to Persons in the World*, 184.

60 De Sales, 184.

61 De Sales, *Introduction to the Devout Life*, 48. For more on the mutual presence of infused virtue and acquired vice, see Michael S. Sherwin, OP, "Infused Virtues and the Effects of Acquired Vice: A Test Case for the Thomistic Theory of Infused Cardinal Virtues," *The Thomist* 73, no. 1 (2009): 29–52.

provides moral resources for discerning active participation in a family's social interdependence. Those entrusted with care of their families can consider the categories of cooperation, appropriation, and commitment to the common good so as to decrease cooperation with evil and increase cooperation with good.

In addition to avoiding sin and cooperating in good actions, commitment to God or to any good inevitably involves a sacrifice of other goods. Families may need to live frugally to avoid distractions and so that they can have the resources of time and money needed for what is most central in life. Families also may sacrifice goods to render greater service to God, family, and neighbor. Simplicity, however, is more than avoiding evil, pursuing good, and sacrificing for what is most central. Simplicity also involves the integration of all things in Christ. This process of integration is challenging and never complete on earth. To assist this process of integration, families can pray, offer their work to God, cultivate hearts of gratitude, and see analogies of God in the created world. By living lives united in God's love, individuals can counteract the negative influences of consumerism on their families but also reflect fruitfully on how to actively engage the social interdependence of their families. A further element of that social interdependence is a family's responsibility to engage in social ministry, to which I turn in the next chapter.

7

Navigating Family Responsibilities and Social Ministry

So far, I have reflected on the internally social character of the family, the social interdependence of the family with other social communities, and how families can navigate social engagement. In this final chapter, I reflect more explicitly on the responsibility of the family to respond to the urgent personal and structural needs of those outside of the family. Christ calls everyone to serve the poor, a call formulated in the Catholic social principle calling the faithful to give preferential care for the poor. Since families are interdependent with other social communities, the family's call to serve the poor will involve caring for them in those interdependent social communities. However, the relationship between family responsibilities and broader social needs presents two challenges. First, social needs are seemingly endless, and a family's resources are limited. How do families determine who to help and how? Second, individuals have unique responsibilities to their family members by virtue of marriage vows, conception, and adoption. How do individuals integrate and balance responsibilities to family members with responsibilities to others in need?

In moving toward an answer to these challenges, I highlight the integration and tension that can exist between giving preferential care to the poor and the order of charity that highlights preferential care to one's family. Once again, I employ the infused virtue of simplicity; that is, a way of life united in God's love as a framework for reflecting this integration and tension. In infused simplicity, one can ask how one's service contributes to or harms a way of life that is united in God's love. Focusing on one's nuclear family in a way that neglects the needs of those in one's interdependent communities will not contribute to a unity of life insofar as it prevents one from relating well with others (Luke 14:12–14). Similarly, focusing on social ministry in a way that harms one's relationship with one's spouse, children, or parents will not contribute to a unity of life insofar as one's commitment to social ministry harms one's familial relationships (1 Tim. 5:8). As Aquinas proposes, the order of charity demands that one gives the preference of love to family relationships since those relationships are permanent and multi-layered.[1] Spouses are responsible for fulfilling their marriage vows. Parents are responsible for caring for their children. Children are responsible for showing reverence to their parents and grandparents. By extension, individuals have responsibilities toward aunts, uncles, and cousins. Remembering the infused virtue of simplicity and the order of charity, I will work from the family outward to reflect on different forms of social ministry available to families and on how those forms of ministry present opportunities and risks for living the order of charity and a life united in God's love.

In reflecting on the relationship between family responsibilities and social ministry, one encounters two obstacles to achieving clarity. First, in the absence of an integrated account of family responsibilities and social ministry, one is left to choose between the two. Families can center their lives on social ministry, rejecting or downplaying family relationships in favor of the human family. Alternatively, they can center their lives on their family relationships, developing a private refuge for self-fulfillment out of which they may choose to engage in occasional and indirect forms of social assistance. Neither model is satisfactory. The former is more suited to consecrated religious whose communities focus on service to the poor or to families who have an inspiring but rare calling. The latter seems to overlook the full demands of the Gospel concerning care for the poor. I propose that a fruitful framework for analyzing a family's commitment to broader social ministry must balance family responsibilities with the challenge of the Gospel to serve the poor.

The second obstacle to clarity concerns how one discusses social ministry. The temptation is to be either too vague or too specific. Church leaders and Catholic social ethicists often make insightful but vague statements about the family's responsibility to care for the poor. Many families are sympathetic to the need to meet this challenge, but they do not know how to apply that responsibility in their lives, and so they feel guilty whenever they are unable to participate in various forms of social ministry. Meanwhile, they overlook opportunities that are suited to their lives. The other temptation in discussing social ministry is for individuals or groups to feel compelled to address one specific social issue and then to make that issue the

1 Thomas Aquinas, *Summa Theologiae*, ed. and trans. R. J. Batten, OP, vol. 34, *Charity* (New York: McGraw-Hill, 1975), II.II, q. 26, a. 8, p. 143.

standard for fulfilling the Gospel call to serve the poor. They insist that other families should participate in this form of social ministry, and judge those who do not as failing to live the Gospel. They overlook the fact that different families must serve different social needs. While some issues are a higher priority from the point of view of the whole community, an individual family may have other priorities based on their own circumstances. The needs of people throughout the world are humanly insatiable and inconceivable in their variety and quantity. Yet, however they do so, families must respond to the Gospel call to serve the poor.

In this chapter, I seek to show the various ways that family responsibilities can integrate and stand in tension with social ministry. My focus is twofold. The first emphasis, that everyone has a (theologically rooted) responsibility to serve the poor, is discussed more briefly. I make the point that since families are interdependent with other social communities, this responsibility extends to those outside one's family. The other emphasis, working from the first, is on developing categories to help families think about how they already serve the poor and how they could serve them. I develop these categories to highlight how the family is a basic social unit but also to help individuals with family commitments think about social ministry so that the choice does not seem so all or nothing. I describe the social resources that families often possess, clarifying the various unrecognized ways family responsibilities integrate with service to society. Further, by highlighting various categories of social ministry available to families, I seek to provide terminology to help them discern their social involvement. Finally, by clarifying the possibilities of integration and tension that exist with different forms of social ministry, I seek to explain the complicated relationship between family responsibilities and broader social ministry. The relationship is richer than integration or entrenched opposition. Individuals should not shame families for failing to support any particular social initiative or failing to center their lives on social ministry. Still, the Gospel calls families to something more than being private refuges for the pursuit of self-fulfillment, or even performing occasional, indirect service to the poor.

My central claim is that Christian families must commit to acting for the poor and supporting just social structures but that the framework for this commitment needs to account for family responsibilities. First, I argue theologically that commitment to act for the poor is essential to the Christian faith. Parents with children are not exempt from the call of Christ.

Using this framework, I reflect on the relationship between family commitments and social ministry. I begin by focusing on ways in which commitment to family responsibilities moves families toward broader social ministry. Then, I reflect on different ways families can serve the needs of those in the broader communities by working from the family outward. Families can expand their embodied communities inward to include those whose needs are often overlooked or outward by expanding the edges of their social spheres. Moving beyond a family's immediate communities, families can provide indirect aid to those with more urgent or life-threatening needs. Families also can engage in direct but occasional aid or direct and consistent aid that is removed from one's embodied communities. Finally, some families can focus their lives on social ministry and serve the poor by living with the poor they serve. For this final section, I use the example of families involved in the Catholic Worker movement to note the possibilities of integration and tension that exist with such a bold commitment to broader social ministry. In the conclusion, I note how family responsibilities and different family circumstances will determine an individual family's ability to serve the poor. The choice for families is between different forms of social ministry, not between engaging in such ministry or not engaging in it.

CHRISTIAN FAITH REQUIRES CARE FOR THE POOR

Many people in our society, regardless of their religious convictions, try to help the poor and needy. There are various motivations that might lead them to engage in social service. Some may do so for social approval, "so that they may be praised by others" (Matt. 6:2). Some might do so to fulfill service requirements for a youth organization (such as scouting) or an occupation. Some might engage in service projects in order to belong to a community, to share fellowship with friends who also serve. One might use the opportunity of a service project to have a personally enlightening and enriching experience, the good feeling that often comes from pursuing the good and seeing the gratitude of those one serves. The Christian faith offers unique motivations in addition to these.

Every Christian has a responsibility to care for the poor and vulnerable. This responsibility is rooted in the central tenets of Christian faith: one finds motivation for caring for the poor in the gift of creation, in the gift of God's love and redemption, in Christ's identification with the poor, and in eschatology. The foundation for caring for others is the fact that none of us made ourselves. The term *creatio ex nihilo* highlights that all good things come from God and that these good things were given to humanity as a whole.[2] In teaching his disciples why they must love their enemies, Christ appeals to the experience of nature as God's creation—"the heavenly Father makes his sun rise on the bad and the good and causes rain to fall on the just and the unjust. . . . So be perfect, just as your heavenly Father is perfect" (Matt. 5:45, 48).

Through Christ, God offers His love to each individual, and Christian faith seeks to accept and respond fittingly to that love. To respond fittingly to God and His love, one must live in His love (John 15:9). Any other response falls short. To live in His love is to "love one another as I have loved you" (John 15:12). Since God has compassion for the suffering of humanity, one cannot live in God's love while being indifferent to that suffering. Christ reveals to humanity the opportunity to live in God's love for eternity. This eternal fellowship is shared with God and all of those who live in God's love. By way of participation and anticipation, those who seek to live in God's love on earth must share God's love with everyone, a love that is concretely manifested toward the men and women that they encounter.

Christ reveals in the gift of redemption that every human person is impoverished and in need of God's assistance and that God provides His assistance even at the cost of the incarnation and crucifixion. The apostle Paul, in begging the Corinthians to send money to the poor of other churches, observes, "For you know the generous act of our Lord Jesus Christ, that though he was rich, yet for your sakes he became poor, so that by his poverty you might become rich" (2 Cor. 8:9). Christians help others in their need because Christ first helped them in their need. Freely you have received, Christ says, so freely give back (Matt. 5:8). Any gift that one offers to another to alleviate his or her poverty is something that one has first received as a gift of creation, a gift that has been given to all of humanity.

Christ models social ministry by extending God's love beyond the household and caring for the poor and vulnerable. When the poor moved toward him, "he had compassion for them, because they were like sheep without a shepherd" (Mark 6:34). He instructed his followers that by performing good deeds they could "store up treasures in heaven" (Matt. 6:20).

2 Pontifical Council for Justice and Peace, *Compendium of the Social Doctrine of the Church* (Washington, DC: United States Conference of Catholic Bishops, 2004), 171.

One cannot purchase a ticket to the Kingdom of God with money or fine things, but instead is responsible for using one's portion of creation to meet human needs. Christ urged his followers to invite to their banquets not those of high position, but those poor whom God loves (Luke 14:13), and told them that for this "you will be repaid at the resurrection of the righteous" (Luke 14:14). In the parable of Lazarus and the rich man, he provided a picture of the experience of the afterlife for the rich as being determined by how they treated the poor (Luke 16:19–31).

Jesus counted Himself among the poor, to whom belong the kingdom of heaven. He lived simply, observing during his ministry that "foxes have holes, and birds of the air have nests; but the Son of Man has nowhere to lay his head" (Matt. 8:20). He identifies with the poor most dramatically through his suffering and death and in the parable of the judgment (Matt. 25:31–46). Christ's haunting words, "Whatever you did for one of these least brothers of mine, you did for me," highlight that God became human and endured various forms of poverty. Some people helped him in his need and others did not. Christ's incarnation and identification with the poor challenges Christians to see the *imago Dei*—to see infinite value and dignity—in the face of all, but especially the poor, whose dignity is often overlooked. The connection between care for the poor and eternal fulfillment is not arbitrary. The parable describes an essential feature of the Kingdom of God—to participate in it, one must live in God's love and to live in God's love is to love everyone, including the poor and vulnerable.[3]

These theological foundations for social ministry to the poor stand in stark contrast to the framework of isolation-based conceptions of marriage and family. If family life is merely a context for seeking self-fulfillment, then care for the poor is something we can choose if we think we will find fulfillment in that work; in other words, it is one hobby among many. Hanlon Rubio writes, "Working for social justice seems to be an option for some Catholics, one possible way to live out one's faith rather than an essential part of life in an interdependent community."[4] As an occasional and optional opportunity, one might conceive of social ministry in primarily self-referential terms. Serving the poor will complete required service hours

3 Brent Waters stresses that the Church and those committed to singleness serve as an eschatological reminder for families that union with God is the ultimate good. Brent Waters, *The Family in Christian Social and Political Thought* (New York: Oxford University Press, 2007).

4 Julie Hanlon Rubio, *Family Ethics: Practices for Christians* (Washington, DC: Georgetown University Press, 2010), 198.

or will broaden my horizons and help me to be more thankful. Social ministry becomes yet another instance in which the poor and vulnerable are used as instruments for the benefit of others. The temporary needs of the poor may be met in the form of food or clothing, but their humanity has not been touched, and their long-term situation remains the same. The Christian faith instead demands that the needs of the poor be met with the face of Christ's love.[5]

The magisterial documents related to social ethics and family ethics consistently note the need for families to care for the poor outside of their basic social unit. This is an overlooked element of magisterial teaching. One sees the theme highlighted especially in the last two apostolic exhortations on the family. Pope John Paul II, in *Familiaris Consortio*, repeatedly emphasizes the need for families to go outside their own communion to care for the poor: "The Christian family is thus called upon to offer everyone a witness of generous and disinterested dedication to social matters through a 'preferential option' for the poor and disadvantaged. Therefore, advancing in its following of the Lord by special love for all the poor, it must have special concern for the hungry, the poor, the old, the sick, drug victims and those who have no family."[6]

Similarly, Pope Francis presents the need for families to care for the poor outside the family as a pervading theme. He writes,

> The family is thus an agent of pastoral activity through its explicit proclamation of the Gospel and its legacy of varied forms of witness, namely solidarity with the poor, openness to a diversity of people, the protection of creation, moral and material solidarity with other families, including those most in need, commitment to the promotion of the common good and the transformation of unjust social structures, beginning in the territory in which the family lives, through the practice of the corporal and spiritual works of mercy.[7]

Francis connects Eucharistic fellowship with care for the poor in his commentary on 1 Corinthians 11:17–34. In this passage, Saint Paul is addressing

5 John Paul II, Apostolic Exhortation *Familiaris Consortio* (November 22, 1981), 64.

6 John Paul II, 47; see also 44, 64.

7 Pope Francis, Postsynodal Apostolic Exhortation *Amoris Laetitia* (March 19, 2016), 290; Francis is quoting from Synod of Bishops, Fourteenth Extraordinary General Assembly, *Relatio Finalis* (October 24, 2015), 93. See also Francis, *Amoris Laetitia*, 181, 183, 324.

the question of table fellowship with the Corinthian Christians. He is concerned that some people are going hungry while others are eating and drinking to excess. In response, Paul challenges his readers to share the Lord's supper in remembrance of Christ, stating that one should "examine himself" before eating the bread and drinking the cup (1 Cor. 11:28). Francis interprets this call to self-examination as an invitation "to open the doors of the family to greater fellowship with the underprivileged, and in this way to receive the sacrament of that eucharistic love which makes us one body."[8]

CATEGORIES FOR SOCIAL INVOLVEMENT

The Gospel challenges Christians to serve the poor, and families are not exempt from this call. Families, however, need an articulation of social ministry that helps them to see how it can be integrated with family commitments. One needs an account of social ministry that is both challenging and fitting for those who have significant family responsibilities. As John Paul II writes, the Church must help families "to harmonize the intimacy of home life with the generous shared work of building up the church and society."[9] Recognizing that each family is unique and distinct, and that no one framework will speak to all families, I present four categories for thinking about family involvement in social ministry: social service flowing from family relationships, service to those in a family's embodied communities, caring for those with urgent needs outside of a family's embodied communities, and centering one's family on social ministry.

Social Service Flowing from Family Relationships

Family commitments often serve as a motivation for social engagement. Reflecting the social interdependence of families, family members, in pursuing a goal or an interest, discover the need for a community of support. Subsequently, individuals make contributions to the community for the sake of a family member or in remembrance of a family member. This category of social ministry presents the clearest example of how family commitments and social ministry can be united in God's love. Some central tasks for helping families think about social ministry outside of family

8 Francis, *Amoris Laetitia*, 185–86. This interpretation is strongly rooted in the original context, in which Paul was correcting the Corinthians who were, in their celebration of the Eucharist, perpetuating divisions stemming from social class.

9 John Paul II, *Familiaris Consortio*, 69.

responsibilities are to help them recognize the forms of social ministry they already engage in and the specific resources each family possesses for participation in broader service, and to show them how their service connects to their faith.

Since the family is interdependent with other social communities, families often serve broader society simply by being families. Families function as the basic social unit when they form their members in social virtues that their members then live out in their schools, work, neighborhoods, parishes, and recreational communities. Centering one's family on a way of life that is united in God's love—and thereby refraining from shallow, materialistic, consumeristic trends—strengthens peers to do the same by providing a living witness and example as well as a nexus for healthier social activities, parties, and so on. This can be as simple as inviting friends who might otherwise be watching television or going shopping to either interactive activities like game nights or sing-alongs or faith-centered events at a parish or school.

Families also can support the good actions of others when they deliberately purchase household goods from companies that implement just working conditions. Such attentiveness to economic decisions can have an impact on broader society, but perhaps more essentially, help families to recognize how their practices and purchases help or harm those who live outside of their social spheres. The temptation to overlook this help and harm is especially tempting in a globalized world where one often does not know where products are made and under what conditions. By being attentive to how their purchases support certain labor practices and attempting to cooperate in the good labor practices of others, families demonstrate that the fulfillment of family responsibilities need not undermine concern for those outside one's family.

Since families are socially interdependent, family commitments often present powerful motivations for social engagement. Often, ministry flows from concern for family members to the broader community. In some forms of social service, individuals begin supporting communities only because a family member is involved, but in serving their communities, they benefit others in the process. A mother might start a youth choir after recognizing that her child has musical interest and talent. A father might coach a youth softball team to ensure that his daughter enjoys the sport and can improve as a player. A husband might make costumes for a play in which his wife is a cast member. Even when the primary motivation for such service is to support an individual family member, insofar as the contribution genuinely improves the community, the individual engaged in such service will serve many others in the process. A youth choir needs a community of singers, and the mother wants them all to sing well so her child has a positive experience and an opportunity to grow musically. Moreover, in her careful concern to cultivate a love of music in her child, the mother develops a capacity to recognize the musical interests and abilities of other children, which she also can cultivate with care. The same is true with the softball coach and the costume-maker. Care for one's family member leads to care for the community, which includes care for those outside one's family in the community. One's primary motivation to care for one's child or wife is often accompanied by benevolent concern for others. Care for family integrates with and motivates care for those outside of one's family.

In other cases, one develops or participates in supportive communities in order to endure a family struggle. A person might launch or support a community that helps individuals grieve the death of loved ones, or participate in a community that supports the families of those who suffer from cancer, or gather with others who have endured divorce or separation. In these cases, a personal encounter in one's family can motivate support for a broader social community. Individuals who benefit from such a community then often continue to support the community even after their crisis has somewhat resolved. Someone whose daughter died can help other parents process and work through the loneliness, anger, and sadness that accompanies the death of a child. A woman whose husband has endured various struggles with cancer can help others deal with the uncertainty and vulnerability of not knowing whether the cancer cells are growing and destroying or remaining static or absent. Someone who has suffered divorce or separation can help others process guilt and anger and make the difficult steps of building a life moving forward. The experience of struggle in one's family puts one in solidarity with others who have endured similar struggles. One who overlooks the connection between family commitments and these forms of ministry will tend to miss either the social contribution of these ministries or the family commitments that motivate the service. These are also excellent examples of a kind of social need that one family is well suited to fulfill while another may not be. A family of faith that has a child with physical disabilities can be far more helpful to parents of other such children than would another well-meaning family less familiar with these challenges and concerns.

Family responsibilities also motivate individuals to engage in political advocacy that impacts family life.[10] Individuals try to build community and advocate for an allocation of resources that can help family members thrive in their communal setting. A father might advocate for neighborhood sidewalks so that his children can walk to and from school safely. A mother might advocate for maternity leave at her workplace or policies that support employees who need to leave work to care for sick children or dying parents so that she can better care for her family. An older sibling might advocate for more disabled parking spots at church so that his younger brother who uses a wheelchair can feel welcome at Mass. Those with family responsibilities know the experience of family life and understand what their family needs to thrive. By their commitment to their own families, they have the experience and the knowledge that gives them insight into and motivation to advocate for family concerns that impact the larger community.

The creation of just family policy requires the insights and efforts of those engaged with family commitments.[11] Political or communal advocacy begins with concern for family members, but then lead to change that benefits various people. Many families stand to benefit from better sidewalks near a school zone. Supportive family work policies would allow workers with family responsibilities to provide better care for their families. More disabled parking spaces would help others with disabilities and would model to the parish community the need to care for those in the body of Christ who struggle with poverty and vulnerability. Thus, political or communal advocacy speaks to the Catholic social tradition's attentiveness to social structures. Families are particularly well suited to advocate on issues that impact their particular lifestyles and concerns.[12]

The last example of social ministry that flows from family concerns is when individuals become personally invested in a social cause out of gratitude for the way the community helped a family member or because the family lacked the resources to care for a family member in her time of need. A grandmother might serve as a school board member in gratitude for the education the school provided for her children or perhaps out of concern

10 Second Vatican Council, Decree on the Apostolate of Lay People *Apostolicam Actuositatem*, 11, in *Vatican Council II: The Conciliar and Post Conciliar Documents*, ed. Austin Flannery, OP (Collegeville, MN: The Liturgical Press, 1984), 779.

11 John Paul II, *Familiaris Consortio*, 44.

12 Second Vatican Council, *Apostolicam Actuositatem*, 11, in Flannery, *Vatican Council II*, 779.

for the way the school neglected her children. A son might dedicate himself to breast cancer research after his grandmother and mother die from complications of the illness. A sister might volunteer at a drug rehab center after her brother's life is positively transformed by the center, or because the center lacked resources when her brother's life was in danger. These forms of ministry are not seeking to help a family member, but the communal support or lack thereof given to a family member motivates an individual to serve and strengthen the community.

By identifying the powerful motivation that family relationships provide, one can recognize the critical role motivation plays in social ministry. If social ministry is merely seen as a moral obligation, then individuals may struggle to find the motivation to do it or may do it in a minimal and half-hearted way. If, however, an individual can relate personally to a ministry, just as they can when the cause relates to a family member, then they will be more willing and able to participate and to do so with vigor and persistence. How often have those who instituted great social change done so because of how the cause related to a family member? One misses this powerful motivation for social ministry when one defines the family as an isolated refuge or sees the relationship between family life and social ministry as a tension of responsibilities.

Often, commitment to social service that relates to a past experience of a family member integrates with family life, helping to strengthen and unite a family. The family member who struggled might appreciate the efforts made to contribute to something so prominent in his life. Support for the relevant cause could rally other family members as well. However, while the motivation to serve comes from familial relationships, the action is not directed toward family members in these examples, possibly causing some tension with family life. If the grandmother's husband thinks the school system is a lost or unworthy cause, he may resent the time and resources his wife dedicates to the school. The son's passion for cancer research might mean that he forgoes marriage altogether. The sister volunteering at the drug rehab center might dedicate time and resources that could be used to provide ongoing support for her brother or to care for her dying parents or adolescent children.

This possibility of tension is present for the other examples as well. The choir director might favor her child with solo opportunities, abusing her position. The softball coach might deny his daughter playing time out of a concern to avoid favoritism, causing resentment that spills over into their interactions at home. The costume-maker might make a mistake on his wife's costume and thereby cause her embarrassment or a sense of being neglected. Individuals who are distraught about family loss or fixated on their own family might strain community dynamics and resources without helping others in the community. Individuals who advocate for sidewalks near a school might anger neighbors or friends who own the land on which the sidewalks would be built. Creating family-friendly workplaces might cause a sense of alienation in employees who do not have significant family responsibilities. Extra disabled parking spaces might often remain empty and inconvenience older parishioners who do not have disabled status, causing tensions between the families of persons with disabilities and others who had previously treated them warmly.

The possibility of these disruptions, however, should not overshadow the various ways in which concern for family members leads individuals to contribute to the common good, and thereby to those involved in the relevant community. In these examples, the integration between family responsibilities and broader social service is often more prominent than any tensions. The integration of family responsibilities and broader social concern in these examples becomes even more accentuated when one redeems these interactions in Christ through the Christian tradition. A life united in God's love will not remain indifferent to singers, softball players, actors, school children, coworkers, fellow parishioners, individuals with cancer, or those who struggle with addiction.

Further, individuals might contribute more fully if they have the language to understand how to do so. Motivations rooted in family relationships help individuals to see how they can serve the common good, practice subsidiarity, and understand the universal destination of goods. The Christian faith highlights the need to care not just for one's family, but for the least of the communal body's members (1 Cor. 12:22–23). The incarnation of Christ shows individuals how embodied, incarnational experience can bring understanding, elicit compassion, cultivate solidarity, manifest love, open dialogue, and establish credibility. The suffering and death of Christ reveal how suffering can open one's life to assisting others as they encounter suffering and death. It buoys up one's efforts when the attempt to help others is difficult and does not yield the immediate rewards that one would like to see.

In this first category, individuals serve the community primarily because of a concern for or experience of a family member. Insofar as the person serving can expand concern for a family member to genuine concern for the common good and others involved in the community, this service is crucial and significant. The motivation of a family member does not undermine the contribution of the service; rather, this service reflects the social strength of family commitments. Love for family members motivates concern for the communities in which family members live. Individuals should be encouraged to engage in social ministry that relates to their family relationships. If individuals who have personal experience and are highly motivated to develop a community or support a cause do nothing, then the community will be deprived of the growth that such service could provide.

Service to Those in a Family's Embodied Communities

At other times, families serve the local community not because of a need within their own family, but because they are members of the broader community, they see a need, and they act to address the need. As a basic social unit often stabilized in a concrete location, families are well situated to recognize and meet the concrete needs of those who live within their social spheres, such as extended family, coworkers, and neighbors. Such ministry reflects the fact that families are a basic social unit. Families have an internally social character, and they also are interdependent with, and therefore responsible for, the local community. While a few families have the resources, political power, or charisma to improve national or international injustices, for most families, as Wendell Berry notes, the "description of a problem as 'planetary' arouses a motivation for which, of necessity, there is no employment."[13] Berry continues:

> The question that *must* be addressed, therefore, is not how to care for the planet, but how to care for each of the planet's millions of human and natural neighborhoods, each of its millions of small pieces and parcels of land, each one of which is in some precious way different from all the others. Our understandable wish to preserve the planet must somehow be reduced to the scale of our competence—that is, to the wish to preserve all of its humble households and neighborhoods.[14]

These smaller forms of service may seem insignificant in relation to international hunger or violence, but they are crucial to those who are in need.

13 Wendell Berry, "Word and Flesh," in *Simpler Living, Compassionate Life*, ed. Michael Schut (Denver: Living the Good News, 1999), 100.

14 Berry, 101.

These embodied needs often are entrusted to the care of families. Individuals with family responsibilities may be the only people who see these needs and the only ones able to address them. In this section, I show why focusing on local, embodied communities is fitting for family service, highlight ways in which families are specifically suited to service that is embodied in a community, and describe other service that families should provide out of a general sense of social responsibility.

Why are families specifically suited to meet local needs? Because families are socially interdependent and integrated with various local communities, and therefore with various people who have various needs, their opportunities for service are endless (even if their time is not). Hanlon Rubio notes that service "to the poor is important not just because it is commanded but because it is needed."[15] Each parent may have living parents, grandparents, siblings, or cousins. Those who work outside of the home have a community of coworkers. Students have classmates. Every family member interacts with friends. David Matzko McCarthy analyzes how families can develop neighborhood economies of gift-giving.[16] Hanlon Rubio reflects on how families have and can build community in one's parish.[17] Through these varied social connections, families, as John Paul II observes, "devote themselves to manifold social service activities, especially in favor of the poor or at any rate for the benefit of all people and situations that cannot be reached by the public authorities' welfare organization."[18] Families can see and respond to personal and social needs that no one else sees.

Often, the challenge that social ethics presents to families is not to solve world hunger but to be intentional about encountering, understanding, and addressing the needs of those within the reach of their lives. Families often fail to recognize and meet these needs. They are sympathetic to helping, but they are too busy or too deep in debt to notice or to help.[19] Meeting the needs of others is particularly challenging when families define themselves as a private refuge over and against other social communities. This ideology

15 Hanlon Rubio, *Family Ethics*, 204.

16 David Matzko McCarthy, *Sex and Love in the Home: A Theology of the Household*, 2nd ed. (London: SCM Press, 2004).

17 Hanlon Rubio, *Family Ethics*, chapter 7. Francis refers to local service as a kind of pastoral activity that begins "in the territory in which the family lives, through the practice of the corporal and spiritual works of mercy" *Amoris Laetitia*, 290.

18 John Paul II, *Familiaris Consortio*, 44.

19 Hanlon Rubio, *Family Ethics*, 198.

of social isolation manifests itself in various ways. Some families focus on providing their children with safety and resources, and they are uncompromising in their refusal to participate in social engagements that might drain resources or present even the possibility of danger (however slight) to their children. Other families socially isolate because they self-identify as religiously righteous and do not want their children tainted by the false ideas or vices of others. Similarly, other families are passionate about questions of social justice or environmentalism, but as a result are intolerant of others whom they perceive as mindlessly accepting consumer practices, unjust social structures, and unfair power dynamics. Still other families wish to socially interact, but they worry that their family is too disruptive and dysfunctional, or that they are not accepted or welcomed by the communities in which they live. In other words, while the idea of serving local needs sounds easy, this service is wrought with obstacles and challenges that families must confront and overcome. The authors of *Gaudium et Spes* articulate the challenges well: while "freedom is often crippled by extreme destitution," it can also "wither in an ivory-tower isolation brought on by overindulgence in the good things of life. It can, however, be strengthened by accepting the inevitable constraints of social life, by undertaking the manifold demands of human fellowship, and by service to the community at large."[20]

Families often possess the resources and strengths necessary to meet local needs. As John Paul II notes, "The social contribution of the family has an original character of its own, one that should be given greater recognition and more decisive encouragement, especially as the children grow up, and actually involving all its members as much as possible."[21] One strength of a family is its social interdependence—a family consists of various members who each have their own social networks. Collectively, families encounter various communities, people, and needs. By being attentive to people, families can recognize, understand, and respond to those diverse needs.

In addition, many families possess a stability that enables them to provide hospitality and to exercise stewardship of their resources. Familial stability is rooted in the permanence of relationships established by marriage, conception, and adoption. The quality of family stability, however, depends

20 Pastoral Constitution on the Church in the Modern World *Gaudium et Spes*, 31, in *Vatican Council II: The Conciliar and Post Conciliar Documents*, ed. Austin Flannery, rev. ed. (Collegeville, MN: Liturgical Press, 1975), 931.

21 John Paul II, *Familiaris Consortio*, 44.

on the character of familial relationships and circumstances. Not all families possess stability—some families move from location to location for employment and others endure divorce and separation. While stability varies from family to family, the presence or absence of stability is more than a consumer choice. Generally, the welfare of spouses and the formation of children benefit from such stability, and the surrounding community certainly does. When the family is a communion of persons, it can sustain geographical moves, although at sometimes significant cost to its involvement in a wider community. Divorce and separation, by contrast, often harm children directly, as well as being a great challenge for involvement in the wider community. One sees the significance of stability when parents seek to settle down as their kids approach school age.

This gift of stability so crucial for the internal character of family life also strengthens families for serving the needs of local communities. The authors of *Gaudium et Spes* argue that the family receives stability "from the human act by which the partners mutually surrender themselves to each other" but that after marriage is established, "for the good of the partners, of the children, and of society this sacred bond no longer depends on human decision alone."[22] Here, the council notes that familial stability is proper to the family as a good for spouses and children, but also that it is a good for society. Individuals secure in the love and support of their spouse or parents can more easily cultivate relationships and thereby genuinely understand the needs of friends and neighbors, including those friends and neighbors suffering through family instability.

One central service flowing from familial stability is the practice of hospitality. Hospitality has a prominent place in the Christian tradition. In ancient Greco-Roman and Jewish contexts, hosts typically provided food, sometimes lodging, water to wash, protection from enemies, and an escort out of town.[23] One sees this pattern when Abraham shows hospitality to the Lord who has taken on the appearance of three men (Gen. 18:1–8). The Israelites understood that God wanted them to be hospitable to foreigners after they had been vulnerable foreigners in Egypt and God had cared for them (Deut. 10:17–19). Jesus extends this tradition of hospitality. He sends out the Twelve to preach and heal, encouraging them to stay with someone

22 Second Vatican Council, *Gaudium et Spes*, 48, in Flannery, *Vatican Council II*, 950.

23 Andrew E. Arterbury, *Entertaining Angels: Early Christian Hospitality in Its Mediterranean Setting* (Sheffield, UK: Sheffield Phoenix Press, 2005), 6.

who extends hospitality, but if no one welcomes them, to shake off the dust from their feet and leave the town (Matt. 10:5–15; Mark 6:7–13; Luke 9:1–6). Jesus proposes that eternal judgment will in part depend on how individuals welcome the stranger (Matt. 25:35, 43). Following this biblical witness, Saint Benedict stresses hospitality in his rule: "All guests who present themselves are to be welcomed as Christ."[24] This monastic hospitality serves as a refuge for many and will enable many of the great medieval pilgrimages.[25] This tradition of Christian hospitality continues today as Catholic leaders stress the need to show hospitality to refugees; Catholic charities are among those most active in making this hospitality possible.

With advances in transportation, welcoming a stranger who is passing through one's land has, in some ways become less crucial. Today, hospitality commonly refers to a broader set of practices, including hosting a party or a meal or even operating an industry of paid workers who provide and serve meals or welcome guests to hotels. Jessica Wrobleski, in her work *The Limits of Hospitality*, defines hospitality as "*a host's willing and gracious reception of a guest into a safe and friendly space*."[26] This broader use of the term retains resonances with the ancient antecedents. Those showing hospitality continue to provide food, rest, and lodging and continue to welcome individuals into new spaces. The guest, however, is rarely passing through to another location. They are guests visiting and then returning home, or they have been uprooted and need help starting anew.

Church documents related to the family frequently highlight the ability and responsibility of families to provide hospitality. The Second Vatican Council's Decree on the Apostolate of Lay People *Apostolicam Actuositatem* argues that the family serves as the primary cell of society when it "offers active hospitality."[27] John Paul II and Francis each dedicate a paragraph on the topic in their respective apostolic exhortations on the family. John Paul II writes, "In a special way the Christian family is called upon to listen to the apostle's recommendation. 'Practice hospitality,' and therefore, imitating Christ's example and sharing in his love, welcome the brother or sister in

24 Saint Benedict, *The Rule of Saint Benedict in English*, ed. Timothy Fry, OSB (Collegeville, MN: The Liturgical Press, 1981), 53.

25 William Cavanaugh, "Migrant, Tourist, Pilgrim, Monk: Mobility and Identity in a Global Age," *Theological Studies* 69, no. 2 (2008): 353–54.

26 Jessica Wrobleski, *The Limits of Hospitality* (Collegeville, MN: Liturgical Press, 2012), 12, italics in original.

27 Second Vatican Council, *Apostolicam Actuositatem*, 11, in Flannery, *Vatican Council II*, 779.

need."[28] In the second to last paragraph of *Amoris Laetitia*, Francis writes, "Led by the Spirit, the family circle is not only open to life by generating it within itself, but also by going forth and spreading life by caring for others and seeking their happiness. This openness finds particular expression in hospitality, which the word of God eloquently encourages: 'Do not neglect to show hospitality to strangers, for thereby some have entertained angels unawares' (Heb 13:2)."[29]

A home community and space that allows spouses and children to test boundaries, to thrive, and to experience love, forgiveness, and joy provides a great gift to family members that can be shared with others. Many families have created a stable community of love that can and ought to welcome and nourish others. Hanlon Rubio writes,

> Not everyone is called or able to live in a poor neighborhood, but surely all Christian families are called to think about how their table can be a place that is welcoming to people in need, whether they welcome a child who is going through a rough time with parents, a recently divorced friend, or a reclusive neighbor. Hospitality is an eating practice that can powerfully shape children's and adults' sense of what it means to be Christian, especially if hospitality is embraced as an opportunity to extend the table to those in need.[30]

Family hospitality can be as small as hosting a friend for dinner or allowing a neighbor's child to stay at one's home for a few minutes after school before her mother gets home from work. In a society suffering from an epidemic of loneliness, these small gestures can in fact be immensely life-giving. Or, hospitality can be something more resource-intensive, like housing and caring for pregnant mothers in need, providing foster care, hosting a foreign exchange student, or even sheltering a refugee family trying to get on their feet. The Catholic Worker movement, which I discuss later in this chapter, has a tradition of having a "Christ room" in one's home reserved at all times for needy guests.[31]

28 John Paul II, *Familiaris Consortio*, 44. The internal quotation cites to Romans 12:13. This material is followed by a reference to Matthew 10:42.

29 Francis, *Amoris Laetitia*, 324.

30 Hanlon Rubio, *Family Ethics*, 146.

31 Dan McKanan, *The Catholic Worker after Dorothy: Practicing the Works of Mercy in a New Generation* (Collegeville, MN: Liturgical Press, 2008), 160–62.

While the stability of family life specifically enables families to provide hospitality, families must prudently discern the limits of their hospitality. Jessica Wrobleski notes that all social ministry, including hospitality, requires that one reflects on boundaries.[32] She focuses on how boundaries can protect the possibility of hospitality: "When boundaries are formed by fear, prejudice, callousness, or anger, they easily become impenetrable walls of hostility rather than limits of hospitality. Even the 'no' of limits must be in some way informed by a 'yes'—a spirit of hospitality—that affirms the other and sets limits in a way that minimizes hostility and violence when and however possible."[33] If hospitality is welcoming someone into a safe space, then limits must be placed on who can be welcomed and how so that the home can remain a safe space for family members and guests. Families must reflect on how guests would integrate into the household community, dangers they might present, assistance they might provide, the current ability of the family to offer a generous and caring welcome, how long the guests will stay, and whether they will have separate or personal space. Families must hold in tension their limits with Christ's call to welcome the least of His brothers and sisters. Even Catholic Worker houses of hospitality ask disruptive residents to leave or separate them from others so that the community can continue to provide hospitality for other guests.

In addition to possessing the resource of stability, families often are well suited to help others who need help with household tasks. Someone who has a lawn mower and the capacity to mow lawns could mow the lawn for an elderly neighbor or for a coworker who will be out of town for a few weeks. Someone might lend tools to a neighbor or help a friend build or repair their house. These same household skills and resources might dispose individuals to serve local organizations like Habitat for Humanity. They can donate furniture when they are downsizing during the empty nest phase or share the home-building skills they have developed while caring for their homes. Individuals also could help others with grocery shopping or cooking or cleaning. Because they manage a house, families possess resources and skills to help others with household tasks.

Other skills relate more specifically to family relationships. Families often are best positioned to help other families. Families might have children's clothes or toys to share with a friend, a cousin, or a neighbor. Parents

32 Wrobleski, *The Limits of Hospitality*, xii.

33 Wrobleski, xii.

or older siblings might provide childcare for other families as needed. Parents can discuss with other parents how they navigate parenting struggles or share knowledge about community events and resources. Since they have shared experiences and needs, they know how to help and assist one another. Hanlon Rubio notes that parishes can help facilitate this inter-family service: "Instead of offering activities that focus solely on entertainment, parishes might encourage parishioners to share tools and skills, start babysitting or food co-ops, plant community gardens, exchange used clothing, care for the sick or elderly in their neighborhoods, or mentor young married couples. These sorts of activities encourage interdependence, simple living, and questioning of middle-class norms.[34] Those with family responsibilities often have the skills, resources, and interests to help other families.

Beyond normal aid that families can provide, they also can assist those in need, especially when the need manifests the lack or breakdown of family relationships. John Paul II writes, "The apostolate of the family will also become wider through works of spiritual and material charity toward other families, especially those most in need of help and support, toward the poor, the sick, the old, the disabled, orphans, widows, spouses that have been abandoned, unmarried mothers and mothers-to-be in difficult situations who are tempted to have recourse to abortion, and so on."[35] In the internal dimensions of a family, members care for the sick, the old, and the disabled. This care can extend to those who have physical, social, and economic needs but lack a stable network of support to address those needs. This care can also, as mentioned above in the context of hospitality, include relieving these individuals' loneliness and providing an experience for them of stable and warm loving relationships at a time when they have experienced deficits or disappointments in their own intimate connections.

In other cases, families can provide ministry that is not specific to the family, but appropriate to the call that all Christians receive to serve. *Apostolicam Actuositatem* notes that families can help run schools.[36] One could add that families can help promote justice and just structures in various locations. Due to the robust social interdependence of families with other

34 Hanlon Rubio, *Family Ethics*, 203.

35 John Paul II, *Familiaris Consortio*, 71.

36 Second Vatican Council, *Apostolicam Actuositatem*, 11, in Flannery, *Vatican Council II*, 779.

social communities, families witness the operations of various just and unjust structures that politicians, social workers, and church leaders do not see. Families can promote justice in the workplace, in neighborhoods, or in a recreational organization. In these and other locations, family members can be *scouts* identifying needs and injustices, *ambassadors* of God's love, and *missionaries* who serve and evangelize.

As members of the laity, spouses and parents should also support politically prudent politicians and just legislation. Insofar as they do not hold formal positions in the Church, laity can advocate for political causes without some of the risks present when those with formal ecclesial positions support partisan causes. Spouses and parents can contribute to political discourse helping to formulate a language and understanding of the common good. They can support or even formulate legislation on issues related to their competence. They can inform themselves about local ballot initiatives or the platforms of city and county political candidates. They can even run for political office.

In serving those within one's embodied communities, families can help those whose needs and wants would otherwise remain hidden and neglected. One can play a game with one's annoying younger brother, say hello to the coworker who seems to talk more to himself than others, or meet the neighbor who seems to wear a permanent frown. One also can expand outward, extending the edges of one's social spheres by reaching out to those who are not seen in one's daily activities without going out of the way, such as visiting a lonely grandparent or inviting over a socially awkward cousin. One can expand from watching out for neighborhood kids and welcoming new neighbors to serving as a legal advocate for local children who suffer from domestic abuse or showing hospitality to refugees settling in a neighboring city. One can expand from supporting coworkers who have experienced a personal crisis, an injury, or an illness to providing mentoring and job training to those who are unemployed. One can expand from building community in one's parish with those who share a similar social status, cultural background, and ecclesial sympathies to finding ways to get to know others in the parish community. For example, if one was born and raised in a parish community, one could expand from one's family and high school friends to teaching ESL or supporting the liturgies and festivals of the parish immigrant community. When expanding out from one's social communities, one's family needs to grow but need not be uprooted and replanted.

Service to Those with Greater Needs Outside of One's Embodied Communities

As we move from social ministry motivated by family commitments to ministry expanding to the local community, we see more tension between family responsibilities and social ministry. And, as we move outside of our embodied communities, social ministry is less connected to personal relationships, including family relationships. Disembodied ministry presents some unique opportunities and risks. The opportunity of ministry outside one's embodied communities is that one might encounter individuals with more urgent needs who would go without absent intervention. These unique struggles in turn can pose challenges to a person's reframing of hardships or priorities. The risk is that since one does not live in the community, one might misunderstand the situation and the needs. A person can also lack a relationship with those being helped. One does not know their journey, their skills and assets, and their obstacles. To overcome such dangers, one needs to invest even more time and resources to understand the far-off situation well enough to develop relationships and genuinely help, but this can draw time and attention away from the local community.

When one's family members have urgent needs, discernment about where to focus social service is easy. Insofar as one has a responsibility for one's family and direct contact with one's family, one bears a unique responsibility to serve those needs. The discernment becomes more difficult when the needs of those outside one's embodied communities are greater or even life-threatening. One way to help the more urgent needs of those outside one's social spheres is to financially support groups or individuals who are meeting the more urgent needs of others. This indirect service requires a trusting relationship with the organization or individual being supported. One trusts that one's donation is being used to genuinely help others. One might, for example, make a financial donation to Catholic Relief Services, inspired by their model of hiring individuals who were born and raised in the communities they seek to help. One might donate clothes or food to the St. Vincent de Paul Society, trusting that they will locate those in most need and accurately assess and address their needs. One might donate furniture to Habitat for Humanity for use in new or renovated homes. In these cases, the individual or organization being supported provides a great service by identifying needs in one location and asking those with resources in another location to help those in need. This systematic organization of charity is often required to meet urgent needs and has a long history in the Church going back to the work of Paul (2 Cor. 8:7–15).

When one provides financial support in indirect support of the poor, one is trusting in an intermediary, and sometimes, there can be legitimate questions about whether even a charitable endeavor built on goodwill actually uses resources efficiently and respectfully serves the recipients of the aid. When those involved in systematic charity attempt to both live with the poor and with those possessing resources, they may struggle to understand each community. One challenge for this indirect assistance is that the supporting individuals often struggle to sustain their motivation for this service. Even if one trusts the intermediary, the lack of contact or understanding of the genuine need means that individuals often donate their unwanted things or participate in occasional food or clothing drives, but their commitment is occasional and conditional.

Some organizations attempt to form a closer connection between those providing indirect aid and those in need. Instead of donating used furniture, one could help build a home with Habitat for Humanity. One may not meet the individual or family that will live in the house or understand their need for a house, but this brings the person serving others closer to the issue. One does not just drop off unwanted furniture and move on with one's life, but rather spends time and shares specific skills to help others. Similarly, one can buy Christmas gifts identified by needy families or advocate for state and national social services or justice in the workplace. In each of these cases, one has some understanding of the human need and is making efforts to help, even though one is not directly involved in meeting the person or addressing a concrete need. One works with some knowledge of the situation but through an intermediary. Such forms of service may be appealing to families who would like to help but are not prepared to uproot from their embodied communities and immerse themselves in the lives of those with needs more urgent than their family's needs. That distance, however, means having to trust in an intermediary and lacking a concrete relationship with the people one seeks to help. Some of these ministries allow family members to serve together; others require an individual to act separately from his family.

Other forms of ministry available to families involve direct forms of aid in which one has some contact with those being helped, but this contact takes place outside one's home and daily life. This direct and removed form of service may be occasional or more consistent. Direct and occasional service could include a daughter serving food to the hungry once a year with her youth group, a father volunteering at a homeless shelter two nights a year, a teenage son going on a regional mission trip with his confirmation class, an uncle and his niece picking up trash off the road with the uncle's workplace, or providing a metro pass, food, or hand warmers for the homeless and hungry that one encounters while taking public transportation. The occasional nature of the service gives individuals flexibility to shift toward family responsibilities when necessary. These forms of service are direct aid to those in need but insofar as they are occasional, the person engaged in the service often does not have a chance to develop a relationship with those being helped.

Other forms of social ministry may be direct and more consistent. A mother might serve food on a weekly basis to the hungry, or a father might volunteer two nights a month at a homeless shelter. The youth group might visit a nursing home on a weekly basis. A family might provide food for the same homeless woman every time they go to the library. A mother and her newborn might visit needy families on behalf of St. Vincent de Paul to develop a relationship with a family in need and thereby help St. Vincent de Paul assess and address their concrete needs. An eighth-grade boy might meet weekly with a second grader who is struggling with school and life through a school mentoring program. A family might provide foster care or show hospitality to refugees seeking to establish themselves in the local community. A father might direct a parish social ministry program or the local Catholic Charities. Some Catholic Worker families fit into this category; when they get married and have kids, they move out of the house of hospitality but live nearby to provide consistent help and support to the community.

These more consistent forms of service provide an opportunity to establish concrete relationships with those one seeks to help. This service also provides some opportunities for integration with family responsibilities. Consistent service can provide crucial witness and formation to one's family that one should care for those in urgent need. If other family members participate in these services, the work can raise important conversations over the dinner table and cultivate gratitude and a willingness to live more simply. Consistent commitment to these ministries, however, also can stand in tension with family responsibilities. If one is committed to serve in a specific way at a specific time, one might have less flexibility for meeting family responsibilities. One might have to miss a child's music concert or basketball game from time to time. If one dedicates free time to social ministry, then one has less time to read, play, pray with children, complete household tasks, or talk to one's spouse about his or her day. Integration with family responsibilities is possible in these more consistent forms of service but individuals and families will need to be intentional about attaining that integration.

Centering One's Family on Social Ministry

The Gospel and the Catholic social tradition highlight that care for the poor is essential to Christian faith and therefore to family life. Some families have responded to the needs of the poor in bold ways, doing missionary work, directing social ministry programs, or generously and tirelessly serving local needs as they emerge. To highlight the possibilities and struggles of families who commit in dedicated or dramatic ways to care for the poor, I turn to the example of Dorothy Day and families involved in the Catholic Worker movement. Family involvement in the Catholic Worker movement provides an insightful case study for reflecting on the inspiring witness that families can provide and also on the tension that can exist between family responsibilities and the Christian call to serve the poor.

The Catholic Worker movement was cofounded by Peter Maurin and Dorothy Day in the United States in the early 1930s. They began with a house of hospitality in which volunteers and homeless men and women would share a house together. The houses of hospitality were and continue to be a location for practicing the works of mercy, especially sheltering the homeless and feeding the hungry. Beyond these works of mercy, some distinctive elements of the houses of hospitality are also roundtable discussions of social questions and ideas, voluntary poverty, and opportunities for prayer. Maurin and Day provided a profound witness of meeting the needs of those before them, and their work has inspired houses of hospitality throughout the world.

My focus in what follows is to analyze the experiences of those who have attempted to live in houses of hospitality or who have been intimately involved in houses of hospitality while raising young children. The consensus among those who have attempted to live in houses of hospitality while raising a family seems to be that generally Catholic Worker volunteers need to substantially alter their service when they marry and have children and that having a family in a house of hospitality is a unique calling that ought to be discerned carefully. In addressing this tension between family responsibilities and houses of hospitality, the idea is not to challenge the inspirational work done in houses of hospitality, but to reflect on the tension that can exist between family responsibilities and uniting one's life around social ministry.

Dorothy Day was a single mother and cofounder of the Catholic Worker movement. She lived in houses of hospitality that cared for the homeless, and she often traveled to raise necessary funds, protest injustice, and support other Catholic Worker communities. Many families have founded or participated in Catholic Worker houses of hospitality. These families have responded to the Gospel's call to care for the poor by sheltering the homeless and performing the works of mercy. Many of these families also report tension between family responsibilities and the crucial ministry done by Catholic Worker houses.

Dorothy Day and her daughter Tamar do not often speak about being a family in a Catholic Worker house, but one can learn about their relationship from interviews and Dorothy's diary. Tamar was seven when Dorothy and Peter Maurin started the Catholic Worker paper and began providing hospitality to the homeless. In addition to her commitment to running houses of hospitality and editing the Catholic Worker, Dorothy traveled often to give talks that would raise funds for their work. When Dorothy traveled, sometimes Tamar would travel with her but often Tamar would remain with other individuals or families involved in the Catholic Worker house. In an interview with Rosalie G. Riegle, Tamar stated,

> It was wonderful to grow up [at the Catholic Worker]. So much enthusiasm! And everybody had found something they really wanted to do, so it was just so . . . hopeful. I loved the spirit of that first ten years. But Dorothy would be away a lot, and I had a hard time with that. I even nick-named her "Be-going." I wanted Dorothy so bad! When she came home, she lit up my room, she lit up my life.
>
> When I went away to boarding school, I always wanted to be home, but at the same time it wasn't good for me there. There were just so many things that were precious to me about Dorothy.[37]

Both Tamar and Dorothy seemed to have felt deeply the tension between the Catholic Worker and their relationship and responsibilities to one another as mother and daughter.[38] Since Dorothy was busy, and the houses

37 Rosalie G. Riegle, *Dorothy Day: Portraits by Those Who Knew Her* (Maryknoll, NY: Orbis Books, 2003), 109.

38 Kate Hennessy, one of Dorothy's granddaughters, details the history of Dorothy's relationship with Tamar in *Dorothy Day: The World Will Be Saved by Beauty* (New York: Scribner, 2017).

of hospitality were not an ideal location for a young girl, Tamar attended various boarding schools starting at the age of eight.[39] When she stayed at the house of hospitality, she would hide gifts that she received from family members under her bed but guests at the house of hospitality would inevitably steal or sell them. Patricia Ann Bryon, who lived at Maryhouse with her young daughter in the seventies, reports that Dorothy told her "to treasure the time I spent with [Patricia's daughter] Jennifer, that if she had to live her life over again, the only thing she would change would be the amount of time she devoted to her daughter."[40]

Many Catholic Worker families feel this tension between family responsibilities and the Gospel call to serve the poor. Dan McKanan relays the crisis of a commune of farming families in Easton, Pennsylvania, the first such commune supported by the New York Catholic Worker community. McKanan notes that the crisis concerned, among other issues, whether resources from the Catholic Worker community should be distributed to families living on the farm. The families argued that they should have the first claim on all the farm's resources. Dorothy, however, saw the communes as a place of retreat for the urban poor and Catholic Workers. McKanan writes, "Day knew, far better than the Easton families, that contributions to the Worker came primarily from people who wanted to help the poor, and she felt responsible for honoring those intentions. Since it cost more to maintain a family than a single volunteer, a predominance of families on the farm threatened the apostolate to the poor."[41]

Day writes that "the majority of young couples who have met through the Worker 'have recognized that in taking a wife and bringing forth children their status in the lay apostolate has changed, that their first obligation has to be to take care of their own and not to ask others to support them.'"[42] Some families modified their involvement with Catholic Worker. Joseph Zarrella, an early volunteer with Day, attempted to start a satellite Catholic Worker house in Tell City, Indiana with his wife, Mary Alice. This house did not come to fruition, but Joseph did help organize furniture workers. Later in life, Joseph would say,

39 Riegle, *Dorothy Day*, 109

40 Riegle, 109.

41 McKanan, *The Catholic Worker after Dorothy*, 154.

42 McKanan, 155.

> You know, I have never considered us as leaving the Catholic Worker when we got married and moved to Tell City. It never rubs off. If you've ever been under Miss Day's influence, you can't shake it. You're haunted. And you have a guilt complex, in many senses, if you don't do something about a situation. So you're always getting in trouble because when issues come up, you've got to take a stand. And it's usually a minority stand, so you rub your friends the wrong way. But after a while, if you do it right, you learn from people and you earn people's respect.
>
> I think the biggest thing you learn from Dorothy is personal responsibility. Personal responsibility and spirituality. One without the other doesn't go. You know, people always think about her in terms of the social issues, but she was a deeply spiritual person. That's what made her so strong on the social issues.[43]

Many Catholic Worker families, like the Zarrellas, adjusted their involvement with the Catholic Worker movement after marriage and children. Some moved to houses or apartments near houses of hospitality, shifting from being full-time Catholic workers to supportive members, while providing occasional hospitality to specific individuals.

In some instances, the parents' responsibility for their children's safety required that they move away from or shift the work of a house of hospitality. Bill Gauchat helped found Blessed Martin House in Cleveland. When Bill married Dorothy Schmitt, they moved to a Catholic Worker farmhouse in Avon, Ohio. They would provide hospitality on the farm, and Bill continued to commute to the urban hospitality house. After a homeless man briefly kidnapped one of their children, Dorothy Gauchat decided she did not want men staying at the farmhouse while her children were living there.[44] The Gauchats later found an inspiring ministry more fitting to their family responsibilities. They established Our Lady of the Wayside, a nonprofit agency providing foster care for children with disabilities.[45]

In an interview, Marcia Timmel offers a compelling argument for family involvement in Catholic Worker houses. While acknowledging that living in a house of hospitality presented risks to her children, she argues that children encounter similar dangers at school or taking walks in a large city. She notes that many of the homeless today are children and families, making

43 Riegle, *Dorothy Day*, 113–14.

44 McKanan, *The Catholic Worker after Dorothy*, 155.

45 McKanan, 155.

family involvement specifically necessary. She also argues that she did not want to raise her children to be self-absorbed and removed from injustice and hardship. Two years later, however, her family decided to move away from the Worker House she was serving after her children were nearly harmed in a neighborhood gunfight.[46]

Similarly, following the birth of his daughter Rozella, Dennis Appel wrote in the Beatitude House newsletter that he thought giving his best to his daughter meant continuing to live in the Catholic Worker house in Guadalupe, California. Thirteen years later, he writes that his family moved into a separate house where they could continue to be involved in the Catholic Worker house. They note that in this somewhat removed position, while their two children have struggled with being different from their peers, they seem to be thriving and navigating their differences well.[47]

Other Catholic Workers remained intimately involved in houses of hospitality even as they were sustaining and adding on new family responsibilities. Mark and Louise Zwick ran multiple Catholic Worker houses while raising their children. While the Zwick children lived in a space separate from the houses of hospitality when they were young, Mark and Louise were engaged in the everyday work of Casa Juan Diego. As they acknowledge in their book, *Mercy Without Borders*, "It hasn't always been easy to balance family life with the busy Catholic Worker."[48] They note that Mark needed to leave the Catholic Worker house in the afternoons to cook dinner for the children. The Zwicks do not share details about their family difficulties in their books; instead, they provide various examples of how their children and grandchildren have helped with their houses of hospitality.[49]

Those families who have been more directly involved with housing the homeless and caring for their guests are quick to warn other families that such work should reflect a unique calling and is not for everyone.[50] They do not sugarcoat the struggles involved, even while they find their work to be intimately connected to the Gospel and service to the Kingdom of God.

46 Rosalie Riegle Troester, ed., *Voices from the Catholic Worker* (Philadelphia: Temple University Press, 1993), 291–93.

47 Gary Cavalier, ed., *Family Life in the Catholic Worker Movement* (Las Vegas: Las Vegas Catholic Worker, 2012), 6–18.

48 Mark Zwick and Louise Zwick, *Mercy without Borders: The Catholic Worker and Immigration* (New York: Paulist Press, 2010), 248.

49 Zwick and Zwick, 248–49.

50 McKanan, *The Catholic Worker after Dorothy*, 166, 174.

Despite these warnings, families have played an increasingly prominent role in the Catholic Worker houses. While many Catholic Worker houses have struggled to maintain stability as individual volunteers moved in and out, houses founded by a family or group of families have tended to be more stable.[51] Ironically, like the first Christians, the task of concretely living out the Gospel's demands to see everyone as part of God's family has relied heavily on the stability and resources provided by specific households.

One can learn a good deal about the tension between family responsibilities and social ministry in the lives and testimony of families who have been intimately involved in the Catholic Worker movement. Like other families who center their family life on social ministry, one sees in the Catholic Worker movement a clear opportunity for families to live the Catholic social principles and the works of mercy, to counteract the pervading influence of consumerism, and to live a life united in love of God and love of neighbor. These practices help one's family to focus on what is ultimately important and thereby integrate well with the goals of a rich family life. By embracing voluntary poverty and sharing meals and living spaces with those they seek to help, Catholic Worker families are helping those who live in their embodied communities. This allows them to develop relationships with the homeless and the hungry and to serve their needs accordingly.

Families have been involved in Catholic Worker houses at different levels. Those who have lived in houses of hospitality or united their lives around service in a house of hospitality often report tension between family responsibilities and social ministry, with some families feeling guilty that they are not more involved in the houses of hospitality, others feeling guilty that they are not more present to their families, and many wishing they could be more present to both. Those families that are more involved in the Catholic Worker movement tend to experience more tension between their social ministry and their family relationships than those who only provide support or assistance. One sees the tension especially for those families who live in houses of hospitality or those who have gone to jail for protesting violence. Spouses and children miss the presence of their spouse or parent. Many Catholic Worker parents also note how their children are anxious about maintaining peer relationships since their life at the Catholic Worker house and their family's commitment to voluntary poverty is so distinct from their peers. Sometimes, family members have safety concerns and

51 McKanan, 174–75.

stress related to forms of hospitality that place them in close contact with strangers. Individuals have a finite amount of time, energy, and material resources. Full-time dedication to a house of hospitality can prevent individuals from fulfilling family responsibilities. Some spouses directly involved in the Catholic Worker movement have divorced and relationships between parents and children have been strained by their service to the homeless and the hungry. In the early years, Day encouraged individuals who were getting married to focus on their family responsibilities. Then, large families attempted to gather and form communities in farming communes. More recently, smaller families direct or assist houses of hospitality, typically in midsized cities.[52] Even those who remain intimately involved and report that their social ministry has enhanced their family life are quick to note that families should not enter such ministry lightly but only after prayer and reflection on the personal and familial costs involved.

CONCLUSION: DISCERNING FAMILIAL INVOLVEMENT IN CARE FOR THE POOR

As a basic social unit, the family is internally social and socially interdependent. These two social dimensions can stand in tension. In the order of charity, individuals have unique responsibilities to their family members due to the stable character of those relationships rooted in marriage vows, conception, and adoption. Still, Christ calls everyone to care for the poor. Since families are socially interdependent, this call to care for the poor extends to the family. The question is how to serve, not whether. Different families in different contexts will engage in care for the poor in different ways depending on their circumstances and resources. In this chapter, I have identified and described four different types of social ministry in which families can engage and reflected on how those ministries can contribute to a way of life united in God's love, a way of life that includes attentiveness to family responsibilities.

First, I highlighted social ministry that flows from family relationships. Often, individuals are motivated to build community structures that support others because of the interest, need, or experience of a family member. Since this form of ministry responds to the needs of a family member, it presents the easiest form of integration with family responsibilities. Insofar as one acts with genuine concern for the needs of others in the community,

52 McKanan, 173.

one serves the community and one's family at the same time. The ministry becomes a way of spending time with or coming to know one's family member but also a way of building community and recognizing and serving the needs of others, especially those who may lack family support.

A second form of ministry is family service to those who live in their embodied communities. Often, each family member has complex relationships with various individuals and communities. In those embodied communities, families are uniquely positioned to recognize and serve specific needs. Parents who have the tools and skills to run a household and raise children can support others in the community who are struggling with similar responsibilities. Family stability, so crucial for the flourishing of spousal love and the development of children, is also a gift to be shared with others in hospitality. These service opportunities provide a way of uniting one's service with one's commitment to family members since both require a similar set of skills and resources.

Third, families can engage in indirect or direct aid to those with more urgent needs who live outside of their embodied communities. Such ministry can integrate with family responsibilities if families discern together how they will support or serve in these capacities. Further, such ministry, while directed to the needs of others, can have the further benefit of putting a family's struggles and ambitions into perspective. However, the movement away from a family's embodied community also presents risks. The aid provided is either indirect and lacking in personal contact or family members are investing significant time and energy away from the family in order to understand and respond to the relevant urgent needs. While the mistake of serving one's family to the neglect of others is the more common risk to charity, when the investment of time and resources in service outside of one's embodied community undermines the performance of family responsibilities, such service harms the order and unity of charity.

Finally, families can unite their lives around social ministry. Families, for example, could engage in missionary work or initiate and run social programs. I examined the inspiring and challenging work of families involved in Catholic Worker houses of hospitality. While the houses of hospitality provide a crucial ministry to those who are homeless, hungry, and lonely, and a lifestyle that communicates to children what is essential in life, most families who have been involved in houses of hospitality have observed that when volunteers marry or have children, their role in the houses of hospitality needs to change substantially. In the order of charity, they have responsibilities toward their spouses and children, and they need to create boundaries of safety, especially for young children.

How do families discern the opportunities for service in which they should engage? How should they discern those that would be harmful to meeting their family responsibilities? Since every family is unique and distinct, there is not a single answer to either question. I propose that a preferential care for the poor, the infused virtue of simplicity, and the order of charity provide some clarity. In the order of charity, individuals have unique responsibilities to their families but the preferential care for the poor and the social interdependence of families highlights the responsibility individuals have to serve those outside of their families. One can ask if one's commitment to family members or service to those beyond one's family is conducive to a way of life that is united in God's love. Do one's family commitments cause one to neglect or do harm to others in one's embodied communities or beyond one's embodied communities? Does one's service lead to neglect of or prevent one from meeting family responsibilities?

In moving from general principles to application, one can benefit from reflecting on intention, family needs, and family dialogue. Assuming that the action of social ministry is good in its object and circumstances, one also needs to consider the intention behind the actions. In social ministry, the one serving should seek to address the needs of another; applying this simple observation can help to reduce tension between family responsibilities and social ministry. In social ministry, individuals should not use those in need as a mere means for families to feel good about themselves, or as a chance to gain broader experiences and perspectives. Neither should social ministry serve as a mere means to escape from difficult family situations. The primary intention in serving the poor should be to meet the needs of the person one seeks to serve.

Among the four forms of social ministry that I have highlighted, the first two tend more easily toward an intentional integration of family responsibilities and a commitment to the poor. The social ministry flows from family needs or expands from a family's embodied experiences. Still, even with these forms of ministry, families can be more or less intentional about finding opportunities to serve and about linking their service to family responsibilities. In the last two forms of social ministry, individuals will need to be more active and intentional about attaining integration with family responsibilities since the ministry is more removed or more demanding of time and resources.

Since families are always growing and developing, individuals will also need to consider family needs in their discernment of social ministry. Some individuals are so overwhelmed with family responsibilities that they struggle to help those outside of their family. Family needs can limit one's ability to engage in a broader ministry to the poor. A woman whose husband has just suffered a stroke that has limited his mental capacity and his ability to move the left side of his body need not volunteer at the homeless shelter. A man whose wife cares for three small children and suffers from postpartum depression need not leave home for a parish mission trip. A single man whose mother is slowly dying from dementia and needs regular care need not lead the charge for more just working conditions in his workplace.

Families need not give to others what they need themselves. In addressing the question of whether one should give alms from one's necessities, Thomas Aquinas writes, "In the first place, we can mean that without it something else cannot exist. Whatever is necessary in this sense, for example, where a man has only just enough to keep himself with his children and dependents alive, should certainly not be given away from his own life and that of his dependents."[53] After offering the sacrifice of one's self for the Church or state as an exception, Aquinas continues:

> In the second place, when we say a thing is necessary, we mean that without it a man cannot have a livelihood in keeping with his own and his dependents' social position. Now there is nothing so fixed and final about the amount that is necessary for a life in keeping with this, that enables one to say there is too much or not enough, even where there has been considerable increase or considerable loss. Yet this being so, it is well to use such necessities for almsgiving, though it is not a matter of precept, but of counsel.[54]

Building on Aquinas here, one need not give from one's own needs, or even more than one's state of life requires, but persons can reflect on the range of acceptable choices available in their state of life and discern whether or not they could live in the lower part of that range so they could be more generous to those in urgent material need.

In some phases of family life, individuals may be more on the recipient end of social ministry. A family dealing with disability or addiction, or

53 Aquinas, *Summa Theologiae*, II.II, Q. 32, a. 6, in Batten, 257.

54 Aquinas, II.II, Q. 32, a. 6, in Batten, 257–59.

divorce or postpartum depression, may have family needs that make broader social ministry difficult or imprudent. In those times of life, individuals may find ways to serve those who are serving them to develop communities of support in which they can help and be helped. By identifying the first two forms of social ministry, those in situations of need can find meaning in living the Gospel call to serve the poor according to the forms of social ministry available to them.

Finally, social ministry should be the fruit of family dialogue and discernment. While certain forms of social ministry may seem to integrate well with family commitments in theory, one needs to consider the thoughts, desires, consciences, and concerns of the members of one's family. If a father feels called to do missionary work or start a house of hospitality or embrace voluntary poverty, he needs to dialogue with his wife and children. The father would need to consider the concerns of his wife and the anxieties of his children, and the wife and children would need to listen to the desires of the father. Through prayer and dialogue, the family may discern a special calling to missionary work or running a house of hospitality. Alternatively, the wife and children may find other ways to support the father's missionary spirit, and the father in listening to his family's concerns and needs may find creative ways to serve those in need without causing undue burden on his family.

Since families are united in stable relationships, the ministry of one family member will likely impact others in the family. Individuals need to be careful that they are not making social commitments that place heavy burdens on family members who are not prepared for such burdens. Those with social zeal need to work with the consciences of their family members, inviting them to pray and grow in small steps, while listening to their needs so they do not overlook family responsibilities. Those who are focused on family responsibilities need to represent family needs in dialogue, but also remember the Gospel call to serve the poor, the social interdependence of families, and remain open to growing in generous service to others.

Family dialogue will be crucial not only for discerning how involved a family should become in social service but also in determining what kinds of social ministry to engage in. If a family finds its time is filled with caring for young children, but they have some disposable income, they can propose and dialogue about what groups and individuals they will support. Families lacking financial resources may discern how they can use their time in service to others. As individuals identify social needs and consider ways of serving those needs, they can dialogue with family members to learn how such ministry might impact and engage others in the family and thereby discern which forms of social ministry seem fitting and appropriate for their life circumstances.

The question concerning social ministry outside of a family is not whether but how. Families have various ways of meeting social needs available to them, and each of these ways will present different opportunities and risks for integration with family responsibilities. Discernment about family involvement in social ministry needs to consider the Gospel call to give preferential care for the poor and the order of charity, which emphasizes familial responsibilities. Families can reflect on whether their commitment or lack of commitment to social ministry reflects a way of life united in God's love. Falsely simple answers would include an exclusive focus on family responsibilities or a denial of family responsibilities in commitment to the broader human family. Some tension between fulfilling family responsibilities and giving preferential care for the poor is inevitable. One will have to be intentional about integrating these commitments through prayerful discernment that considers a family's needs and resources and reflects the fruit of dialogue that considers the zeal and concerns of all the family members.

Conclusion

God, the source of all existence and of each human existence, is a divine communion of persons. From the first moment of conception, human beings stand in relation to God. God creates us and invites us to participate in communion. Human beings are communal beings. They also are embodied. In this embodiment, humans experience limitations in the time and energy available to cultivate communion with others. Their movement toward union with God necessarily passes through specific relationships with those who live in their embodied communities.

The family is a basic social unit. From the moment of conception, human beings stand in a uniquely permanent relationship with their parents and family. Family relationships are formed and expanded through marriage, conception, and adoption, which, taken together, establish permanent relationships that imply mutual responsibilities. For those who have the capacity and commitment to fulfill these responsibilities, the common risk is to focus on one's family to the neglect of those in other social communities. One's own well-being is caught up in the well-being of one's family; one lives with one's family, and so grows accustomed to recognizing and responding to family needs. The tendency to focus on family needs to the neglect of those in other social communities is not merely a symptom of the particularities of modern family life.

Human society traditionally followed a family clan model, in which one's family includes a robust network of extended family connected by marriage and friendship with other families. The family clan is socially determinative. Under this model, one's identity comes from the social status of one's family and one's position in the family's birth order. One learns one's trade in one's family and one's prospects for marriage are determined, maybe even arranged, by that family. The central goal of life is to sustain or increase the social status of one's family. One cares for one's family and those connected to that family, but one generally does not concern oneself with those outside the family clan. It was this family model that Christ challenged so decisively when he said that the family of faith took precedence over the natural family: "Whoever does the will of God is my brother and sister and mother" (Mark 3:35).

Remnants of the clan family model remain in modern society, although they have been strained by social mobility and small family sizes.

Ironically, Catholic families can sometimes maintain this type of clan-based inward focus more easily when they have large families and many relatives. But the more dominant family model that I have been critiquing throughout this book sees the family as an isolated context for individuals to seek self-fulfillment. The family is thereby defined over and against public communities like the workplace or the political sphere. Since families in this model seek isolation, they can do what they want without interference from others and bear few or even no responsibilities to those outside the family. Their needs and their desires are focused on an impersonal "market," from which they take goods and services and to which they offer the service of their labor to get the money they need to pay for those goods and services. Both the family clan model and the socially detached model isolate the family from broader social communities, but they do so in radically different ways. In the family clan model, one serves those in the robust social community that is the clan. In the socially isolated family model, a family is a (possibly unstable) nuclear family that is isolated from the needs, wants, and support of others except through the medium of impersonal forces. When their attempt to satisfy themselves through family relationships or the market fails, these families often are confused about what went wrong. They might seek alternative family relationships or market joys, or they might conclude that family life is a façade promising a fulfillment it cannot deliver.

The family is internally social. As an internally social community, the family possesses various features of social life. A family, for example, has legislators, alliances, an economic system, and a moral ethos. Family relationships and interactions form individuals personally and socially in fundamental ways. Living familial relationships well is difficult—a person seeking easy self-fulfillment in his family is likely to find instead the social complexities and challenges of family life.

The Catholic social tradition possesses theoretical and prudential resources for thinking richly about social life. Since the family is a basic social unit, Catholic social principles, which shed light on the organization of nations and the workplace, also clarify relationships in the social community that is family life. I have attempted to apply the discussion of work found in the papal social encyclical tradition to household labor and reflected on how recent theological discussion of peacemaking might help parents respond to sibling violence. These are but a couple of examples of how the Catholic social tradition can clarify family interactions, and thereby help individuals to alleviate family struggles and cultivate meaningful social interactions in family life. To offer a few other examples, one can see how the principle of human dignity would clarify how to respond to a sibling who gets on one's nerves, or how solidarity would encourage one to cultivate relationships with parents and grandparents who live in a nursing home, or how the right to private property and the universal destination of goods can help parents moderate how different children possess and share the gifts they receive for birthdays or Christmas. Subsidiarity could help inform how a parent helps a daughter with her homework. Distributive justice could clarify how to distribute food at the family meal.

The central reason to apply Catholic social ethics to everyday family interactions is that individuals inevitably struggle with family relationships, and these principles are clarifying and enriching. This application, however, may also have other indirect positive benefits. As a basic social unit, the family forms its members in foundational ways. Formation in the family will overflow into schools, parishes, and workplaces. The application of social principles to family examples also can serve as a simple and effective pedagogical tool for presenting Catholic social ethics. Most individuals can relate to family interactions and so family applications have broad accessibility and applicability.

Even with the application of Catholic social principles, however, family members will continue to have needs and experience hardships. The family clan and isolated family models may struggle with those needs. In a family clan model, individuals will seek to take care of their own, but they will struggle to integrate family members whom they perceive to be obstacles to sustaining or developing a family's social welfare. In the isolated family model, one seeks self-fulfillment in family relationships. When one encounters instead physical need, psychological stress, or moral or spiritual poverty, one may be confused and not know how to respond. The Catholic faith highlights that every person is in need. Our existence is contingent on God. We lack the natural capacity to live the divine communion for which we long, and even the natural capacity that we do have is distorted by sin and disorder. God creates us, redeems us, elevates us, and gives us the grace to respond to His call to eternal fellowship.

God owes us nothing and still he cares for us in our poverty. Christ calls His disciples, who have benefitted from God's mercy, to extend that mercy to others. In the Catholic social tradition, the works of mercy have long provided categories for thinking about how to care for the poor. Living in God's love, Christians extend this love by taking the gifts of God and sharing them or serving as an instrument of those gifts to others.

In family life, one encounters humanity, and therefore poverty. In the embodied community of family life, one encounters physical needs, psychological stress, and spiritual poverty. The works of mercy have application to family interactions. In chapter 3, I reflected on feeding the hungry and caring for the sick. As is the case with the Catholic social principles, it is possible also to reflect on various other applications of the works of mercy to family life. One can visit children imprisoned in their high chairs, car seats, or cribs; or physically disabled family members confined to their beds or wheelchairs; or family members who are in jail because they have made bad decisions or been unjustly convicted. In applying the works of mercy to family life, one might reflect on how to welcome those family members who often seem like strangers inside of the home. The works of mercy challenge us to lovingly educate the ignorant sibling and correct the sinning spouse, but also to bear wrongs patiently. The works of mercy are a way to care for the needs of another while sharing God's love.

The primary reason for applying the works of mercy in family life is that individuals are suffering and often only family members can see and respond to that suffering. Application of the works of mercy to the family is significant also because the biblical presentation of mercy often employs familial language. In that sense, living the works of mercy gives credibility to one's proclamation of Christ's mercy but also brings to life the biblical imagery of the Father's mercy. Highlighting the importance of familial mercy can have a further implication. In the isolated family model, family life is presented as a private context for seeking self-fulfillment. By highlighting human poverty and the need for mercy, one subtly shows that family is not merely for pleasure and fulfillment, but, instead, a social community in which members need mercy. This need for mercy points to God; since God often works through human agents and family members are not always capable of serving individual needs, the family also needs support from broader social communities.

In highlighting the internally social character of family life, one needs to be clear that the family also stands in an interdependent relationship with other social communities. Otherwise, families risk falling into the clan model in which individuals take care of only their own. On both a theological and sociological level, families are interdependent. Christ challenges his disciples to place their family relationships in relation to God and to see the broader human family in which we are all adopted sons and daughters of God. One has unique responsibilities to one's family members, but one's responsibility goes beyond the family.

Families are interdependent with broader social communities. A family benefits from safe neighborhoods, job opportunities, just political systems, social peace, accessible healthcare, and a vibrant parish community. Individual family members have educational and social needs that other family members cannot provide. The Church helps individuals to frame family commitments in relation to the Christian faith and provides families with opportunities for Christian friendship, clarification with respect to scripture and tradition, and access to the grace of the sacraments. Families benefit from broader social communities, and families have responsibilities to serve the common good. Beyond forming individuals who then impact broader social communities, families also can serve as a model for social communion. While families are not immune from injustice, the permanence and intimacy of family life often make it a nucleus of social exchange. One develops relationships with the family and friends of one's spouse and with the parents of one's children's friends. When they live as a communion of persons, families model for society unity, fidelity, stability, sacrifice, and intergenerational communion.

Families can benefit greatly from broader social communities when those communities provide social, educational, and spiritual opportunities for growth and service. Social interdependence, however, can also be harmful for families when the broader social communities are violent, present health risks, or provide a negative moral or spiritual formation. I reflected on the pervasive and powerful formative character of consumerism. Consumerism, understood as a social way of life that devours and exhausts, especially when wedded with a private account of isolated family life, presents various obstacles preventing families from living as a basic unit. In a consumer context, putting family first often means working long hours so that one's family can increase its purchasing power. Market branding forms human desires to feel that happiness will come from material purchases or vacations or drugs, and it influences the way individuals think about conjugal love, marriage, sexual union, and the role of procreation in marriage. Consumerism forms habits of material and social detachment and self-seeking competition that can prevent individuals from recognizing the good of social communion and addressing the social needs of one's family members.

Negative social influences pose challenging dilemmas to those in charge of families. How does one live well a family's social interdependence knowing that broader social influences can be both positive and negative? Since families are socially interdependent, the question is not whether families will socially engage but how. I analyzed the question of familial social engagement through the lens of infused simplicity, that is, a way of life united in God's love. While family is a great good, God alone is a good capable of uniting all other goods. While complete withdrawal from social community is not possible, families will withdraw from those social interactions that are uniquely harmful to communion with God. Many other decisions concerning social engagement will require prudential discernment. The categories of moral cooperation and moral appropriation can help clarify decisions about appropriating the benefits of or cooperating with the evil action of another. Similarly, the common good and moral cooperation clarify how to support the good actions of others. The goal is not merely to avoid sin but to live a life united in God's love. Activities that actively help families move toward an integration of life in God's love include prayer, offering one's work to God, gratitude, and seeing the goods of the world as an analogy of God.

The Gospels, papal social encyclicals, and the last two apostolic exhortations on the family highlight a family's responsibility to care for the poor. Many families are sympathetic to the poor and to this call to serve but struggle to see how social ministry to the poor relates to responsibilities they have to care for their spouses, children, and parents. I propose that one needs an account of social ministry that integrates with family responsibilities.

The stability and socially robust character of families often means that families are specifically suited to serving needs in their various embodied communities. In some instances, the broader social ministry of an individual flows from family relationships or relates to social service that families are specifically suited to address. In other cases, families serve those in their embodied communities, because, like everyone, they see human needs and can address those needs, and so they do so.

When the needs of one's family are greater than those outside of the family community, one should focus on his family. A father working two minimum wage jobs so that his family can pay rent and eat three meals a day may not have the time or financial resources to engage in formal ministries dedicated to the homeless and hungry. His service to the poor is directed towards his wife and children. Still, since families are socially interdependent, families in unique situations of need may find that they are able to build communities of support in which they can help and be helped.

Families who have been stuck in poverty for generations may lack the material resources to donate money to good causes, but they may understand the genuine needs of those enduring similar struggles, and they might be able to help link other families with social resources, or know of some thoughtful ways of improving available ministries.

Sometimes, however, the needs of those who live outside of their embodied communities are greater than the typical needs of those who live in one's social spheres. Despite the risks of helping in disembodied ways, these urgent needs call for a response from those who have the resources to help. Families can provide indirect aid by making contributions to communities or organizations that have direct contact with the poor. Alternatively, families can have direct contact with the poor but in locations distinct from their livelihood. Some individuals will have greater family responsibilities than others. Families with teenagers may be busy moving from event to event, but they could engage in occasional, direct service or take a mission trip. Spouses with an empty nest might be positioned to commit on a more consistent basis to some kind of social ministry. They might regularly visit families struggling with poverty to provide a needs assessment for St. Vincent de Paul or regularly distribute resources to refugee families trying to settle in the area.

Finally, families can center their lives on social ministry, making the lives of the poor their own, insofar as that is possible for someone intentionally choosing a life of downward mobility. Families committed to missionary work or other social initiatives, such as initiating and running a Catholic Worker house of hospitality, provide a bold witness challenging the general tendency for individuals to serve family members to the neglect of those outside one's family. Still, such inspirational service should be viewed as more of an exception than the rule, especially for families with young children. Service requires giving to others in their need, and serving those outside of one's embodied communities requires extra time to understand the genuine needs and extra resources necessary to address those needs.

The variety of options for families reflects the social character and role of families. The choice between these various options is a choice between different kinds of social ministry and not a choice between self-seeking private isolation and social ministry, and the options go beyond occasional, indirect service or centering one's life on social ministry. One family cannot perform every kind of social ministry, and they certainly cannot establish peace throughout the world. Christians of good will have differing yet still acceptable levels of commitment to social ministry. Some families with a strong social conscience may feel guilty for living next to a Catholic Worker house of hospitality rather than in the house of hospitality. Other families will rarely encounter those with urgent material needs and may lose sight of the call to provide indirect financial aid to those in need. In some families, individuals will be unified in their commitment or lack of commitment to serving the poor, but in other families, individuals will have to work harder to attain agreement about social commitment. The oldest daughter of a family may desire to serve the poor more consistently and dramatically while her parents may want her to focus on her education, and her younger siblings may lack interest or ability to serve the poor. A lack of commitment or lack of social virtues does not excuse families from serving the poor, but the varying viewpoints of family members do need to be considered in familial decisions about the relationship between family responsibilities and social service. Those entrusted with the care of their families must discern what forms of social service to engage in. That discernment ought to depend on family needs, dialogue, prayer, and generosity.

A family's capacity to recognize and address needs outside of their family forms a test of integrity for those who argue that social formation in the internally social family flows outward into society. Insofar as the family is social, one can view caring for the poverty of family members as a kind of social ministry. If the family is a basic social unit, then offering preferential care for the poor in the family should form habits that overflow into the broader community. Without this socially life-giving overflow to the wider community, the risk is that the family is simply taking care of their own, drawing from social resources without responsibly contributing to the common good. In recognizing that the family is internally social and socially interdependent, one can see more clearly the unique social needs of one's family. Individuals then can discern more clearly how they will live out the Gospel's pervasive and challenging call to serve the poor, both in the internally social dimension of family life and as part of a family's broader social interdependence.

Bibliography

Adams, Samuel L. *Social and Economic Life in Second Temple Judea*. Louisville: Westminster John Knox Press, 2014.

Alvaré, Helen. *Putting Children's Interests First in U.S. Family Law and Policy: With Power Comes Responsibility*. Cambridge: Cambridge University Press, 2018.

Anderson, Jane. "The Impact of Family Structure on the Health of Children: Effects of Divorce." *The Linacre Quarterly* 81, no. 4 (November 2014): 378–87.

Aquinas, Thomas. *Summa Theologiae*. Edited and translated by R. J. Batten, OP. New York: McGraw-Hill, 1975.

———. *Treatise on Law*. Washington, DC: Regnery Publishing, 1956.

Aristotle. *Aristotle: Selected Works*. Translated by Hippocrates G. Apostle and Lloyd P. Gerson. 3rd ed. Grinnell, IA: The Peripatetic Press, 1991.

———. *The Nicomachean Ethics*. Translated by David Ross. Oxford: Oxford University Press, 1998.

Arterbury, Andrew E. *Entertaining Angels: Early Christian Hospitality in Its Mediterranean Setting*. Sheffield, UK: Sheffield Phoenix Press, 2005.

Balthasar, Hans Urs von. *Explorations in Theology*. Vol. 3, *Creator Spirit*. San Francisco: Ignatius Press, 1993.

Barrera, Albino. *Market Complicity and Christian Ethics*. New York: Cambridge University Press, 2011.

Benedict, Saint. *The Rule of Saint Benedict in English*. Edited by Timothy Fry, OSB. Collegeville, MN: The Liturgical Press, 1981.

Benedict XVI, Pope. *Caritas in Veritate*. Encyclical Letter. June 29, 2009. In *Catholic Social Thought: The Documentary Heritage*. Edited by David J. O'Brien and Thomas A. Shannon, 526–86. Rev. ed. Maryknoll, NY: Orbis Books, 2016.

Benestad, Brian. *Church, State, and Society: An Introduction to Catholic Social Doctrine*. Washington, DC: The Catholic University of America Press, 2011.

Bennett, Jana Marguerite. *Water Is Thicker Than Blood: An Augustinian Theology of Marriage and Singleness*. Oxford: Oxford University Press, 2008.

Berry, Wendell. "Word and Flesh." In *Simpler Living, Compassionate Life*, edited by Michael Schut, 99–103. Denver: Living the Good News, 1999.

Botana, Federico. *The Works of Mercy in Italian Medieval Art (c. 1050–c. 1400)*. Medieval Church Studies, 20. Turnhout, Belgium: Brepols, 2011.

Bourg, Florence Caffrey. *Where Two or Three are Gathered: Christian Families as Domestic Churches*. Notre Dame, IN: University of Notre Dame Press, 2004.

Cahill, Lisa Sowle. *Blessed are the Peacemakers: Pacifism, Just War, and Peacebuilding*. Minneapolis: Fortress Press, 2019.

———. *Family: A Christian Social Perspective*. Minneapolis: Fortress Press, 2000.

Carmona, Victor, "Mixed-Status Families, Solidarity, and *Lo Cotidiano*." In *Sex, Love, and Families: Catholic Perspectives*, edited by Jason King and Julie Hanlon Rubio, 199–210. Collegeville, MN: Liturgical Press, 2020.

Casarella, Peter, ed. *Jesus Christ: The New Face of Social Progress*. Grand Rapids, MI: William B. Eerdmans, 2015.

Catechism of the Catholic Church. 2nd ed. Washington, DC: United States Catholic Conference, 1997.

Cavalier, Gary, ed. *Family Life in the Catholic Worker Movement*. Las Vegas: Las Vegas Catholic Worker, 2012.

Cavanaugh, William T. *Being Consumed: Economics and Christian Desire*. Grand Rapids, MI: William B. Eerdmans, 2008.

———. "Migrant, Tourist, Pilgrim, Monk: Mobility and Identity in a Global Age." *Theological Studies* 69, no. 2 (2008): 340–56.

Chautard, Jean-Baptiste, OCSO. *The Spirit of Simplicity*. Translated and annotated by Thomas Merton. Notre Dame, IN: Ave Maria Press, 2017.

Cherlin, Andrew J. *The Marriage-Go-Round: The State of Marriage and the Family in America Today*. New York: Alfred A. Knopf, 2009.

Cloutier, David. *Love, Reason, and God's Story: An Introduction to Sexual Ethics*. Winona, MN: Anselm Academic, 2008.

———. *The Vice of Luxury*. Washington, DC: Georgetown University Press, 2015.

Cloutier, David, and William C. Mattison III. "The Resurgence of Virtue in Recent Moral Theology." *Journal of Moral Theology* 3, no. 1 (January 2014): 228–59.

Conwell, Yeates, Kimberly Van Orden, and Eric D. Caine. "Suicide in Older Adults." *Psychiatric Clinics of North America* 34, no. 2 (June 2011): 451–68.

Cronin, Blaise. "Eros Unbound: Pornography and the Internet." In *The Internet and American Business*, edited by William Aspray and Paul E. Ceruzzi, 508–533. Cambridge, MA: MIT Press, 2008.

Daniels, Kimberly, and Joyce C. Abma. "Current Contraceptive Status among Women Aged 15–49: United States, 2017–2019." NCHS Data Brief, No. 388, October 2020. https://www.cdc.gov/nchs/data/databriefs/db388-H.pdf.

Daniels, Kimberly, Jill Daugherty, Jo Jones, and William Mosher. "Current Contraceptive Use and Variation by Selected Characteristics among Women Aged 15–44: United States, 2011–13." National Health Statistics Report No. 86, November 10, 2015. https://www.cdc.gov/nchs/data/nhsr/nhsr086.pdf.

Day, Dorothy. *Selected Writings*. Edited by Robert Ellsberg. Maryknoll, NY: Orbis Books, 1992.

Degler, Carl. *At Odds: Women and the Family in America from the Revolution to the Present.* Oxford: Oxford University Press, 1980.

Dennis, Marie, ed. *Choosing Peace: The Catholic Church Returns to Gospel Nonviolence*. Maryknoll, NY: Orbis Books, 2018.

De Sales, Francis. *Introduction to the Devout Life*. Translated by John K. Ryan. New York: Image Books, 1989.

———. *Letters to Persons in the World*. Translated by Henry Benedict Mackey, OSB. New York: Benziger Brothers, 1900.

———. "On Simplicity and Religious Prudence." In *The Spiritual Conferences*, translated by Abbot Gasquet and Canon Mackey, OSB, 212–33. Westminster, MD: The Newman Bookshop, 1943.

———. *Treatise on the Love of God*. Translated by Henry Benedict Mackey, OSB. Westminster, MD: The Newman Bookshop, 1945.

Dumitrascu, Nicu, ed. *Christian Family and Contemporary Society*. New York: Bloomsbury, 2015.

Edwards, Jim. "FDA Issues Blood-Clot Warning for Bayer Birth Control Pills . . . and Bayer Cheers." CBS News website. https://www.cbsnews.com/news/fda-issues-blood-clot-warning-for-bayer-birth-control-pills-and-bayer-cheers/

Essler, Samuel, Natalie Christner, and Markus Paulus. "Longitudinal Relations between Parental Strain, Parent-Child Relationship Quality, and Child Well-Being during the Unfolding COVID-19 Pandemic." *Child Psychiatry and Human Development* 52 (August 2021): 995–1011.

Finley, Mitch, and Kathy Finley, *Christian Families in the Real World: Reflections on a Spirituality for the Domestic Church*. Chicago: The Thomas More Press, 1984.

Finn, James, ed. *Private Virtue and Public Policy: Catholic Thought and National Life*. New Brunswick, NJ: Transaction Publishers, 1990.

Francis, Pope. *Amoris Laetitia*. Apostolic Exhortation. March 19, 2016.

———. *Evangelii Gaudium*. Apostolic Exhortation. November 24, 2013.

——— *Fratelli Tutti*. Encyclical Letter. October 3, 2020.

———. "Homily on the Feast of the Baptism of the Lord." January 11, 2015.

———. "Interview with Pope Francis." December 2013. *La Stampa*. http://www.lastampa.it/2013/12/14/esteri/vatican-insider/en/never-be-afraid-of-tenderness-5BqUfVs9r7W1CJIMuHqNeI/pagina.html

———. *Laudato si'*. Encyclical Letter. May 24, 2015.

———. "Message for the 24th World Day of the Sick – 2016." September 15, 2015.

———. *Misericordiae Vultus*. Bull of Indiction. April 11, 2015.

———. *On the Family*. Translated by *L'Osservatore Romano*. San Francisco: Ignatius Press, 2015.

———. "Works of Mercy." Audience. June 30, 2016.

Furfey, Paul. *Fire on the Earth*. New York: Macmillan, 1936.

Grabowski, John S. *Sex and Virtue: An Introduction to Sexual Ethics*. Washington, DC: The Catholic University of America Press, 2003.

Grant, Brian W. *The Social Structure of Christian Families: A Historical Perspective*. St. Louis: Chalice Press, 2000.

Hadas, Edward. *Counsels of Imperfection: Thinking through Catholic Social Teaching*. Washington, DC: The Catholic University of America Press, 2021.

Hauerwas, Stanley. "The Family as a School for Character." In *Perspectives on Marriage: A Reader*, edited by Kieran Scott and Michael Warren. Oxford: Oxford University Press, 1993.

———. *The Hauerwas Reader*. Edited by John Berkman and Michael Cartwright. Durham: Duke University Press, 2001.

Hennessy, Kate. *Dorothy Day: The World Will Be Saved by Beauty*. New York: Scribner, 2017.

Hildebrand, Dietrich von. *The Nature of Love*. Translated by John F. Crosby and John Henry Crosby. South Bend, IN: St. Augustine's Press, 2009.

———. *Transformation in Christ*. San Francisco: Ignatius Press, 1990.

Hilgers, Thomas W. *The Naprotechnology Revolution: Unleashing the Power in a Women's Cycle*. New York: Beaufort Books, 2010.

Himes, Kenneth R., OFM. "Consumerism and Christian Ethics." *Theological Studies* 68, no. 1 (2007): 132–53.

———. "Peacebuilding and Catholic Social Teaching." In Schreiter, Appleby, and Powers, *Peacebuilding*, 265–99.

Horowitz, Juliana, Nikki Graf, and Gretchen Livingston. "Marriage and Cohabitation in the U.S." November 6, 2023. https://www.pewresearch.org/social-trends/2019/11/06/marriage-and-cohabitation-in-the-u-s/.

Jacobs, Andrew S. "'Let Him Guard Pietas': Early Christian Exegesis and the Ascetic Family." *Journal of Early Christian Studies* 11, no. 3 (2003): 265–81.

Jatlaoui, Tara C., Alexander Ewing, Michele B. Mandel, Katherine B. Simmons, Danielle B. Suchdev, Denise J. Jamieson, and Karen Pazol. "Abortion Surveillance—United States, 2013." Centers for Disease Control and Prevention, Morbidity and Mortality Weekly Report, November 25, 2016. https://www.cdc.gov/mmwr/volumes/65/ss/ss6512a1.htm

John Paul II, Pope. *Centesimus Annus*. Encyclical Letter. May 1, 1991.

———. *Christifideles Laici*. Apostolic Exhortation. December 30, 1988.

———. *Dives in Misericordiae*. Encyclical Letter. November 30, 1980.

———. *Familiaris Consortio*. Apostolic Exhortation. November 22, 1981.

———. *Laborem Exercens*, Encyclical Letter. September 14, 1981. In *Catholic Social Thought: The Documentary History*, 378–421. Edited by David J. O'Brien and Thomas A. Shannon. Rev. ed. Maryknoll, NY: Orbis Books, 2016.

———. *Man and Woman He Created Them*. Translated by Michael Waldstein. Boston: Pauline Books, 2006.

———. *Veritatis Splendor*. Encyclical Letter. August 6, 1993.

Kasper, Walter. *Mercy: The Essence of the Gospel and the Key to Christian Life*. Mahwah, NJ: Paulist Press, 2014.

Kavanaugh, John F. *Following Christ in a Consumer Society*. Maryknoll, NY: Orbis Books, 2006.

Kaveny, M. Cathleen. "Appropriation of Evil: Cooperation's Mirror Image." *Theological Studies* 61, no. 2 (2000): 280–313.

Keenan, James. *The Works of Mercy: The Heart of Catholicism*. 2nd ed. Lanham, MD: Sheed and Ward, 2008.

Kierkegaard, Soren. *Works of Love: Some Christian Reflections in the Form of Discourses*. Translated by Howard and Edna Hong. New York: Harper and Row, 1962.

King, Jason. *Faith with Benefits: Hookup Culture on Catholic Campuses*. Oxford: Oxford University Press, 2016.

———. "A Theology of Dating for a Culture of Abuse." In *Leaving and Coming Home: New Wineskins for Catholic Sexual Ethics*, edited by David Cloutier, 29–46. Eugene, OR: Cascade Books, 2010.

Kiselica, Mark S., and Mandy Morrill-Richards. "Sibling Maltreatment: The Forgotten Abuse." *Journal of Counseling and Development* 85, no. 2 (Spring 2007): 148–60.

Konieczny, Mary Ellen. *The Spirit's Tether: Family, Work, and Religion among American Catholics*. New York: Oxford University Press, 2013.

Lally, Maria. "Fertility Exploitation: The Couples Paying a High Price for Wanting a Baby." *Telegraph*. June 26, 2017. http://www.telegraph.co.uk/women/family/fertility-exploitation-couples-paying-high-price-wanting-baby/.

Lamidi, Esther O., Wendy D. Manning, and Susan L. Brown. "Change in the Stability of First Premarital Cohabitation among Women in the United States, 1983–2013." *Demography* 56 (2019): 427–50.

Lasch, Christopher. *Haven in a Heartless World: The Family Besieged*. New York: Basic Books, 1977.

Leo XIII, Pope. *Rerum Novarum*. Encyclical Letter. May 15, 1891. In *Catholic Social Thought: The Documentary Heritage*, 14–40. Edited by David J. O'Brien and Thomas A. Shannon. Rev. ed. Maryknoll, NY: Orbis Books, 2016.

Letourneau, Nicole, and Martha Hart. *Parenting and Child Development: Issues and Answers*. East Sussex, UK: Waterside Press, 2020.

Lewis, C. S. *The Abolition of Man*. New York: The Macmillan Company, 1947.

Littlejohn, W. Bradford. "Addicted to Novelty: The Vice of Curiosity in a Digital Age." *Journal of the Society of Christian Ethics* 37, no. 1 (Spring/Summer 2017): 179–96.

Lonergan, Bernard. Review of *Marriage*, by Dietrich von Hildebrand. In *Shorter Papers*. Vol. 20 of *Collected Works of Bernard Lonergan*, edited by Frederick Crowe and Robert Doran, 153–56. Toronto: University of Toronto Press, 2007.

Love, Maryann Cusimano. "What Kind of Peace Do We Seek? Emerging Norms of Peacebuilding in Key Political Institutions." In Robert J. Schreiter, R. Scott Appleby, and Gerard F. Powers, *Peacebuilding*, 56–91.

Lysaught, M. Therese, ed. *Catholic Bioethics and Social Justice: The Praxis of US Health Care in a Globalized World*. Collegeville, MN: Liturgical Press, 2018.

Massaro, Thomas. *Living Justice: Catholic Social Teaching in Action*. 3rd ed. Lanham, MD: Rowman and Littlefield, 2016.

Mattison, William C., III. "The Beatitudes and Moral Theology: A Virtue Ethics Approach." *Nova et Vetera*, 11, no. 3 (2013): 819–48.

———. *Introducing Moral Theology: True Happiness and the Virtues*. Grand Rapids, MI: Brazos Press, 2008.

McCarthy, David Matzko. "Becoming One Flesh: Marriage, Remarriage and Sex." In *The Blackwell Companion to Christian Ethics*, edited by Stanley M. Hauerwas and Samuel Wells, 276–88. Oxford: Blackwell, 2004.

———. *The Good Life: Genuine Christianity for the Middle Class*. Grand Rapids, MI: Brazos, 2004.

———. *Sex and Love in the Home: A Theology of the Household*. 2nd ed. London: SCM Press, 2004.

McKanan, Dan. *The Catholic Worker after Dorothy: Practicing the Works of Mercy in a New Generation*. Collegeville, MN: Liturgical Press, 2008.

Miller, Claire Cain. "Americans Are Having Fewer Babies: They Told Us Why." *New York Times*, July 5, 2018.

Miller, Donald. *Concepts of Family Life: From Vatican II through "Christifideles Laici."* San Francisco: Catholic Scholars Press, 1997.

Montessori, Maria. *The Absorbent Mind*. Translated by Claude A. Claremont. New York: Holt, Rinehart, and Winston, 1967.

Moody, Anne. *The Children Money Can Buy: Stories from the Frontlines of Foster Care and Adoption*. Lanham, MD: Rowman and Littlefield, 2018.

Noye, Irénée. "Miséricorde (Oeuvres de)." In *Dictionairre de Spiritualité*, 10: 1327–49. Paris: Beauchesne, 1980.

Omer, Haim. "Helping Parents Deal with Children's Acute Disciplinary Problems without Escalation: The Principle of Nonviolent Resistance." *Family Process* 40, no. 1 (2001): 53–66.

———. *Nonviolent Resistance: A New Approach to Violent and Self-Destructive Children*. New York: Cambridge University Press, 2004.

Omer, Haim, and Eli R. Lebowitz, "Nonviolent Resistance: Helping Caregivers Reduce Problematic Behaviors in Children and Adolescents." *Journal of Marital and Family Therapy* 42, no. 4 (October 2016): 688–99.

Omer, Haim, Irit Schorr-Sapir, and Uri Weinblatt. "Nonviolent Resistance and Violence Against Siblings." *Journal of Family Therapy* 30, no. 4 (2008): 450–64.

Osborne, Thomas. "The Threefold Referral of Acts to the Ultimate End in Thomas Aquinas and His Commentators." *Angelicum*, 85, no. 3 (2008): 715–36.

Paul VI, Pope. *Humanae Vitae*. Encyclical Letter. July 25, 1968.

———. *Populorum Progressio*. Encyclical Letter. March 26, 1967.

Pieper, Josef. *Leisure: The Basis of Culture*. Translated by Gerald Malsbary. South Bend, IN: St. Augustine's Press, 1998.

———. *Only the Lover Sings: Art and Contemplation*. Translated by Lothar Krauth. San Francisco: Ignatius Press, 1990.

Pinckaers, Servais. *The Sources of Christian Ethics*. Translated by Sr. Mary Thomas Noble, OP. Washington, DC: The Catholic University of America Press, 1995.

Pius XI, Pope. *Divini Illius Magistri*. Encyclical Letter. December 31, 1929.

Pohl, Christine D. *Making Room: Recovering Hospitality as a Christian Tradition*. Grand Rapids, MI: William B. Eerdmans, 1999.

Pontifical Council for Justice and Peace. *Compendium for the Social Doctrine of the Church*. Washington, DC: United States Conference of Catholic Bishops, 2005.

Putnam, Robert. *Our Kids: The American Dream in Crisis*. New York: Simon and Schuster, 2015.

Riegle, Rosalie G. *Dorothy Day: Portraits by Those Who Knew Her*. Maryknoll, NY: Orbis Books, 2003.

Riegle Troester, Rosalie, ed. *Voices from the Catholic Worker*. Philadelphia: Temple University Press, 1993.

Roche, Mary M. Doyle. *Children, Consumerism, and the Common Good*. Lanham, MD: Lexington Books, 2009.

———. *Schools of Solidarity: Families and Catholic Social Teaching*. Collegeville, MN: Liturgical Press, 2015.

Rosato, Donna. "How High-Tech Baby Making Fuels the Infertility Market Boom." *Time*. July 8, 2014.

Rubio, Julie Hanlon. *A Christian Theology of Marriage and Family*. New York: Paulist Press, 2003.

———. "Cooperation with Evil Reconsidered: The Moral Duty of Resistance." *Theological Studies* 78, no. 1 (2017): 96–120.

———."Does Family Conflict with Community?" *Theological Studies* 58, no. 4 (December 1997): 597–617.

———. "The Dual Vocation of Christian Parents." *Theological Studies* 63, no. 4 (December 2002): 786–812.

———. *Family Ethics: Practices for Christians*. Washington, DC: Georgetown University Press, 2010.

———. *Hope for Common Ground: Mediating the Personal and the Political in a Divided Church*. Washington, DC: Georgetown University Press, 2016.

Scales, Stephen, Adam Potthast, and Linda Oravecz, eds. *The Ethics of the Family*. Newcastle, UK: Cambridge Scholars Publishing, 2010.

Schaefer, Jame. *Theological Foundations for Environment Ethics: Reconstructing Patristic and Medieval Concepts*. Washington DC: Georgetown University Press, 2009.

Schemenauer, Kevin. "Hating One's Family: Reading Luke 14:26 in the Context of Luke's Gospel." In *Human Families: Identities, Relationships, and Responsibilities*, edited by Jacob M. Kohlhaas and Mary M. Doyle Roche, 100–11. College Theology Society Annual Volume, 66. Maryknoll, NY: Orbis Books, 2021.

———."The Infused Virtue of Simplicity: St. Francis de Sales and Dietrich von Hildebrand." *Logos* 20, no. 3 (2017): 95–121.

———. "The Works of Mercy: Francis and the Family." *Journal of Moral Theology*, 6, no. 2 (June 2017): 32–47.

Schiraldi, Glenn R. *The Adverse Childhood Experiences Recovery Workbook*. Oakland: New Harbinger Publications, 2021.

Schor, Juliet B. *Born to Buy*. New York: Scribner, 2004.

———. *The Overspent American: Upscaling, Downshifting, and the New Consumer*. New York: Basic Books, 1998.

———. *The Overworked American: The Unexpected Decline of Leisure*. New York: Basic Books, 1992.

———. "The Viacom Generation: The Consumer Child and the Corporate Parent." In *At the Heart of Work and Family*, edited by Anita Ilta Garey and Karen V. Hansen, 206–16. New Brunswick, NJ: Rutgers University Press, 2011.

Schreiter, Robert J., R. Scott Appleby, and Gerard F. Powers, eds. *Peacebuilding: Catholic Theology, Ethics, and Praxis*. Maryknoll, NY: Orbis Books, 2010.

Sears, Neil. "The £25m IVF Doctor: Clinic's Profits Fuel Criticism of the 'Human Life Industry.'" *Daily Mail*. May 13, 2012. http://www.dailymail.co.uk/news/article-2143934/The-25m-IVF-doctor-Clinics-profits-fuel-criticism-human-life-industry.html.

Second Vatican Council. *Apostolicam Actuositatem*. In *Vatican Council II: The Conciliar and Post Conciliar Documents*. Edited by Austin Flannery. Rev. ed. Collegeville, MN: Liturgical Press, 1975.

———. *Dignitatis Humanae*. In *Vatican Council II: The Conciliar and Post Conciliar Documents*. Edited by Austin Flannery. Rev. ed. Collegeville, MN: Liturgical Press, 1975.

———. *Gaudium et Spes*. In *Vatican Council II: The Conciliar and Post Conciliar Documents*. Edited by Austin Flannery. Rev. ed. Collegeville, MN: Liturgical Press, 1975.

———. *Gravissimum educationis*. In *Vatican Council II: The Conciliar and Post Conciliar Documents*. Edited by Austin Flannery. Rev. ed. Collegeville, MN: Liturgical Press, 1975.

Sherwin, Michael S., OP. "Infused Virtues and the Effects of Acquired Vice: A Test Case for the Thomistic Theory of Infused Cardinal Virtues." *The Thomist* 73, no. 1 (2009): 29–52.

Simon, Yves. *Work, Society, and Culture*. Edited by Vukan Kuic. New York: Fordham University Press, 1971.

Singer, Natasha. "Health Concerns Over Popular Contraceptives." *New York Times*, September 25, 2009.

Smith, Janet. *Humanae Vitae: A Generation Later*. Washington, DC: The Catholic University of America Press, 1991.

Stassen, Glen H., ed. *Just Peacemaking: The New Paradigm for the Ethics of Peace and War*. Rev. ed. Cleveland: The Pilgrim Press, 2008.

Taha, Nadia. "Opting Out of Parenthood, with Finances in Mind." *New York Times*, November 13, 2012.

United States Census Bureau. "Table MS-2. Estimated Median Age at First Marriage, by Sex: 1890 to the Present." https://www.census.gov/data/tables/time-series/demo/families/marital.html.

United States Conference of Catholic Bishops. "Corporal Works of Mercy." https://www.usccb.org/beliefs-and-teachings/how-we-teach/new-evangelization/jubilee-of-mercy/the-corporal-works-of-mercy.

———. *Ethical and Religious Directives for Catholic Health Care Services*. 6th ed. Washington, DC: United States Conference of Catholic Bishops, 2018.

———. *Marriage: Love and Life in the Divine Plan*. Washington, DC: United States Conference of Catholic Bishops, 2010.

Vasko, Elisabeth T. "'Mad Mothers, Bad Mothers': Resisting Stigma and Embracing Grace as Dis-ease." *Journal of the Society of Christian Ethics* 37, no. 1 (Spring/Summer 2017): 141–59.

Vaverek, Timothy. "Christian Asceticism: Breaking Consumerism's Destructive Hold." *Houston Catholic Worker* 21, no. 1 (January 2001): 1–7.

Volf, Miroslav. *Work in the Spirit: Toward a Theology of Work*. New York: Oxford University Press, 1991.

Votruba-Drzal, Elizabeth, and Eric Dearing, eds. *The Wiley Handbook of Early Childhood Development Programs, Practices, and Policies*. Malden, MA: John Wiley and Sons, 2017.

Ward, Terence. *The Guardian of Mercy*. New York: Arcade, 2016.

Waters, Brent. *The Family in Christian Social and Political Thought*. New York: Oxford University Press, 2007.

Wilson, Gary. *Your Brain on Porn: Internet Pornography and the Emerging Science of Addiction*. Margate, UK: Commonwealth, 2014.

Witt, John. *Church, State, and Family: Reconciling Traditional Teachings and Modern Liberties*. New York: Cambridge University Press, 2019.

Wrobleski, Jessica. *The Limits of Hospitality*. Collegeville, MN: Liturgical Press, 2012.

Zwick, Mark, and Louise Zwick. *Mercy without Borders: The Catholic Worker and Immigration*. New York: Paulist Press, 2010.

Index

Also from The Catholic University of America Press

Handbook of Catholic Social Teaching: A Guide for Christians in the World Today
Edited by Martin Schlag. Foreword by Peter K.A. Turkson

A Catechism for Family Life: Insights from Catholic Teaching on Love, Marriage, Sex, and Parenting
Edited by Sarah Bartel and John S. Grabowski

Vocation to Virtue: Christian Marriage as a Consecrated Life
by Kent Lasnoski

Counsels of Imperfection: Thinking through Catholic Social Teaching
by Edward Hadas

Church, State, and Society: An Introduction to Catholic Social Doctrine
by J. Brian Benestad

Rethinking Cooperation with Evil: A Virtue-Based Approach
by Ryan Connors

Biblical and Theological Foundations of the Family: The Domestic Church
by Joseph C. Atkinson

Recovering Origins: A Unique Healing Program for Adult Children of Divorce
by Margaret Harper McCarthy. Foreword by Carl A. Anderson

Blood in the Fields: Óscar Romero, Catholic Social Teaching, and Land Reform
by Matthew Philipp Whelan

The Theology of Marriage: Personalism, Doctrine, and Canon Law
by Cormac Burke. Foreword by Janet E. Smith

Mysteries of the Lord's Prayer: Wisdom from the Early Church
by John Gavin. Foreword by George Weigel

The Light of Christ: An Introduction to Catholicism
by Thomas Joseph White, OP

Naming Our Sins: How Recognizing the Seven Deadly Vices Can Renew the Sacrament of Reconciliation
Edited by Jana M. Bennett and David Cloutier

Aquinas and the Theology of the Body: The Thomistic Foundations of John Paul II's Anthropology
by Thomas Petri, OP